070.435
F35i

142197

DATE DUE			

The International
News Services

The Twentieth Century Fund is an independent research foundation which undertakes policy studies of economic, political, and social institutions and issues. The Fund was founded in 1919 and endowed by Edward A. Filene.

The International News Services

A TWENTIETH CENTURY FUND REPORT

by Jonathan Fenby

Schocken Books · New York

First published by Schocken Books 1986
10 9 8 7 6 5 4 3 2 1   86 87 88 89
Copyright © 1986 by The Twentieth Century Fund
All rights reserved

Library of Congress Cataloging in Publication Data
Fenby, Jonathan.
International news services.
(A Twentieth Century Fund report)
Bibliography: p.
Includes index.
1. News agencies. I. Title. II. Series.
PN4717.A1F46 1986   070.4'35   85–2023

Design by Cynthia Basil
Manufactured in the United States of America
ISBN 0–8052–3995–2

To my parents

Contents

Foreword

Control over news and information has been a continuing source of conflict between the developing and developed countries. Most developing countries have long resented what they consider to be the monopoly over the flow of news by Western news agencies. Despite many economic and political differences, the so-called Third World has maintained an impressive unity in its demands for a "new world information order," largely because it sees the existing system as a particularly grating vestige of colonialism.

Because communications has long been one of the major interests of the Twentieth Century Fund, we have been concerned about the issues posed by demands for a new information order. In the late 1970s, the Fund convened an independent Task Force to consider ways in which to bridge the gap separating journalism as practiced in the advanced Western democracies, with its emphasis on freedom to print and broadcast news, and in the Third World, where governments frequently have a major role in deciding what constitutes news and how it ought to be disseminated. The Task Force, which brought together distinguished journalists from around the world, acknowledged the imbalance in the flow of news. It pointed out that this imbalance was not due to any antidemocratic bias or ethnocentric conspiracy. Rather, it was because the Western world is so much more significant and powerful in global affairs, with the result that it makes "news" much more often than does the developing world. The Task Force then went on to point out that a free flow of news is as critical to the developing countries as it is to the developed, and proposed a series of constructive measures to encourage a better balance.

Unfortunately, few of the developing countries have been willing to take remedial action. On the contrary, they have persisted in seeking redress in such international agencies as UNESCO, and in pressing for control over reportage by restricting foreign journalists through accreditation procedures or other measures that curtail freedom. They have also made a target out of the major international news agencies—the Associated Press, United Press International, Reuters, and Agence France-Presse—which together account for more than 80 percent of the international news diet of the non-Communist nations.

The Fund decided that an examination of these agencies—the so-called "wire services"—which are the principal wholesalers of news in both the West and the Third World, was in order. Are they, as some critics charge, the handmaidens of their governments? Do they slant the news? Indulge in sensationalism? Demonstrate an anti-development bias? And what about their accountability? Are they responsible? Do they serve the public? Their shareholders? How do they decide what makes news? And how do they respond to political pressures in foreign areas? Do they impose self-censorship or risk harassment or expulsion of their correspondents?

The range of questions made it obvious that a comprehensive analysis would be a complicated and difficult task. Our search for a candidate was consequently a long one, but was finally rewarded when Jonathan Fenby, an English journalist who had worked for Reuters, most recently as editor of its world news service, and who had been a member of Reuters' executive committee, was persuaded to undertake the assignment. Fenby reviews the history and current role of the wire services, demonstrating how they are structured financially and editorially and how they operate. He goes on to describe the steps taken by all four wire services to meet the complaints of their Third World customers. And he provides a sober assessment of the prospects for resolving the conflict between the West and the Third World.

Jonathan Fenby has provided a fascinating and remarkably objective account of the wholesalers of news that are in large part responsible for what we know about the world. The Fund is grateful to him for illuminating a particularly contentious and critical problem.

M. J. Rossant, Director
Twentieth Century Fund
April 1985

Acknowledgments

This book aims to present a group portrait of four of the world's most important suppliers of information, the major international news agencies. I have drawn, in part, on my own experiences during fourteen years with one of those agencies. Throughout, I have tried to approach the subject as objectively and impartially as possible, basing myself on interviews, factual evidence, documentation, and analysis of agency services.

In all, I spoke to about 150 people while carrying out research for this book. It would be invidious to single out a few of them for mention here. The notes at the back of the book refer to help I received from printed sources and unpublished records of the agencies' histories. I would like to acknowledge my special debt, however, to the late Stanley Swinton for his lengthy and ultimately successful efforts on my behalf at the Associated Press. To all the other people, inside and outside the agencies, who helped me, I express my thanks for their time, patience, and knowledge-sharing, aware that a fair number of them will not agree with at least part of what I have written.

This book was made possible by the Twentieth Century Fund. Apart from underwriting the project, Fund staff played a valuable editorial role. The Fund's director, Murray Rossant, was a source of support and a valuable sounding board for half-formed ideas from the time we first discussed the project in the midst of a London traffic jam. James A. Smith sympathetically helped to keep the research and the draft version of the manuscript on track. Margaret Gwynne was a pleasantly painstaking editor. My thanks to them and to other members of the Fund's staff who helped the project along.

As always, my deep appreciation to the patience of my family in what turned out to be a longer undertaking than initially envisaged. As well as putting up with the invasion of our home by seemingly endless boxes of research papers and reels of agency tapes, my wife

The International News Services. . . . .

made a major contribution to the statistical analysis and to the compilation of the tables in chapters 5, 7, 11, and 12.

Jonathan Fenby
Bonn
March 1985

The International News Services

CHAPTER 1

News of the World

The world has never been more abundantly informed about itself. Computers, satellites, and high-speed data links have revolutionized communications in the past three decades. Information transmitted at ever-greater speed and volume across national frontiers conjures up the image of a global village whose inhabitants are linked, thanks to scientific progress, as never before. Dazzling though the technical advances of the past thirty years have been, the image is misleading in suggesting the existence of a worldwide community sharing the same kinds of interests and information as inhabitants of villages do. Progress has affected the means of transmitting information rather than the information itself. Satellites and video screens do not originate messages or decide their contents; that is done by, and for, people whose outlook is considerably less global than the communications systems they use.

This is particularly true of news. Press and broadcasting organizations use new technologies to send and receive reports from all over the globe, free from the wordage restraints and delays that hampered reporting in the days when dispatches were transmitted laboriously via cable. A single high-speed burst over a satellite circuit can move tens of thousands of words in the time a telex machine used to take to send a hundred. Live television broadcasts show events as they are happening on the other side of the globe; news photographs are in print around the world within a few hours of having been shot. Intercontinental radio interviews have long been taken for granted.

The media of the world are so firmly established in the gallery of late-twentieth-century institutions that they are assumed to have a collective existence above and beyond their constituent newspapers and broadcasting stations. Since they deal in international as well as domestic news, this existence is assumed to have an international aspect; indeed, politicians and commentators speak of "the international press" as though it were a single, clearly definable entity acting along uniform lines. But this is akin to speaking of "the international aircraft" or "the international sociologist." Like aircraft and sociologists, newspapers have certain common characteristics, many of which they share with broadcasting organizations. They exist to pass on to the public a selection of the information available to them, and the selection process determines what portion of the daily flow of information is classed as news. But the idea that newspapers and broadcast organizations operate collectively on an international scale is spurious. The criteria applied in selecting information immediately set individual media organizations apart from one another. Their news may come from all over the world, but—with the exception of a few publications and government-financed international radio stations—it is selected and presented with particular national audiences in mind. Each newspaper and broadcasting station sees the globe through a local prism.

For the commercial media, which live by selling their news and advertising space, this is the result of the efforts of editors and reporters to give audiences what they want. Public demand, as evaluated—rightly or wrongly—by journalists, is the most important element in determining news selection, and a basic assumption of most news organizations is that no national audience is very interested in the rest of the world, apart from spectacular developments and events affecting it directly. This is an assumption that the public has never contradicted. Newspapers with the highest circulation devote the least space to foreign news; in Britain, for example, the two best-selling dailies give more than 90 percent of their news columns to domestic events, and even the "quality" national newspapers print at least twice as much domestic as foreign news.[1]

Such figures actually overestimate the amount of truly international news the public receives, since a substantial proportion of news from abroad is related more to domestic concerns than to the outside world. The journeys of a nation's leaders, the misadventures of its traveling citizens, and the performances of home sports teams in foreign competitions are covered for their domestic interest, not as a part of a wider international picture; Paris newspapers, for example, reported an earthquake in Algeria in 1980 under headlines reassuring readers that there were no French victims. Selfless regard for the rest of the world is rare. Most commercial news media both reinforce and feed off the public's more immediate concerns, presenting foreign events in terms of stereotypes and prejudices that buttress parochialism and national divisions.

4

Western news organizations, which make up the bulk of the world's commercial media, have developed in recent years in ways that mitigate even more strongly against an international approach to reporting the world's news. When a poll taken for the American Society of Newspaper Editors highlights consumer demands for more self-oriented features, more neighborhood news, and personalized journalism, most of the media—except for the few organizations that regard international news as an integral part of their characters and are willing to pay the price—are not going to feel any need to run large and expensive foreign reporting operations. "It becomes such a matter of great cost that [it] gets harder and harder to convince the businessmen who publish the paper it's worth it," in the words of one American foreign editor. Money can be used much more profitably to develop local news, features, self-help, and life-style sections, which attract readers in a very direct manner. After all, who can tell whether a superior reporting service from Africa actually sells a single additional copy or an inch of advertising space?

It is not surprising that, when economic pressures on the press mounted in the United States and Western Europe in the 1960s, foreign coverage was widely regarded as an area that could be cut back without alienating readers. In 1963, U.S. publications employed 919 full-time staff overseas. By the mid-1970s, the total was down to 676. The decline stopped when mergers, technical modernization, and sharper management raised press profitability. The late 1970s may have seen a slight increase in the number of American foreign correspondents from the low point in the middle of that decade, but the total remained well below the level of the early 1960s. While technology was advancing by leaps and bounds, the number of men and women using it to inform their home countries about the world was dropping substantially.

Across the Atlantic, the London *Daily Express,* which had prided itself on its corps of foreign correspondents in the days when it sold four million copies a day, entered the 1980s with no foreign staff reporters outside the United States and circulation hovering around two million. Between 1960 and 1980, the number of British staff correspondents in Paris halved. In 1982, the editor of the London *Times,* singling out the people and the departments that had won him a top journalism award, found room on his long list for just one foreign correspondent, while highlighting the contribution made by the newspaper's entertainment listings, parliamentary shorthand reporters, and sports staff.

The strong impact of visual reporting leads easily to an over-estimation of television's role as a carrier of international information. Television may epitomize the advances in communications technology in the past thirty years, but its place as a provider and interpreter of foreign news is restricted by its internal organization and its need to appeal to a mass market. Domestic concerns dominate the limited time given to news by television stations. Only the biggest foreign stories break through. The presumed parochialism of the audience is not the sole reason for this; international events are often difficult to report in visual terms. Moving pictures can show ministers arriving at conferences, but they cannot weigh the issues being discussed. Explanation takes time, which television generally does not have. The availability of film footage conditions news judgments, and filming is easier and cheaper close to home than in a jungle on the other side of the world.

The domestic pull is at least as strong at most radio stations, where coverage resources are even more limited than those of television or the press. While radio news broadcasts are more frequent than those on television, the time allotted to them is usually extremely limited. How much can a news reader explain about the evolution of a crisis in the Middle East or a change of government in Japan in a thirty-second item on a three-minute newscast? And how much do his listeners really want to know?

The demands of audiences are less important in the controlled news systems of authoritarian states than in the commercial media of democracies. This does not mean that the news is any more internationally minded; furthering national interests, and especially the position of the ruling group, is the predominant aim. Reports are selected and phrased according to state requirements as laid down by those in authority, if not actually provided by the government itself. Information of little general interest or importance is printed or broadcast at length if it advances the government's interests. Foreign events pass through a national filter that ensures that friends are presented in a favorable light and enemies are damned. Reporting the world becomes a function of domestic politics as surely as the commercial media's approach is a function of the domestic audience. Whatever the system, national considerations rule.

The world's media are not only fragmented by national boundaries, they are also spread extremely unevenly around the globe. The bald statistics look impressive: 10,000 newspapers sell 420 million copies a day; 1 billion radio receivers and 400 million television sets are in regular use.[2] Never have so many people had such an opportunity to learn what is going on around them. But that opportunity remains concentrated in the industrialized world, despite images of Bushmen listening to transistor radios and illiterate Asian villagers crowding around communal television sets. North America, Europe, and Japan account for 83 percent of the newspapers sold each day, 80 percent of radio receivers, and 88 percent of television sets. The number of newspapers in 36 black African countries fell by 40 percent to 67 between 1965 and the late 1970s. Ten of those countries, with a combined population of 23.5 million, had no daily newspapers at all; nine others had one each.[3] Locked into a framework of national units, the distribution of the world's media is as lopsided as the distribution of its wealth and power.

Four organizations rise above this uneven distribution of the means by which the world is informed about itself. Collecting and distributing news on a worldwide scale, four major international news agencies are the town criers for the world. It has been estimated that they account for 80 percent of the immediate international news circulating around the planet each day. Their services are indispensable to the biggest as well as the smallest newspapers, to major television networks as well as tiny local radio stations. They distribute their news to rich and poor countries alike, to dictatorships and democracies. They are little-known to the general public, and generally work on a wholesale basis, selling their services to newspapers and broadcasters that select what they want to retail to their reading, viewing, or listening audiences. The agencies disclaim the exercise of power; they owe responsibility only to their clients and to their own standards. Nevertheless, they have become the center of a decade-long international debate that has resulted in their being branded as monopolistic agents of Western domination of underdeveloped nations.[4]

Together the four major news agencies constitute the nearest thing there is to an international news network. An understanding of what they are, how they operate, and what they seek to do is essential to an understanding of how the world is informed in the 1980s.

The Big Four . . . .

The four major international news services—Reuters, the Associated Press (AP), United Press International (UPI), and Agence France-Presse (AFP)—have the same basic purpose as the 103 national news agencies around the world: the collection of news on

7

behalf of recipients who are thus able to get more information more quickly and more cheaply than they could if they depended upon their own resources. What sets the "Big Four" apart from the rest is the worldwide scope of their operations and their independence from external control—either from governments or from powerful clients.

Based in the United States and Western Europe, Reuters, the AP, UPI, and AFP span the whole range of general-interest news reporting from summit conferences to college sports, from airline crashes to humorous fillers. Each works independently of the others, but much of their information covers the same events in broadly similar style. Their main concern is for the speedy reporting of immediate news, known in the trade as "spot news." In addition, they provide feature articles, explanatory background pieces, descriptive accounts of places and people, and other material ranging from Hollywood gossip to weather forecasts. In their wholesale role, they supply news and features to the press, radio, and television, but they also sell their services directly to government departments, companies, international organizations, and anyone else who needs a twenty-four-hour service of immediate news and is willing to pay the price.

In addition to their general-interest textual files, the major agencies have built up a series of other services during their 150 years of existence. The two American agencies, the AP and UPI, have dominated the supply of international news pictures around the world, though their monopoly is now being challenged by the two European-based services. London-based Reuters is a shareholder in one major international television newsfilm agency, and UPI held a stake in another for sixteen years. The AP, UPI, and the French AFP are the basic domestic news-reporting organizations in their respective countries. Reuters, followed at considerable distance by the American agencies, has developed into a major supplier of specialized financial and commodity news to banks, foreign exchange dealers, companies, and official institutions, which has increasingly set it apart from its competitors.

Despite this wide range of activities, the supply of textual news to the international media remains the core of the agencies' international operations as a whole, and is the main subject of this book. A subscriber taking all four agency services would, in many areas of the world, receive more than 300,000 words a day in English, French, Spanish, German, or Arabic. Since one twenty-four-hour file of international news may run to 90,000 words—far too much for any newspaper or broadcasting station to use or for any government to store in its files—the agencies do not expect the bulk of their output to be used by most subscribers. Important stories will of course be picked up all over the world, but many others are transmitted to meet the local needs of a few clients. This does not mean that the agencies are conforming to the parochial patterns of most of their subscribers; to the contrary, they meet the needs not of just one national audience but of *each* national audience, one after another. Their concern for local requirements is worldwide.

The four agencies exist to serve markets, whether it is the global market for news of an event of international interest or the restricted market for coverage of a story of local or national significance. Their international operations are conducted on a commercial basis, although—paradoxically—they frequently operate in ways not calculated to maximize profits. Their prime concern is with the rich media markets of the United States, Western Europe, and Japan, and increasingly with the business community, which requires fast information services that can be used to make money. While the agencies' commercial nature orients them toward the more prosperous parts of the world, their scope remains as global as governments and economics allow them to be. Their raison d'être is to report and sell their news wherever they can, but this effort has pushed them into a degree of competition and uneconomical operations no truly commercial enterprise would accept. The result has been a substantial disproportion between the responsibilities the four agencies have assumed and the resources at their disposal, a disequilibrium that contributes significantly to the inadequacies of today's world information flow. The agencies are all too easily assumed to have powers and responsibilities that in fact they have never had—and do not seek. Little effort has been expended to date on painting a more accurate picture of just what the Big Four are and what they are not.

As worldwide collectors and suppliers of news, the four agencies are surprisingly frail. Their total combined staffs, at home and abroad, amount to only around 10,000 employees, of which some 4500 work outside the home countries of their respective agencies. Well under half this overseas total consists of journalists; the rest are technical, managerial, and sales staff. As a result, the agencies are ill-equipped to cover the whole world in any depth. Correspondents are concentrated in those places where news of greatest interest to the widest range of clients occurs. The result of this application of the commercial market approach to news is that an agency may well have

9

more staff reporters in a single major European country than in the whole of black Africa. With all four competing agencies following the same pattern, the geographical imbalance of their combined reporting sources is huge.

Similarities among the Big Four agencies enable critics to see them as a monolithic bloc, made all the more sinister by their common values and U.S.–Western European headquarters. But each of the four puts more store by its independence than by any professional clannishness. As editor of Reuters' world service from 1974 to 1977, this writer never met the chief editors at the AP or UPI. Each agency stands on its own, even if it shares a philosophy of independent news-gathering and distribution with the other three. The "gang of four" is a collection of highly individualistic organizations with differing strengths and weaknesses.

The two U.S. agencies, the AP and UPI, compete fiercely in domestic as well as in international news services. In France, AFP dominates the provision of domestic news to the media, but in Britain, Reuters not only does not distribute domestic news, it does not even sell its foreign news directly to the press outside London. Abroad, all four agencies compete energetically in Europe, Asia, and South Africa. In the Middle East, Reuters and AFP run Arabic-language services, while the two U.S. agencies confine themselves to English-language distribution. In black Africa, AFP predominates in French-speaking areas and Reuters in Anglophone countries. Latin America is largely a preserve of the U.S. agencies. Each service sells in the home territory of the others.

Apart from such geographical differences, the agencies also differ in the activities they undertake that are not directly concerned with supplying textual general news to the media. Reuters, established as the leading supplier of news to the business world, earns the vast majority of its revenue outside Britain, while the other agencies draw most of their income from their home countries. News photographs have long been an integral part of AP and UPI operations, but neither European agency went into international pictures on a major scale until 1984. The two U.S. services provide comprehensive text and audio reports for radio stations; AFP does so only on an ad hoc basis; Reuters closed down its service of voice reports for radio stations at the end of the 1970s.

There are differences, too, in forms of ownership. The AP is a cooperative. UPI, a private company, changed hands in 1982 and again moved to modify ownership in 1985. Reuters is a limited-liability British company that was owned mainly by the national and provincial press of the United Kingdom until June 1984, when the big profits earned by its business news services led its owners to decide to float the firm on the London and New York stock exchanges, but with stiff restrictions aimed at ensuring that control would remain with the original proprietors. AFP enjoys the barely fathomable status of a public French organization guaranteed by a parliamentary statute.

These differences have done nothing to affect the portrayal of the four agencies as a group of more or less conscious conspirators exercising worldwide hegemony over the flow of information. To outside critics, it appears inconceivable that four such organizations could exist without being part of a wider scheme to achieve the geopolitical aims of the countries in which they are based. The similarities in their operations, their common North Atlantic background, their reticence and self-protectiveness—all contribute to the picture of the major agencies as the handmaidens of Western domination of the world.

For many years, the agencies functioned happily in semianonymity. They would still prefer to be viewed simply as professional organizations whose journeymen employees pursue a self-imposed code of accuracy and impartiality in the interests of their subscribers—whatever the obstacles put in their way by repressive governments, closed frontiers, expulsions, or refusals to divulge information. (As agency executives point out in private, many of their most vocal critics represent countries that do the least to foster the free flow of information.) But this view of the agencies is today both overly simplistic and outdated; the debate about the way the world is informed has become increasingly politicized. No longer does the subject of information concern only the members of one closed profession; any four organizations that supply 80 percent of the instant international news circulating around the world cannot help but be drawn into a debate that—while they may think it unfair—underscores the importance of their role in today's world.

The World Information Debate . . . .

The current debate on the dissemination of information around the world stems from the poorer nations' realization that the ending of colonialism has not lessened their reliance on the industrialized countries, any more than their political independence has acted as an automatic spur to internal progress or external power. As long as this situation exists, the debate is likely to continue.

The weakness of newly independent nations is most evident in political and economic terms. Their numerical strength has not modified the East-West power balance. Much talk about the need to forge new North-South relationships has so far led to few concrete results. Political and economic power remains firmly rooted in the Northern Hemisphere. The nations of the South find their importance as raw-materials producers unmatched by any real growth in wealth or influence. As the 1980 Independent Commission on International Development Issues (the Brandt commission) noted:

> All the efforts of international organizations and the meetings of the major powers have not been able to give hope to developing countries of escaping from poverty, or to reshape and revive the international economy to make it more responsive to the needs of both developing and industrialised countries.[5]

While economic weakness and political impotence have constituted their main concern, the developing nations grew increasingly anxious in the 1970s about what they saw as their growing dependence on Western nations in the field of culture. Alien influences, they believed, were swamping national identities and sucking them into a cultural system directed from a few rich countries for motives of commercial profit. In its most obvious form, the cultural invasion from the West could be summed up in pictures of children in Africa wearing Mickey Mouse T-shirts or poor Asian villagers watching the adventures of *Starsky and Hutch* on their communal television sets. At a deeper level lay the fear that Western films, television programs, and consumer goods could create a pattern of dependence that would make it even more difficult for poor and weak nations to develop properly on their own terms and to escape their subordinate position in the world. To some, it seemed that free exchange of cultural information and products would result only in the wiping out of essential parts of the national identities of poor countries by seductive ideas, images, and behavior models exported from the West. It was not simply a matter of books, movies, or music; Amadou Mahtar M'Bow, director-general of the United Nations Educational, Scientific, and Cultural Organization (UNESCO), sweepingly characterized culture as "the sum total of people's creative activities, its methods of production and of appropriation of material assets, its form of organization, its beliefs and sufferings, its work and leisure, its dreams and success.'' Such an approach made the defense of a country's culture from harmful foreign influences a key element in the preservation of national identity.[6]

Concern about cultural dependence quite naturally spilled over into concern about communications—including the previously largely neglected subject of the communication of news. Given its obvious political and economic impact, it was surprising that the international news flow had not been identified earlier by leaders of the developing nations as one possible cause of their problems. Internally, most of these leaders, after gaining power, had shown that they fully understood the significance of news by ensuring that their countries' press and broadcasting services fostered national objectives. Having often used the press as a weapon in the struggle for independence, they were well aware of its political potential. International news, on the other hand, did not come under scrutiny in any serious way until the early 1970s. Once it had emerged as a subject for concern, however, it soon became firmly established as a major topic of meetings at UNESCO and other forums designed to chart ways in which the unbalanced world could be made into a better place for more of its member states. By the 1980s, officials at UNESCO headquarters in Paris and in most of the organization's member states spoke of the need for a new world information order as an accepted fact of life, a needed accompaniment to new political and economic orders.

Their reasoning was simple. The developing world's case for a fairer deal appeared to them self-evident, yet it was getting nowhere. Ninety percent of the globe's manufacturing capacity remained in the North, while some thirty countries of the South had an average per capita annual income of under $200. The director-general of the Food and Agriculture Organization (FAO) warned that the number of undernourished and hungry people in Africa could double in the first half of the 1980s. The extent of such disparities, and the urgent need to do something about them, was not fully appreciated in the rich nations, to which would fall the responsibility of making the necessary concessions. It must be that the poor nations' case was being presented poorly—or not being presented at all. The developing countries were suffering from portrayal as incapable, corrupt, and coup-ridden, unworthy of help and largely responsible for their own predicaments. A distorting mirror had been set up between the poor and the rich countries by the media of the industrialized world, it was argued.

If an information failure could be blamed for a failure in international understanding, it could be blamed as well for the inability
of the developing nations to form an effective, united front on anything but the most general principles. Despite their broad common
concerns and interests, the developing nations often seemed to be
more divided than united. This, the new theorists of world information
believed, could be chalked up to a lack of accurate and sympathetic
information circulating among the developing countries. Not only
was the Western-dominated information system producing hostile
reporting of the poor nations for the media of the industrialized world,
it was propagating a similar picture to the developing nations themselves. If the peoples of the poor nations adopted Western forms of
behavior and abandoned traditional cultures in favor of imported,
commercial models, this, again, could be attributed to the lack of
strong information and entertainment systems within their societies.
The distorting mirror reached worldwide, and the need for a new
world information system appeared inescapable.

To create such a system, the strengthening of poor countries' access
to communications technologies was of obvious importance, but on
its own this would be insufficient. What was needed was a system
under which the contents of messages transmitted and received by
poor states would be specifically designed to aid their national development, strengthen the unity of the nonaligned movement, and
protect national cultures and societies from alien ideological domination. Information could no longer be regarded as a commercial
commodity, with its collection and distribution decided by the marketplace where unevenly distributed demands had led to distortions that
were now to be swept away. Instead, information was seen as a tool
to be used for the predetermined purposes of its originators. It should
be regulated according to their wider aims. Meeting in Lima, Peru,
in 1975, foreign ministers from the association of nonaligned nations,
known as "Group 77" from its original membership total, set the
tone by calling for concerted action "to exchange and disseminate
information on mutual national achievements." They urged "measures to accelerate the process of collective acquisition of communications satellites and to prepare a code of conduct which regulates
their utilisation." From the start, regulation and promotion of political
purposes went hand in hand.

The following year, nonaligned leaders deplored "a situation of
dependence and domination in which the majority of countries are

reduced to being passive recipients of biased, inadequate and distorted information.'' Meeting in Sri Lanka, they further declared that

> the emancipation and development of national information media is an integral part of the overall struggle for political, economic and social independence for a large majority of the peoples of the world who should not be denied the right to inform and be informed objectively and correctly. Self-reliance in sources of information is as important as technological self-reliance since dependence in the field of information in turn retards the very achievement of political and economic growth.

The extent to which all nonaligned nations went along fully with the more vocal advocates of a new world information order is questionable, but any doubts harbored at Lima or at subsequent meetings were kept private as the information debate gathered steam. Suggestions that there might be divergent views within Group 77, now consisting of more than a hundred nations, were dismissed as Western maneuvering and proof of the need to regulate the press to ensure that it behaved responsibly.[7] The picture was clearly drawn: the Western media, lacking sympathy with the developing nations, were (consciously or not) bolstering the inequalities of the world through their reporting. The countries of the Northern Hemisphere were exercising ''an information dictatorship'' over the South, as a leading advocate of change, Christopher Nascimento of Guyana, told UNESCO's general conference in November 1983.

The question of state dictatorship of national media, which has become a fact of life in a country like Guyana, was brushed aside. M'Bow of UNESCO refused to answer reporters' questions after one of the organization's conferences when he was asked about the absence of press freedom in UNESCO member states. Critics of the existing state of affairs had no time for Western eulogies of the commercial media systems of North America, Western Europe, and Japan. Pointing to the United States, Nascimento told the UNESCO conference:

> ''Pluralism'' and ''free expression'' cannot be convincingly preached by a country in which single commercial monopoly ownership and control of the daily newspaper exists in 96% of its cities and three major commercial networks dominate television viewing.

Not only were the Western media held to be hypocritical, their news approach, with its concentration on what would immediately interest the public, was judged to be ill-suited to the job of explaining the gradual development of economically emerging societies. Reporters from social, professional, and cultural backgrounds in North America or Western Europe could not possibly understand Africa, Latin America, or Asia, and were bound to present superficial reports. The Western emphasis on the journalism of exception, in which the unusual is reported and the routine ignored, led to the highlighting of a few spectacular but unfortunate events and a disregard for more positive but less dramatic aspects of the development of poor nations, according to critics of Western news "imperialism." A revolution in the way the poor nations were reported, both in the rest of the world and among themselves, was required.

Western media organizations were broadly ready to admit that their coverage of the developing world was less than perfect, but this did not mean that they were prepared to accept the criticisms and conclusions of advocates of a new world information order. "The Third World doesn't understand how the northern press works, but we did ignore them for too long," remarked Katharine Graham of the *Washington Post* in 1984. Henri Pigeat, chairman of AFP, recognizes "the legitimate demand of newly-formed states to develop their national communications resources," but he immediately adds:

> Unfortunately, political and ideological factors quickly obscured what should in fact have been a mutually enriching exchange. The result has been a conflict in which the agencies were easily singled out as scapegoats: valued freedoms have been ignored and, alas, often threatened.

As will be seen, the reporting by the major suppliers of news from the developing world is a great deal less negative than critics surmised. Nor do major news agencies force-feed poor nations with as much unwanted, "culturally alien" news as was often supposed. But it was still the case that the world was told more about what was going on in the richer democracies than in the poor South or the Communist nations. There were good reasons for this state of affairs, as will be seen in later chapters, relating to the availability of information, market demands, communications facilities, and the simple fact that decisions made in Washington or a major West European capital are likely to be more important to more people around the globe than events in a small, weak country in Africa, Asia, or Latin America.

Western editors do not like to parade such reasoning in public. In the atmosphere generated by debates in UNESCO and similar bodies, it is difficult to stand up and say baldly that a large number of countries in the world are of only marginal interest to the audiences who determine news choices for most independent newspapers and broadcasting stations. At the same time, Western news organizations felt a need to join in the information debate. Otherwise, they feared that the stage would be monopolized by those who wanted to make news part of a drive to reorder the world.

This was an understandable concern, but the debate was flawed from the start by the reluctance of spokesmen for the press in democratic countries to state clearly that their whole approach to reporting the world had little or nothing to do with achieving greater equity between nations or a more quantitatively balanced news flow. To have said that they considered the press the best judge of its own responsibilities would have been to invite condemnation as a self-regulating oligarchy that needed to be brought to heel in the interests of international understanding. Western media, feeling on the defensive from the start of the information debate in the mid-1970s, were in no mood to court such condemnation.

This meant that the long-running discussion on the way the world was informed was conducted in terms laid down by the proponents of change. The need for a new "order" gained wide acceptance, even by those who disliked the word and doubted whether much good would result from its translation into practice. The debate shifted from whether a new order was needed into whether such an order should be imposed or should evolve gradually. UNESCO met criticisms of its supposed partiality for governmental, "statist" ideas by challenging its accusers to find any document that showed it encouraging state control of the media. (Skeptics might have pointed to the time and effort it took to get UNESCO conferences to adopt such apparently straightforward steps as condemnation of censorship or recognition of the watchdog role of the media.)

UNESCO's protestations were beside the point. The basic problem was that the discussion of a new world information order, carried out largely by government representatives and members of state-influenced news organizations, went into an area where, in the democratic press tradition, government had no business intervening. This did not necessarily mean bad faith on the part of those who wanted to draw up guidelines for the reordering of the world's media. But the two sides were never on the same wavelength, and a failure of commu-

17

nication could only result, which was ironic enough in view of the subject under discussion. To take one example, the 1970s and 1980s saw sporadic suggestions that international journalists working in danger zones might be issued with special press cards to assure their safety. For humanitarians outside the media, this seemed a naturally good idea. For journalists who knew how little such cards would do to stop a sniper shooting or a mine detonating, such cards might seem an irrelevance. To those concerned about press freedom, they could appear a dangerous measure, since they would be issued by a licensing authority that would then have the power to decide which journalists merited protection and which, by the refusal of a card, should be classed as nonjournalists.

The underlying gap between the UNESCO approach and the democratic press tradition was a factor in pushing the Reagan administration into giving one year's notice of withdrawal from the Paris-based UN agency at the end of 1983. The charges that UNESCO had become "politicized" and that it was badly managed, particularly in budgetary affairs, were also high on the list of complaints that led the United States to go through with its withdrawal decision at the end of 1984. Similar reasons lay behind Britain's decision to give one year's notice of withdrawal from UNESCO unless it saw significant improvement by the end of 1985. Other Western European countries such as West Germany, Holland, Switzerland, and Denmark also expressed unhappiness with the way UNESCO was run and with its catchall program, which seemed too thinly spread, too ideological, and not sufficiently monitored for concrete results. In February 1985, Japan, the second biggest contributor to UNESCO after the U.S. withdrawal, warned that it would have to reconsider its relations with the organization if reforms were not introduced by the end of the year.

In response to the complaints, UNESCO director-general M'Bow and his supporters pointed their fingers, in part, at the Western press. Speaking during a meeting of UNESCO's executive board in February 1985, M'Bow spoke of "an unprecedented press campaign that certain journalists have led against the organisation and its director-general, dishonouring their profession by the methods they have used and the channels they have chosen." M'Bow said he and UNESCO had been the target of rumors and inventions that had not even spared his family or his religious convictions. UNESCO hired a Washington public relations firm to act on its behalf, for $15,000 a month. This was paid from a special fund which received some of its money from

18

UNESCO's share in the proceeds of records sold in France to raise cash for cancer research. Asked about the ethics of this, UNESCO spokesmen contented themselves with saying that they were not breaking any regulations. In February 1985, UNESCO suspended the compilation of its long-standing daily review of international press reports and comment about the organization. It was a cost-cutting measure, but it could be taken as symbolic of the divorce that had grown up between Western news media and the UN agency meant to promote international intellectual progress.

M'Bow's reactions to critical reporting had been particularly sharpened by a series of detailed articles published by the French newspaper *Le Monde* at the end of 1984. The director-general, himself, sent a lengthy, but none too precise, refutation to *Le Monde,* accompanied by point-by-point answers from one of his assistants to the main criticisms in the newspaper's series. *Le Monde* ran detailed answers to the answers and seemed to come out on top of the argument. What was striking was the lengths to which M'Bow went in this exchange. It appeared that, while he had come to expect criticism from the press in the United States and Britain, he was taken aback to find that he and UNESCO could no longer command the sympathy of a newspaper known for its traditional support of causes championed by his organization.

The threats which the Western press saw in the new world information order promoted by UNESCO have made newspapers pay fresh attention to the Paris-based organization. UNESCO's 51-nation executive board, which previously attracted little attention outside devoted followers of the organization, attracted regular coverage from the early 1980s on. UNESCO's internal workings became the subject of front-page stories in the *International Herald Tribune,* which made a point of tracking the organization's moves closely and giving them prominent coverage. In the United States, what was regarded as UNESCO's hostility toward the Western press model became the yardstick by which the UN agency was generally judged. Elaborating on the reasons for U.S. withdrawal, the assistant secretary of state for multinational organizations, Gregory Newell, said that UNESCO's support for "statist theories," which stress governmental control over individual rights, was shown by the drive for a new information and communications order. "Their programs," he added, "have been focused on codes, ethics, licensing of journalists and basically all that translates into government censorship and government control of the media."

Newell could go too far. His charge, at a press conference in March 1984, that there had been no development of communications by UNESCO in practical, concrete terms was unfounded, since UNESCO had established a program to back concrete practical communications projects, following a Carter administration initiative. UNESCO could, equally, point to the fact that it had pulled back from suggestions of establishing an international press card, a change endorsed by an internal report, not made public by M'Bow, which concluded that the working conditions of journalists was not a suitable subject for the Paris-based organization.

Such arguments were as likely to be effective as the workings of the Western press were likely to be understood by M'Bow, who, speaking to the present writer, once lumped together the Soviet news agency, TASS, and the British Broadcasting Corporation as similar state organizations. Everybody might agree, as a matter of principle, that practical measures to develop information media in poor countries were a good thing. But the philosophical differences between supporters of independent, commercial media practices in democracies and those who see news as being too important to be left to the marketplace are so basic that real agreement is impossible. Advocates of the Western media model are bound to feel increasingly frustrated at trying to navigate within channels whose borders were determined by recognition of state interests.

As a British spokesman, Lord Nicholas Gordon Lennox, warned a UNESCO conference in 1982: "Our own experience has shown that attempts to fix principles or guidelines in this area, far from providing a basis for common understanding, are likely to divide nations from one another." That sensible observation did nothing to diminish the conviction of a majority of UNESCO member states that, in M'Bow's words during a visit to Nigeria a month after receiving the U.S. notice of withdrawal, "from now on, the arrival of a new world information and communication order, whatever its nature might be, seems to be an irreversible process."

The search for culprits for the failings of the old information order quickly latched onto the main international news agencies. Although not usually identified by name, the Big Four were soon the prime targets of a stream of speeches and declarations denouncing the monopolistic grip on the world's information exercised by what M'Bow described as "a tightly-knit group of professionals or technocrats who hold populations so to speak at their mercy and can direct if not manipulate them at will." [8]

While emphatically denying such allegations, the four major agencies cannot escape the fact that they are suspect, as both reporters and distributors of news, to those who see a need for a fundamental change in the world information system. The agencies share in all those aspects of the Western-originated approach to news that many governments in the Third World find so objectionable, such as oversimplification, lack of detailed explanation, and highlighting of the exceptional. Indeed, because of the speed at which they work and the pressures arising from their limited resources, they can seem to represent the Western system at its most extreme. A newspaper correspondent posted to an African country can leave the capital for a week or two to produce in-depth reports on development projects; a news agency reporter usually has to stay in the city to report on the daily flow of immediate events. The newspaper correspondent writes his in-depth reports knowing that they are assured of a place in the single paper he works for; the agency reporter has to produce a news report that is immediately understandable and attractive to thousands of subscribers with hundreds of other demands on their time and interests.

The agencies' worldwide distribution exacerbates their exposure. For the most part, reports from foreign correspondents of newspapers or broadcasting stations reach only national audiences, and usually only part of those audiences. Stories from the four main agencies, on the other hand, go to the media, governments, international organizations, and other subscribers all over the world. Not only is their distribution uniquely wide, it is also extremely fast. A government in Asia may not learn for days about a newspaper correspondent's dispatches transmitted to the United States, printed there, and relayed back by the country's embassy in Washington. A news-agency story is likely to come up on the teleprinter in the government's information office within an hour of being filed or even, in cases of urgent news, within minutes. The speed of transmission does not alter the contents of the message, but it can easily heighten the sensitivity of a government that sees reports of a coup attempt on its teleprinters even as rebel soldiers are storming the presidential palace.[9]

It is therefore inevitable that the major agencies have become central figures in the continuing debate about the way the world is informed, and especially about the flow of news to and from developing countries. In the process, they have come to be regarded as bearing responsibilities they have never claimed and as having duties

21

akin to those of governmental or humanitarian international organizations. Yet despite the criticism that has developed in the past decade, no alternative has emerged. A dozen national news agencies produce news services especially for international distribution; others send their domestic news files overseas in exchange deals between national agencies. The main motivation is political, most overtly in the case of TASS of the Soviet Union and the Chinese agency, Hsinhua, but also in the foreign distribution activities of national agencies in Western Europe.

Even a cursory reading of the world's press makes it plain that neither the state agencies of the major Communist powers nor the domestic agencies of countries like West Germany, Japan, Spain, or Italy come anywhere near to attracting an international clientele similar to that taken for granted by the Big Four. Nor is there any sign that they are likely to do so in the future. Indeed, there is little indication that the more commercially minded of the smaller international agencies *want* to expand on a major scale, since the global market for the kind of services that they, and the Big Four, produce is already saturated. The question for the 1980s, therefore, is not whether major new sources of international news will emerge, but whether the existing four major services will continue in the role they have played so far. Already there are distinct signs of changing outlooks and emphases as economic realities lead the Big Four to revise historical assumptions. Whatever its outcome, the current debate on the flow of world news and the simultaneous development of the major agencies will have a significant bearing on the information that modern technology sends racing around the globe.

CHAPTER 2 ....

Origins

The nature of the major news agencies was fixed at the start of their history.[1] Their appearance has changed radically over 150 years, but their basic characteristics were established in the era of carrier pigeons and hand-delivered bulletins. An editorial philosophy that professed objectivity and neutrality was a precondition for survival; from the beginning, the agencies had to be one thing to all people, operating within the status quo and avoiding involvement in the events they reported.

On the business side, the major news agencies began to defy commercial logic in their first decades, and have gone on doing so ever since. Their long-range inability to make an acceptable profit from selling news of general interest internationally was obvious by 1870. So was the agencies' determination to continue with an inherently loss-making operation, an ethos that still marks them more than a century later.

The European entrepreneurs and New York newspaper bosses who founded the first agencies between 1835 and 1850 did not intend it to be that way. Their aims in establishing the Agence Havas in France, the Associated Press in New York, Wolff's agency in Berlin, and Reuters in London were clear and businesslike: the Europeans were out to make money, the New Yorkers to cut news-gathering costs. High-minded thoughts of making the world a better-informed place in order to promote international understanding did not enter their calculations.

The Europeans reasoned that, as newspapers grew in numbers and circulation, there would be room for wholesalers of news, each acting on behalf of a large number of separate publications. By selling the same items of news many times over to regular clients, the agencies would be able to offer attractive subscription rates, well below what coverage would cost newspapers acting on their own. The resulting high volume and a steadily expanding market would cover the agencies' expenses and produce a worthwhile profit margin as well.

In New York, the founders of the AP were spurred to action by a recurrent item on their newspapers' expenditure sheets: the costs of bringing foreign news down from Nova Scotia and the far northern U.S. ports, where it arrived packed in canisters aboard boats sailing from Europe. Telegraph tolls were high. Since the news each paper got was much the same, the competitive advantages were small. In 1848, thirteen years after the establishment in Paris of Agence Havas, the first European agency, the leaders of the New York press pooled their resources in a cooperative venture to save money by transmitting foreign news jointly from the northern ports.[2]

Their Associated Press, which soon began to handle domestic news as well, was in every way a child of the press. It belonged to the newspapers that used its services. Member papers exchanged news and jointly met the association's costs; competing nonmembers were not permitted access to the service. Later generations of AP executives would hail this as the purest form of news agency, in which the press served itself cooperatively with no concern other than mutual professionalism. More realistically, the main attraction of cooperation in the association's early days was the news monopoly it offered its members.

In Europe, on the other hand, the founders of the major agencies came from outside the press. Charles-Louis Havas was a translator, Bernhard Wolff, a doctor, and Paul Julius Reuter, a book publisher, before they embarked on news-agency work. The services they created were sold to newspapers, but their companies remained independent of the press. Subscribers enjoyed none of the control that AP members exercised over the running of their agency. Far from excluding possible subscribers, the Europeans' aim was to sell their news as widely as possible. Lacking the AP's cooperative financing, they were constantly in search of fresh revenues and displayed all the diversity typical of nineteenth-century venture capitalism. Charles-Louis Havas had made and lost a fortune as a contractor to Napoleon's armies before his translation work led him to found the first modern news agency. Later in the century, the first Baron Reuter combined running the world's biggest news agency with negotiating a concession to exploit Persia's mineral rights.[3] For such men, establishing a news service, fascinating as it might be, was a way of exercising a talent for business. News was a means, not an end.

Despite the different forms that their agencies took, the founders in New York and Europe shared some basic assumptions. Without these, the agencies either would not have been launched at all or would have taken on a very different shape. Basic to the establishment of the nineteenth-century news services was the belief that a single satisfactory report could be provided to a large number of recipients whose politics, editorial values, and publication schedules differed widely. It is a belief that remains critical to the agencies today, and it lies at the root of much of the criticism of the major news services in the 1980s. The agencies do not issue one service for conservative newspapers and another for the left. They distribute a single account of each event. This has been a constant of agency operations for 150 years. When Charles-Louis Havas set up his agency in 1835, he supplied the same items to reactionaries and reformists alike. Today, his successors at Agence France-Presse provide the same coverage for subscribers in Peking and Pretoria.

To achieve such wide acceptability, the agencies avoid overt partiality. Demonstrably correct information is their stock in trade. Traditionally, they report at a reduced level of responsibility, attributing their information to spokesmen, the press, or other sources. They avoid making judgments and steer clear of doubt and ambiguity. Though their founders did not use the word, objectivity is the philosophical basis for their enterprises—or, failing that, widely acceptable neutrality.

Early on, this approach conferred on the agencies a particular legitimacy as independent suppliers of the world's news, free of the distorting mirror of opinion. It also had the outstanding commercial advantage of enabling them to reach a far wider market than would have been possible with a more partisan approach. By remaining neutral, quoting others, and avoiding political entanglement, the agency founders could reasonably hope to avoid alienating either subscribers or cooperative members. Their news could go to newspapers of all persuasions, and there would be no incentive for political parties or interest groups to form agencies of their own. Official complaints and pressure could more easily be met if the services were able to show that they simply reported demonstrably correct facts and put forth no opinions of their own. Ideally, they would be invisible, inert transmission channels between sources of information and paying clients or agency members. The lower their profile, the wider their potential audience.

The news services came into being at a time of expansion in the press on both sides of the Atlantic. It was assumed that the newspaper industry would continue to provide the growing, structured market essential for the development of wide-ranging international agencies. The AP was protected by its cooperative financing, but the profit-seeking European agencies soon found it hard to balance the costs of their fast-developing coverage with available new sources of revenue. Reporting expenditure was likely to increase unexpectedly under the pressure of events. Cable tolls were high. International revenues, on the other hand, were limited by geographical, linguistic, and economic factors—and by competition among the major commercial agencies. Before long, it became clear that the scale on which the agencies reported was incompatible with the economics their clients had come to take for granted. Problems that were to return to haunt the agencies in the 1970s and 1980s were already very much alive more than a century earlier. The founders' optimistic equation proved to be lopsided in practice.

Despite such difficulties, the European style of private, commercial news agencies was to dominate the world for a century after the establishment of the Agence Havas in Paris in 1835, leaving the cooperative model isolated on the other side of the Atlantic. The reasons were partly geographical and political, partly institutional. Europe was still the center of the world. The attention of the United States was focused on internal development and away from the preoccupation with international power politics that characterized the European countries and their news agencies. The New York AP was content to receive its foreign news through the European agencies and to supply them with its coverage of the United States for distribution abroad. The cooperative's one international move—to send a representative to London to select European copy close to the source—was prompted by competition from a breakaway press association in Chicago rather than by any inherent feeling that the AP should be present overseas.

Apart from the continental insularity of nineteenth-century America, the AP faced a basic institutional problem if it was going to develop into a world agency. Its cooperative structure was workable within a single nation, but how well would it function if the association began to gather and distribute news of its own internationally? For the European agencies, there was no such difficulty; they sold their services wherever they found buyers. But if the AP cooperative were to spread to include European members, this would inevitably produce major changes in the character of the agency, wresting it out of the monopolistic control of its North American newspapers.

Such questions are unlikely to have troubled the early directors of the AP, who were more concerned with fighting off challenges from aggrieved nonmembers and building up a professional journalistic service than with international expansion. Their hold on European agency copy sent to North America was complete, and there was no competition in sight strong enough to induce them to report the rest of the world's news on their own. Such a comfortable position could only reinforce the essentially inward-looking character of their association, and leave the world open to the Europeans.

Havas: The First Founder . . . .

Foreign news, appropriately enough, inspired Charles-Louis Havas to set up his agency. He had enjoyed a connection with the press in his early days of glory under Napoleon, owning shares in the major newspaper of the day, the *Gazette de France,* but this had been a strictly secondary interest compared with his money-making activities as a financier and supplier to the imperial army. After Napoleon's defeat at Waterloo ruined him, Havas was thrown back on using his extensive linguistic knowledge to translate extracts from foreign newspapers for the French press and private clients. By 1832, he had built up enough of a reputation to launch a regular news bulletin under the motto ''Fast and Good.'' Three years later, having absorbed several competitors, he opened the Agence Havas.

The idea of distributing information bulletins was by no means new. In the Middle Ages, European merchant houses had sent their clients newsletters reporting the latest significant events. What was different about Havas was that he supplied his information to the press, to be passed on to the public as the newspapers saw fit. He maintained deliveries to some private clients, but his prime targets were the French newspapers, which were enjoying a period of expansion and international-mindedness in the early, liberal years of King Louis Philippe's rule. Then, as now, most newspapers lacked the resources and organization to collect foreign news themselves on a regular basis. But they could not let their coverage of the world go by default. With his daily service of foreign news, to which he added reports of official French pronouncements, Havas filled the gap.

A mere bulletin service was not enough for the new agency. Receiving foreign newspapers in Paris, selecting and translating significant items, and then distributing them to subscribers was a slow and cumbersome business. To increase speed and efficiency, Havas appointed representatives in the main European capitals to monitor the press on the spot and provide Paris with texts and summaries already translated into French. To get the reports of these first international agency correspondents to Paris as quickly as possible, Havas used a combination of mail coaches, couriers, carrier pigeons, and, after its introduction in France in the 1840s, the telegraph. His pre-cable arrangements enabled him to supply the Paris papers at noon with information from the morning's Belgian press. News from London followed at 3:00 P.M.

The French press reacted enthusiastically, and by 1840 the Havas service went to all the Paris newspapers, as well as to government offices and commercial companies. Havas delivered to the provinces by mail coach. He launched into foreign distribution by buying an agency that sold German-language news across the Rhine. The value of the service was officially recognized when a copy of his overnight report was ordered for the prime minister to ensure that he started each day properly informed.

The favorable opinion of the government was important for the new agency. Journalism was still a chancy profession in much of continental Europe; in France alone, 520 judicial actions against journalists were initiated between 1830 and 1834. Governments had come to appreciate the political power of the press. Days of liberalization were followed by nights of repression. To a man of Havas's basic commercial motivation, there was no point in running a news agency only to risk being shut down by stepping out of line. In any case, Havas had no political drum to beat as he developed the earliest application of news-agency neutrality. Avoiding official disfavor became a cardinal consideration. In part this could be achieved by ensuring that the agency reported only what others said or wrote and keeping itself back from the battlefront. But it is also apparent that Havas felt a need to conform to the status quo regardless of what administration was in power. It was a tendency that was to run all through news-agency history.

How carefully Charles-Louis Havas actually selected his news to please successive French governments is unclear. What is certain is that, in addition to avoiding repression and harassment, he drew useful nonpress revenue from the services he sold to government offices and departmental prefectures. In theory, such sales need not have affected the agency's editorial judgments. In practice, as his successors discovered a century later, governments frequently found it difficult to disclaim the right to oversee reports in return for their financial support. Other European agencies would make this blatantly apparent later in the nineteenth century, and, given the links between the press and politicians in France at the time, it would be surprising if Havas had not paid some editorial price for the revenue he earned from the state. The administration certainly believed there was a link; an official note of 1841 referred to the agency as being "placed under the auspices" of the Interior Ministry. At about the same time, Balzac delivered his opinion that "M. Havas has seen many governments, he venerates the Fact and professes little admiration for Principles; so he has served all governments with equal faithfulness." Havas probably took the novelist's criticism as a compliment.[4]

Money and protection were not all that French governments had to offer the young agency. Havas's bulletins were given preferential treatment in the mails, and the agency enjoyed similar privileges when the telegraph system was introduced in France as a state monopoly. Such technical assistance was particularly important because of the advances in communications that marked the mid-nineteenth century. The growth of international news agencies would have been impossible without the extension of the telegraph system, both within nations and, more importantly, across Europe. Initially, however, the cable was used only for reporting the news; distribution by telegraph was far too expensive.

As it was, the costs of transmitting lengthy newspaper extracts and reports from Havas's own correspondents abroad began to weigh on the agency's finances. Clients had come to expect more and more information, delivered faster and faster. What had been a breakthrough in 1835 was taken for granted by the time Charles-Louis Havas handed over the reins of the agency to his sons in 1853. The daily bulletin now consisted of three sheets of four columns each, covering foreign and domestic events, stock market news, and official announcements. Special sheets were rushed into print when important news broke. The Crimean War of 1853–56 provided the agency with a series of sensational scoops and one spectacular mistake when, on the evidence of a Tartar riding from the battlefield, Havas wrongly announced the fall of the great Russian fortress at Sevastopol. Such was the agency's standing that the report was immediately accepted. This was only the first of several occasions on which news-agency errors produced premature outbreaks of wartime rejoicing.

Still, the agency's future looked secure. Newspapers were increasingly crediting its reports by name in special columns of "telegraphic dispatches." Two hundred provincial publications received the service at midcentury, while foreign sales now stretched far beyond the Rhineland to Rome and St. Petersburg. But the Second Empire of Napoleon III brought an official crackdown on the press in the 1850s, and the surviving newspapers appear to have been unable, or unwilling, to bear the costs that Havas was incurring with its telegraphic reporting from all over Europe. Revenue from selling news was no longer enough to keep the company going. Havas was forced to look for other sources of funds, establishing another pattern that was to run through news-agency history.

Charles-Louis Havas's sons took the agency into advertising. The move was prompted by self-protection as well as the need for money; a competing agency had appeared, offering newspapers a free news bulletin if they would let it handle the sale of their advertising space. In 1857, Havas came to an agreement with the competitor, and the two established a joint company based on simple but highly effective principles. Newspapers needed the news Havas supplied. They also needed advertisements. An organization that could supply both on a national basis had a winning formula. Under the new arrangement, newspapers received the Havas service in return for their agreement that the advertising enterprise of Havas, Fauchey, Laffite, Bullier would handle the nonlocal publicity that appeared in their columns. The advertising firm paid the news agency a percentage of its profits. Havas and its associates thus became the prime suppliers of both news and advertising to the French press.

The news agency used its fresh income to expand overseas, particularly into Latin America. It maintained a legally separate status from the advertising company, but the financial interdependence of the two, and their joint power over the French press, made Havas into an organization of formidable authority. But while the new arrangement appeared to solve the problem of financing news collection, it also contained long-term dangers. By introducing an element of subsidy, albeit an in-house one, it undermined the direct equation between news costs and revenues. Havas's earnings now no longer depended on the sale of its news services alone, but on the performance of advertising salesmen in Clermont-Ferrand or Lille as well. If the advertising agency revenue fell below expectations, expenditures for news coverage would be restricted. If it boomed, the men in charge of the joint enterprise might well conclude that it was more profitable to run an advertising business than to devote their energies to the uncertainties of covering current events. As attractive as it looked at the time, the 1857 diversification sowed the seeds for the agency's eventual moral and financial decline.

Germany and Britain: Wolff and Reuter . . . .

Napoleon III's censorship and the escalating cost of telegraphic coverage were not the only reasons for Havas's financial problems in the 1850s. The agency was also facing international competition for the first time. Two men, both of whom learned their craft at the French agency's offices near the Paris Bourse, emerged as Havas's rivals. Bernhard Wolff and Paul Julius Reuter had gone to Paris separately after compromising themselves with the German authorities in the revolutionary year of 1848. Each quickly absorbed the lessons Havas had to teach and returned home to put them into practice.

Initially, Wolff was the more successful. While in Paris, he had developed an interest in the stock market, and on his return to Berlin in 1849 he abandoned his medical career to establish a service of commercial and financial news. Taking advantage of the German states' telegraph systems, Wolff soon spread his service throughout Prussia and its neighbors. In 1855 he added political and other noneconomic news, establishing himself as the dominant provider of information to the German press.

Reuter had a slower start. Before returning to Germany, he tried to initiate a Paris news bulletin in competition with Havas. It flopped. Next, he traveled to the German border city of Aachen, where he set up a telegraphic "institute" to receive news over the state line from Berlin. From the start, Reuter insisted on one basic principle: that all clients should receive the news at the same time. Critics suggested that this was a rule that Havas, ready to give priority treatment to subscribers who paid over the odds, did not always observe. But Reuter made a virtue of his virtue, going as far as to lock his Aachen clients in his office when the Berlin stock market prices arrived so that they would all get the news simultaneously.

When the telegraphic line from Paris was extended to Brussels, Reuter set up, between the German and Belgian cableheads, a carrier pigeon system that became a legend. He was by no means the first man to use pigeons to carry news; Havas had done so in France, as had the AP in the United States. But the carrier pigeons became so strongly identified with the name of Reuter that one of his distant descendants expressed surprise at not seeing a commemorative bird or two in the agency's newsroom 125 years later.

Technological progress soon caught up with Reuter. The Belgian, French, and German telegraph lines were joined at the end of 1850, making Reuter and his pigeons redundant. Wolff's Berlin Telegraph Company dominated Germany, and Reuter had to look elsewhere. "When Mrs. Reuter . . . complained to me about this destruction of their business," the German telegraphic pioneer Werner Seimens recalled, "I advised the pair to go to London and to start a cable agency there." [5] The timing was perfect. Reuter established his London office just in time to take advantage of the opening of the first telegraph cable between Britain and France. Skeptics thought the line would be destroyed by a stray ship's anchor or snapped in the jaws of a deep-water fish. Reuter was sanguine, and his motto "follow the cable" was put into practice when the Dover-Calais service began at the end of 1851. London, the world's commercial center, was now linked by telegraph with the cable systems of continental Europe.

The free-trade atmosphere in Britain at midcentury suited Reuter admirably. As in Aachen, his initial business was with the financial community, not the press; the London newspapers, used to getting foreign news from their own sources, resisted his approaches. *The Times,* which dominated the press of the day, was particularly hostile, fearing that a foreign news agency would undermine the predominant position of its own large and well-organized international reporting network. Financial operators in the city of London, however, quickly realized the benefits to be drawn from Reuters' network of agents spread across the Continent. Reuter reports on the Crimean War did not appear in the British press, but the agency's messenger was cheered in the stock exchange.[6]

Shunned by London newspapers, Reuter branched out across the Channel, establishing offices in Calais and Ostend and forwarding news culled from official British cables to the continental press. Finally, in 1858, one British newspaper, the *Morning Advertiser,* agreed to take his service, paying £30 a month. Other newspapers followed suit, and by the end of the year, even *The Times* had signed up. Reuter made sure that his agency received maximum publicity from its new subscribers; his agreement with *The Times* included a clause under which the newspaper paid half as much for copy attributed to Reuter as for dispatches printed without a credit.

As sensible businessmen faced with the uncertainties inherent in pioneering a new type of enterprise, Havas, Wolff, and Reuter appreciated the value of cooperation. Much of the foreign news they were transmitting was similar, but they were paying separate high cable costs to receive it from their correspondents. To reduce costs, the three agencies signed an exchange agreement in 1856, which allowed each service to depend on the others for coverage of their home countries. The agreement initially involved only financial news, but was extended to include news of general interest after Reuter had signed up the bulk of the British national press. Meeting in Paris in 1859, the three agency heads also agreed to set up joint offices wherever this would be to their advantage, and to "grant each other mutual assistance for the extension and exploitation of telegraphic services, in such a way as to ward off attempts at competition, and to increase services according to the needs of the public, the press, and the development of the electric lines." The Paris pact prohibited the distribution of "political news" by each agency in the home territories of the others, and bound the signatories "to obtain their services in the status quo in which they now find themselves." [7]

As logical as this agreement was, it proved ineffective in maintaining the status quo. The attractions of competition were too great, producing bouts of rivalry that ended in the relegation of Wolff to the position of junior partner and the establishment of the British and French agencies in the dominant international position they were to enjoy for half a century. The most disruptive force was the most entrepreneurial of the agency bosses, Paul Julius Reuter. He was by now firmly established in Britain, having increased his reputation by such innovations as getting an advance copy of a major speech by Napoleon III and running it while the emperor was still speaking.

Unlike Havas and Wolff, Reuter did not distribute domestic news in his home country. A good part of his attention remained firmly fixed on the Continent. After buying an agency in Amsterdam and setting up a joint Belgian operation with Havas, Reuter acquired a concession on a cable link between England and the North German state of Hanover. He used this both to carry messages for others and to deliver commercial news to trading companies in the Baltic ports. This incursion into Wolff's home territory was highly profitable; the third-party transmissions alone earned Reuter a profit of £2000 a month. Then politics entered the picture. Prussia's military victory against Austria in 1866 established its predominance over states like Hanover. Acting as Wolff's patrons, the Berlin authorities made life increasingly difficult for Reuter, who finally closed down all his German operations except for a service to Hamburg, where his news was irreplaceable for companies involved in world trade.

While successfully repelling Reuter in the north, Wolff was faced with a threat from Havas in Berlin itself. The French agency drew up plans in 1865 to open an office in the Prussian capital. France was in an expansive imperial mood; Havas had already made an agreement with the newly formed Italian news agency, Stefani, for an exchange of services. Now, it offered to buy Wolff, a step that would have enabled it to dominate all of Europe.

Wolff felt unable to resist the Havas advances without official help. Kaiser William was sympathetic; possession of a major news agency was becoming a matter of national pride. The kaiser suggested that Wolff address himself to "respected and patriotic financiers," and a consortium was duly formed, headed by Bismarck's banker associate, Gerson Bleichröder. Through a holding company, Continental Telegraph, the consortium pumped capital into Wolff's agency, providing the backing it needed to withstand Havas. Wolff, retained as general manager, served under two chairmen appointed by Bleichröder's group. The German agency had undergone its first decisive change: it was now firmly in the hands of bankers allied with the authoritarian rulers of Prussia.[8]

This official sympathy and financial backing from men of power enabled Wolff's agency to engage in a burst of international competitiveness. It spurned a suggestion by Reuter that the three agencies share the cost of bringing messages across the Atlantic from the New York AP. Instead, the Germans concluded a contract with a rival AP operating in the Midwest. For a short time, there was the prospect of a major agency battle being fought across the ocean, with Havas, Reuter, and the New York AP challenged by the Midwesterners and the Prussians. But the battle ended almost before it had started when the two AP groups patched up their quarrel, depriving Wolff of its transatlantic ally and restoring the New York AP's monopoly of European agency news.

In the Baltic, meanwhile, Reuter was proving incorrigible. From his Hamburg base, he signed agreements to distribute news in Bremen and Denmark. Early in 1869, Bismarck was warned that Reuter and Havas were joining forces to encroach upon the wider German market. In April, the French and British agencies challenged Wolff by threatening to dissolve the news exchange agreement. The international political dimensions involved were reflected in an appeal by one of the Prussian agency's leading figures, Richard Wentzel, for government help as "a matter of serving the fatherland and checking enemy agitation."

After some hesitation, Wolff and the Berlin government concluded a secret agreement in June 1869, which gave the agency state financial assistance and priority for its cables on the Prussian telegraph network. In return, state officials had the right to screen Wolff's political dispatches and to demand the dismissal of any of the staff they considered unsatisfactory. This arrangement, concealed from public knowledge, enabled Continental-Wolff, as the agency was generally known, to repel Havas and Reuter. The price was its metamorphosis into an instrument of German state policy. While the other two agencies reflected the attitudes and aspirations of their home countries, Continental-Wolff was part of German government apparatus. This role does not appear to have caused the editors and managers in Berlin any pain. In 1878, State Secretary Ernst von Bülow noted approvingly that the agency "has always subordinated itself to the political influence of the government in the most loyal and, for the latter, most convenient fashion. It asks the government about every doubtful telegram and unconditionally follows the government's instructions." [9]

Excluded from Germany by the state takeover of Wolff, Havas and Reuter promptly changed tack. A year after threatening to dissolve the tripartite news exchange pact, the French and British agencies signed a much-expanded cooperation agreement with the German service. The aim, Paul Julius Reuter advised his shareholders, was "to avoid expensive competition." [10] In the process, he and the managers of Havas ensured that Continental-Wolff was restricted to Northern and Eastern Europe. The rest of the world, outside of the United States, belonged to the British and French. It was, said a general manager of the AP, the greatest monopoly in the world. [11]

The Cartel . . . .

The agreement reached among the three European agencies in 1870 was accompanied by a grandiose imperial gesture. The signatories drew a series of lines through a map of the world, marking off their protected preserves. Within its area, each enjoyed a monopoly on sales of foreign news and provided coverage for the other two services. A pattern was established that was to last until the 1920s, and that still affects the scope of agency operations in wide areas of the world. [12]

By splitting up distribution areas, as well as perpetuating their news exchange, the three agencies hoped to solve the problem of balancing costs and revenues. The elimination of competition would enable each to control its reporting expenditures more closely and to fix subscription rates at remunerative levels. Reuters took Britain and its empire, China, Japan, and the Straits Settlements around Singapore. Havas was granted France and its colonies, Spain, Italy, Portugal, and Latin America. Continental-Wolff was restricted to Germany, Russia, and Scandinavia, and had to pay the other two agencies a proportion of its revenue in return for receiving their services. Reuters and Havas were free to expand as they wished into any territories not specified in the agreement; the German agency was allowed to do so only in association with at least one of its partners.

The theory behind the cartel was impeccable, particularly for its British and French members, moving the ever-ebullient Reuter to suggest a further step: the three agencies should consider merging under a holding company. The reaction of Havas is not known, but the directors of Continental-Wolff were favorable to the idea. The banker Bleichröder, however, was not, nor was Bismarck. The idea was dropped, but Reuters and Havas subsequently entered into a bilateral agreement to share profits and run a number of joint offices.[13] This venture lasted for six years, until Reuters compromised its profitability by embarking on an ill-judged attempt to set up a private transatlantic message service. Cooperation had its limits.

While financial details have not survived, what evidence there is suggests that the cartel never lived up to its financial promise. Some of the reserved areas, such as Reuters' domain in India, proved lucrative, but others had only a few poor newspapers that could not afford appropriate subscription levels. Getting paid at all was a recurrent problem in some parts of the world, and reporting was becoming increasingly expensive. Imperial adventures had to be covered on a suitably jingoistic scale. The development of the popular press at the end of the century added to the range of stories the agencies were expected to provide. The worldwide telegraph network built up in the second half of the century enabled the agencies to report much more quickly and to distribute by cable, but the cost was correspondingly high.[14]

By the end of the century, the pattern of dependence on alternate sources of income had become well established. Havas had its advertising agency revenue; Continental-Wolff was firmly in the pay of the German state; Reuters, now under the direction of the founder's son, Herbert, earned money by running a remittance service between Britain, Australia, and South Africa, and drew steady income from the commercial news services with which Paul Julius Reuter had started. The contrasts between these money-making activities and the perils of the news business were such that shareholders rose from time to time at Reuters' annual general meetings to ask when the company was going to be run so as to produce an acceptable profit. "I am sorry to have again to make the admission that news gathering and distribution is an unremunerative business," the chairman told them in 1908. "Did we not fortunately possess other sources of revenue, we could not possibly afford for news telegrams what we at present spend." [15]

Dividends may not have been high all the time, but Reuters had little to complain about. The cartel period saw it firmly established as the leading international agency.[16] Unlike the other services, Reuters did not distribute domestic news in its own country, nor did it send foreign news directly to the provincial press. Both functions were performed by the internal British agency, the Press Association, which agreed not to subscribe to any other international news service and which provided Reuters with its reports of British events.[17] Although its activities in Britain were thus limited, Reuters made the most of the advantages that the British Empire offered. In addition to services for newspapers, it developed commodity and financial reports that were telegraphed between Britain, South Africa, India, and the Far East, and became vital for traders and speculators. Its founder, who had once run the agency's overnight service from a hut in his garden, was awarded a barony by a small German state which was recognized in Britain, and was referred to by Queen Victoria as a man who "generally knows."

Although it proved to be less than a gold mine, the cartel still bought great advantages to the three partners, and was duly renewed in 1890. It froze the agency world in a pattern that prevented uncomfortable competition. The growing number of national news agencies in Europe found it impossible to expand beyond their frontiers, blocked both by the cartel's domination of the market and by their own dependence on the big three's services for a comprehensive picture of the world. An attempt by the Russian finance minister, Count Sergei Yulievich Witte, to break through the cartel's stranglehold at the turn of the century showed just how powerful the partners were.

Witte was angered by Continental-Wolff's refusal to issue stories that failed to coincide with German interests. Such stories, he noted, were of importance to Russia, but there was no way the Russian Telegraph Agency could receive them, since it depended on the German agency for its foreign news. So Witte set up his own news organization, the Trade Telegraph Agency, to ensure that Russia got the commercial news he thought essential for the modernization of the country. The agency quickly ran up against Reuters' entrenched position in the financial and commodity fields. The London-based agency also virtually monopolized reporting from the Far East, a major zone of Russian interest. Havas outshone anything the Trade Telegraph Agency could provide from Russia's western ally and banker, France. Continental-Wolff's control of Germany was such that Witte's agency was unable to engage any correspondents of its own there. Agencies in the smaller European countries tightly tied to the cartel could not envisage agreements with the Russian upstart. Against such odds, Witte's bid for independence collapsed, and his agency merged with Continental-Wolff's Russian client. As the Interior Ministry in St. Petersburg noted in 1904, a Russian agency, even with government backing and finance, "is not able either to acquire equality in the union of foreign telegraph agencies . . . or to obtain direct relationships with the foreign press." [18]

The Turn of the Century: AP and UP . . . .

While the Russians made an effort to challenge the cartel, the AP in New York maintained a faithfully subservient relationship with it. The AP's international quiescence was understandable, given the turmoil it faced at home. [19]

The last two decades of the nineteenth century witnessed a series of battles among the New York association, a renascent group of Midwestern publishers, and various privately run agencies. Discontent with the AP grew, particularly in the face of vigorous competition from the main commercial agency, United Press (UP), whose success prompted two Midwestern members of the AP's governing committee to investigate what was wrong in New York. Their discovery was scandalous: in return for stock in United Press, the men in charge of the New York AP had been giving the private agency access to the cooperative's news.

The discrediting of the New York management left the Midwesterners to take over the running of the AP. In 1892, they established the Associated Press of Illinois with sixty-five charter members. A link with the European cartel was essential for the health of the reformed cooperative, but Reuters had a nasty shock in store for the AP and its new general manager, Melville E. Stone. In 1893, the London agency signed similar agreements with the Chicago AP and UP, which had kept going despite the scandal. Each of the U.S. services would have access to cartel news in London in return for annual payments of £3500 and the supply of their own news to Reuters.[20]

The duopoly did not last long. Under Stone's determined leadership, and after the expenditure of $1 million, the AP forced UP out of business. Baron Herbert Reuter sent a congratulatory telegram to Chicago. The AP had regained its monopoly of cartel news in the United States.

Melville Stone, a Methodist minister's son who instructed staff not to cover such subjects as abortions, disease, infanticide, incest, seductions, social events, or baseball, saw the now-dominant cooperative as much more than a convenient way of sharing news-gathering costs. "A press, to be free, must be one which should gather news for itself," he proclaimed. "A national co-operative news-gathering organization, owned by the newspapers and by them alone, selling no news, making no profits, paying no dividends, simply the agent and servant of the newspapers, was the thing." [21] One of his close associates, Charles Sanford Diehl, described the AP as "wholly American, in its origin, in its nature and in its scope. . . . It represents more nearly the warp and woof of the great Republic than any other agency or prop of government." Both men must have reveled in Mark Twain's assertion that "there are only two forces that can carry light to all corners of the globe—the sun in the heavens and the Associated Press."

Twain not only ignored the distinctly unglobal scale of the AP's news distribution; he also neglected the cooperative's restrictive nature. Access to whatever "light" the AP shed was still confined to its members; existing members could blackball any competitors they wished. On top of that, the cooperative's rules prohibited members from receiving other news services. So seriously did the association take this dictum that, when an Illinois court ruled it unenforceable, the AP moved its headquarters to New York. There, it found suitably protected status for its rules by registering as what Stone described as "a social club." [22]

Although remaining dependent on the cartel for its regular flow of foreign news, the AP began to report abroad on its own account at the turn of the century. It sent a team of correspondents to cover the Spanish-American War, and a dozen reporters, including some intrepid Russians, to the Russo-Japanese conflict of 1905. Stone expanded his staff of permanent reporters in Europe and managed to break through the censorship regulations in St. Petersburg. The cartel agencies did not object, since they faced no competition from the AP in their territories; Herbert Reuter even persuaded Havas to allow the AP to distribute its service in the French agency's preserve of Central America and the Caribbean.

The American agency posed no threat as yet. But Baron Reuter was impressed by the scale of the resources the AP mobilized for its coverage of the Spanish-American War, which cost the cooperative $284,210; such sums were beyond any of the European agencies. "There is no such affiliation of newspapers, as in the Associated Press, to jointly bear such a self-imposed burden in Europe," the baron remarked. "It is an illustration of the power and force of the American Republic to coordinate and use its total strength in any direction it may desire."

The cartel might not have worried about the AP, but the populist American publisher E. W. Scripps did. Most of his newspapers were excluded from the AP by existing members. Even if they had been admitted, they would not have been particularly well served, since the majority of the Scripps newspapers were afternoon publications while the AP was geared to the needs of the morning press. Scripps had been a UP subscriber and, when it folded, built up his own news service. After buying the Publishers Press Association, another private agency, Scripps established in 1907 what would prove to be a durable rival to the AP, the United Press Associations. "I do not believe in monopolies," Scripps wrote. "I believe that monopolies suffer more than their victims in the long run. I did not believe that it would be good for journalism in this country that there should be one big news trust such as the founders of the Associated Press fully expected to build up." [23]

If the AP had been less restrictive, it might have become a long-lasting monopoly. But the growing number of newspapers that wanted an agency service and were excluded from the cooperative made it inevitable that an alternate service would come into being. Scripps's agency survived where other AP rivals had died because there was now a large enough body of nonmembers of the cooperative to sustain a second national service. It was also powerfully aided by Scripps's willingness to underwrite its initial losses. "The early days would have been critical had it not been for the fact that I owned so many of the newspapers that were its clients that its financing was a simple matter," he later explained.

> All I had to do was, first, to calculate the monthly expenses necessary for conducting the United Press; second, to add up the amount of money received each month from clients other than my own newspapers; and, finally, to cause my own newspapers to pay assessments so that their aggregate would be sufficient, taken together with the receipts from other clients, to pay the whole monthly expense. After the first year or two, the receipts exceeded the disbursements.[24]

From the start, UP was determinedly commercial. Its reporting budget was low, and its journalists and technicians showed a genius for cost-cutting improvisation. The agency generated a can-do esprit de corps that contrasted sharply with the AP's canonical style. Roy Howard, the journalist-salesman who ran the agency for Scripps, instructed his staff to forget about the AP and its conservative, wordy approach to news. "We've got to do things that have never been done before," he told them.

> Remember what you wanted but didn't get from a wire service when you were a telegraph editor. Ask every telegraph editor you see what he wants but doesn't get. Don't worry too much about the publisher or the editor—keep in touch with the man who handles the wire report in the newspaper office. Study the way Pulitzer and Hearst humanize the news in their papers. Get interviews with people in the news. People are usually more interesting than the things they are doing. Dramatize them.[25]

This new approach to agency reporting, aimed primarily at the afternoon papers ignored by the AP, soon proved successful. By 1909, two years after its founding, UP had 392 clients and showed a small profit. In 1912, its subscribers numbered 491, only 150 fewer than the AP membership.

Impressive as its growth was, UP faced a problem when it came to foreign news. The AP's monopoly of the cartel service meant that Scripps and Howard had to finance their own network of correspondents abroad. This was a costly process, and UP was unable to compete successfully with the resources of the three European agencies. In 1912, however, Herbert Reuter showed, for the second time, that he was not indissolubly wedded to the AP. He initiated talks with Howard in London, expressing particular interest in UP's ability to provide U.S. stock market news. Howard returned home to discuss the Reuter approach at a conference of executives and leading clients in Chicago.

The conferees rejected any link with the cartel. One objection was that it would associate them with agencies such as Continental-Wolff that were used by their governments as channels for official news, a practice that was also causing the AP some concern. More important to Scripps and Howard was their awareness that an agreement with the cartel would prevent UP from selling its service outside the United States. Having established their agency at home, they saw no reason why they should not distribute news abroad wherever they liked. "I want to see the United Press develop as a world-wide agency," Howard declared. The cartel's death knell had begun to sound.

From Cartel
to Competition

For many people involved in journalism, and far more who are not professionally concerned, news agencies appear to be bureaucratic machines that, by and large, run themselves. Identified only by their initials or one-word names, they do not represent news with a human face. The personalities of the executives in charge seem of little importance; whoever is in the driver's seat, the agencies roll on in their sober, straightforward manner.

Within the agency world itself, however, personalities are often of very great importance; anonymous determinism is not always, or even usually, the prevailing ethos. The personal characteristics of Charles-Louis Havas and, even more so, of Paul Julius Reuter were of key importance for the development of their agencies. In the period between the two world wars, the personalities of the heads of Reuters, the Associated Press, and United Press were critical in the breakup of the cartel and the shaping of the pattern that took its place.

The Proconsul..................................

At Reuters, Baron Herbert sought relief from the agency's financial problems at the start of the century by building up a banking business.[1] The founder's son cut an unusual figure, bicycling for two hours in the park each morning before going to his office, eating mounds of bananas, and showing as much interest in his hobby of higher mathematics as in the more mundane business of managing a news agency. With the banking initiative he appeared to have scored a great coup. In 1913, the company reported gross revenues of almost £1 million—quadruple the 1912 figure—and a profit of £46,046. A banking branch was opened in Australia, and the bank's London manager plunged into investments in continental Europe.

The outbreak of World War I put a stop to this gold mine. The European investments were lost; the bank's revenues slumped. At the same time, the war closed off markets for Reuters' news and escalated reporting costs. Profits dropped to £14,849 in 1914 and £8,791 the next year. In April 1915, Baron Herbert Reuter, heart-broken over the death of his wife only three days earlier, shot himself dead. Eighteen months later, his only son, an equally unworldly character who had resigned his army commission to fight as a private, was killed in France while carrying wounded men to safety. The direct Reuter male line was extinguished.

The future of the agency was thrown into doubt. As a publicly owned company, it was open to takeover bids. The Marconi telegraph firm, which ran a service of news gathered from radio monitoring, prepared a £500,000 offer. It was forestalled by Reuters' ambitious manager for South Africa, Roderick Jones, who had rushed back to London. In association with the agency's chairman, Mark Napier, Jones lined up four bankers to back a successful takeover.

When Napier died in 1919, Jones became chairman as well as managing director. Seven years later, after tortuous negotiations, he arranged to sell his shares to the Press Association domestic agency, and Reuters became the property of the British provincial press. The change of ownership made no difference; from 1915 to 1941, Reuters was Jones and Jones was Reuters. It was not a state of affairs that did the agency any good.

Sir Roderick Jones—he was knighted in 1918—was always eager to impress. He lived and worked like an imperial proconsul. A small man with a taste for large houses, he wore the ties of smart schools he had not attended and spoke of military service in snobbish guards regiments from which his lack of height would have debarred him. When Jones left Reuters' offices in the evening, a messenger was sent ahead to jump on the rubber pad in the street controlling a nearby set of traffic lights to ensure that they were green for the chairman's Rolls-Royce. In his South African days, Jones had been heard up-braiding a servant for having failed to iron his bootlaces. According to one of his closest associates, his first name was really George, not the more impressive Roderick.

Such personal foibles are important because they reflect the attitude that dominated Jones's conduct of Reuters. He ran the agency like an autocrat, treating it as his personal possession and regarding its staff as lackeys. The Press Association ownership, apart from having provided Jones with a useful sum of money for his shares, had the great advantage of giving him a board he could easily overawe. Newspaper managers from the British provinces were unlikely to question the wisdom of this self-appointed great man of the world whose vision stretched around the globe.

At the end of World War I, Reuters was still in a strong position as the unquestioned leader of the cartel. After Germany's defeat, Continental-Wolff was restricted to German-speaking areas of Europe, and the managers of Havas showed more interest in advertising and investing in domestic media than in maintaining a strong world role. Reuters thus had a golden opportunity to deal with the inevitable challenge of the U.S. agencies from a position of international strength. But Jones saw himself and his agency in exclusively British terms. During the war, he had combined part-ownership of Reuters with a high post in the Ministry of Information, and in peacetime he continued to see himself as a propagator of British values and of "the British prestige abroad which the publication of news over Reuters' name in manifold tongues, and Reuters' activities in general, tended to promote." His motivation is summed up in the reason for starting to distribute Reuter news in Latin America: an inquiry from the Prince of Wales "to ascertain whether Reuters could not do something to change the deplorable British news situation in the Argentine, Brazil and the other South American Republics." [2]

UP Challenges the Cartel . . . .

Jones's first international opponent was a man of very different character. Roy Howard was a hustling, bustling journalist and salesman, willing to go anywhere and do anything to expand UP. Howard's ardor had not been checked by his having committed one of the greatest errors in agency history: he reported the 1918 Armistice four days before it was signed, sending the story from France on the basis of information given to him by an American admiral. Later, the UP boss speculated that the news had been planted by a German agent. The error may have been enormous, but only one UP client canceled the service as a result. Howard went right on selling, drumming into his staff that it was working for an international news agency.

World War I caused UP to expand its network of foreign correspondents considerably, and its overseas distribution spread to France, Australia, New Zealand, and Japan. Most important of all, it broke into Latin America in 1914. Under the prewar arrangements of the cartel, Latin America had been a backwater for the world agencies, run by Havas in a not particularly energetic manner despite the presence of some strong newspapers, notably in Argentina. In 1914, the Buenos Aires daily *La Nación* contacted the AP in New York with a request for coverage of German war communiqués it was not getting from Havas. Faithful to his agreement with the cartel, Melville Stone forwarded the request to Paris. As he explained later to his board, "I said to them [Havas] one day: 'Why on earth don't you send from Paris the German official statements?' They said: 'We are French; we cannot do it.' "

The Havas refusal meant that the AP could do nothing about *La Nación*'s request. The newspaper turned to UP. Howard had no problem supplying German communiqués and anything else *La Nación* wanted. An arrangement was worked out under which UP and *La Nación* pooled their services and sold the results jointly throughout Latin America. The annual profit reached $150,000 before *La Nación*, with ambitions to operate alone, made the agreement unworkable. UP then approached the other main Buenos Aires newspaper, *La Prensa,* and signed a contract that greatly strengthened its international position.

In addition to UP's service, *La Prensa* wanted extensive special coverage, notably of European events, which particularly interested it. The paper was willing to pay heavily for this—up to $500,000 a year—and to let UP use such material freely outside Latin America. With *La Prensa* acting as its partial banker, UP stepped up its international reporting. The attention it devoted to Latin America in its regular-service news report attracted a growing network of clients.

. . . and AP Follows . . . .

Havas, preoccupied with war, the advertising business, and the losses of its news service, was in no condition to compete effectively with UP in Latin America, particularly since cable charges were far higher from Paris than from New York. The AP, on the other hand, had little choice but to do battle with UP. Not only was UP leaping ahead as a supplier of international news abroad; its foreign reporting network was providing coverage for the United States that outdid anything the AP could get through the cartel. The cooperative could mount special operations to cover major foreign events; it spent $2.6 million reporting World War I. But it received no corresponding foreign revenues. To prevent UP from becoming the major U.S.–based agency both at home and overseas, the AP would have to break free of the cartel.

Melville Stone was not the man to make the break. Although well aware of the problems the cartel posed for the cooperative, he still respected the alliance, which had given the AP a dominant foreign news position in the United States for so long. But Stone was nearing the end of his tenure as general manager, and the rising man in the AP had a very different outlook and a very different view of the European agencies. Kent Cooper had quite as much self-confidence as either Roy Howard or Sir Roderick Jones, and, like them, he identified totally with the agency he headed from 1925 to 1948. In his spare time, he composed light musical tunes on the violin, but the AP was his life.

Cooper was no journalist. He wrote only one story for the association in his life, and made his initial mark as a communications specialist before World War I. But he proclaimed war on the cartel in the interest of "true and unbiased news—the highest original moral concept ever developed in America and given to the world." By his own account, Cooper's crusade was sparked by *La Nación*'s cable to the AP asking for German war communiqués. When he learned the AP had been forced to turn down the request, he

> felt that The Associated Press by its contract was a party to the suppression of legitimate news in many countries. The natural corollary to this was that it was not defensible for The Associated Press to continue a contract whereby it guaranteed any agency a monopoly of a nation outside its own national territory, or even in its home territory if by so doing it kept people of that nation in the dark.

AP standards should prevail everywhere; "access at the source to the news of all nations should be denied to no one." [3]

In addition, Cooper accused Reuters of spreading a false and sensational picture of the United States around the world through its selection of news from the AP files—a criticism repeated in mirror image today by those who charge the major agencies with dealing only in negative reporting of the developing nations. Unlike today's proponents of a new world information order, however, Cooper had a pressing business reason for his crusade, in the form of the UP. The private agency, he told the AP board, "can never assail the position of the Associated Press in its home territory unless they come to this home territory with a superior world news service.'' That was exactly what UP was doing, while the AP was saddled with what Cooper called "the deficiencies of its allies.''

Even if UP had never existed, Cooper would probably have tried to shake off the restrictions imposed from London; such was his innovative character and faith in the cooperative's moral leadership. With Roy Howard continually building up the rival service at home and abroad, it was inevitable that the AP would be impelled to fight for the same liberty of action.

Cooper went on the offensive well before he took over from Stone as general manager. While the original UP–*La Nación* arrangement was falling apart in 1918, the AP was approached by the newspaper's director, Jorge Mitre, described by Cooper as a charming, courteous figure and by the UP historian as a dark, temperamental man who probably carried a gun. After Cooper traveled to Latin America to assess the situation personally, the AP decided to admit *La Nación* as a member. Cooper negotiated an agreement with Havas that gave the AP a free hand in Latin America. In return, the French agency had access to the AP service and was compensated for lost revenue. By the spring of 1919, the AP had twenty-five subscribers in Latin America and was building up a reporting network there.

The Cartel Crumbles . . . .

Havas's acceptance of the AP move into Latin America was symptomatic of the general decline in the French agency's world standing between the wars, and of its desire to avoid an expensive battle with the Americans. As a result, Reuters was left to carry on the battle for the cartel largely single-handedly. UP was growing steadily stronger. By 1930, it claimed more than one thousand clients in forty-five countries. Its bright, aggressive service reached even Britain via British United Press (BUP), operated by the agency's subsidiary with its legal home in Canada. Jones's concern at the inroads made by BUP in Reuters' home territory was such that at one point he drew up an abortive plan to buy the Canadian subsidiary.

Elsewhere in Europe, some of the bigger national agencies were becoming restive, primarily for political reasons. Russia's agency, first called ROSTA and later TASS, had set a worrying precedent by concluding an agreement with UP. It did not last long, but the example was not lost on the ruler of another authoritarian state, Mussolini, who was keen for Italy's Stefani agency to distribute its fascist version of the news outside Italy. Sir Roderick remained adamant: national agencies receiving the cartel service were not allowed to sell abroad. The rumblings of discontent went on. In the British dominions, several national news agencies debated the idea of forming an imperial cooperative that might supplant Reuters in some of its most remunerative areas.

The crunch came in Japan, a country whose press supported a number of expansionist-minded news agencies.[4] One of these, Kokusai Tsushin-sha (International News Agency), had been pressing Reuters to be allowed to sell its service overseas ever since its foundation in 1913. The Far East was an important revenue source for Reuters and Jones headed the Japanese off until 1926, when the agency's chief, Yukichi Iwanaga, agreed with the AP on the need to break the Reuters stranglehold. Under Melville Stone, the AP had refused to help the Japanese because of the cartel restrictions. Kent Cooper threw his weight behind Iwanaga, who reorganized his agency into an AP–style cooperative under the name Rengo.

To gain time, Jones made a small concession: he allowed Rengo to sell its news in Shanghai. But this had little effect, for Iwanaga was intent on gaining real freedom of action for Rengo. He had two solid business reasons for wanting to get out from under Reuters' skirts: devaluations of the yen were making the sterling-based Reuter subscription rates very costly, and Rengo's main rival, the UP client agency Dentsu, was benefiting from the private American agency's expansion in the Pacific and China.

In 1930, Iwanaga and Cooper agreed in principle that Rengo should take the AP service and distribute it in Japan. At the end of the year, Cooper formally gave notice on the agreement which linked the AP to the European agencies. This was not intended as a complete divorce; the AP hoped to maintain bilateral links with Reuters, Havas, and Wolff. Cooper insisted that each party should be free to sell as it wished, and that any national agency should be able to buy whichever international service it wanted. There would be no more reserved geographical zones; open competition would replace the cartel, and the AP would at last be able to challenge UP worldwide.

Reuters had no alternative but to agree to the broad outlines of the AP proposal. Whatever Jones did, Cooper was clearly going to implement his declaration of independence. The Reuters chairman tried to salvage what he could from the wreck of the cartel. He made it clear that he expected to be consulted before the AP undertook any moves into traditional Reuters territory, but his expectations were soon dashed. The AP and Rengo concluded a bilateral agreement without informing Reuters.

After an unsuccessful attempt to use diplomatic pressure to abort the AP–Rengo contract, Jones turned to UP. A few years earlier, he had written to Cooper extolling the virtues of "a joint and active front against our common rival, the United Press." In the changed circumstances of the early 1930s, he held talks with UP president Karl Bickel about joining forces against the AP. Bickel, Jones reported back to his board, "would most cordially welcome an alliance with Reuters." He said Roy Howard, who had gone into running newspapers but remained UP's father figure, was of the same opinion. Whatever he told his board, even Jones could hardly have believed that UP would consider joining anything remotely resembling the old cartel.

After talking to UP, the Reuters chairman next turned to Japan, where Iwanaga was eager to avoid being seen as the initiator of a break between the AP and Reuters. Given Cooper's determination to have a free hand, the Rengo chief need not have been worried about bearing any moral blame. But his concern was such that he allowed Jones to talk him into a new contract which restricted Rengo's distribution to Japan while cutting the Reuters subscription rate substantially.

His confidence thus restored, Jones denounced the recent agreement with the AP and sent Cooper the draft of a new "four-party treaty." The proposals from London excluded the AP from Europe and involved a large differential payment to Reuters. After some inconclusive transatlantic exchanges, the cooperative's president, Frank Noyes, wrote to Jones to convey his board's conclusion that "our point of view is so entirely divergent from that expressed and reiterated by you that the two cannot be reconciled." The AP, accordingly, accepted Reuters' denunciation of the agreement between them and ignored the rest of Jones's proposals.

Reuters was out on a limb. Havas was distinctly unhappy about Jones's tactics. Having lost heavily on news operations in 1932, it had no wish to be caught in an all-out war with two American agencies. European national agencies, already hard-hit by competition from the low subscription rates that UP offered newspapers and radios, preferred cooperation with the AP to confrontation. Cooper exploited their worries adroitly, writing a series of letters proclaiming how preposterous it was that "an exorbitant and unwarranted demand from Reuters" should prevent them from working with the AP.

The imperial proconsul in London saw his support crumbling away. The previously faithful German agency began to agitate for an unfettered world role as Hitler and Goebbels turned it into a Nazi propaganda machine. From Rome, Stefani offered to supply its service free of charge to newspapers in Asia and Latin America. East European national agencies were demanding reduced subscription rates, or were simply letting their debts pile up under the impact of the Depression. To top it all, Reuters' main news division was running at an increasing loss. In 1934, Sir Roderick Jones sailed for New York. There, he formally buried the cartel by signing a new agreement giving the AP freedom to distribute its news wherever it wanted— even in Britain.

1934–41: New Directions . . . .

The cartel left its mark on the news-agency world. It had established the pattern of a small group of major services distributing international news through client national agencies as well as selling directly to newspapers and broadcasters. Today, traces of this pattern can be found reflected in the geographical strengths and weaknesses among the Big Four, most notably in Africa and Asia but also in the continuation of the dominant position in Latin America taken by the U.S. agencies in their first blow against the European monopoly. The cartel had also helped to ensure that foreign-based agencies stayed out of the United States until the late 1960s.

Despite these hangovers, a new environment for news services was created in 1934. The model of unrestrained competition pioneered by UP became the norm, as the American agencies began to move into a position of equality with the Europeans. But it was not quite the new dawn that Kent Cooper had proclaimed so insistently. The AP found itself distributing its services to European national agencies it had previously denounced as suspect state organizations. The cooperative ideal was retained as an American prerogative; the AP conducted its international distribution through a series of local subsidiaries working on the same commercial basis as Reuters, Havas, or UP.

The major advantage AP members got out of the new situation was an improved foreign report, written and edited to conform to their needs. The cooperative could have done this long before, had it so wished; nothing in its agreements with the cartel prevented the AP from sending its own correspondents abroad, but so long as it had been barred from distributing internationally, that option had looked like an unacceptably uneconomic proposition. Now, operating commercially outside the United States, the AP could join UP in trying to make the basic news-agency financial equation work.

With the exception of Latin America and Japan, the American agencies do not appear to have been any more successful than their European predecessors at accomplishing this. Subscription levels, particularly in Europe, were depressed by economic conditions. UP's rate cutting, which brought accusations of dumping, dragged down the fees that the other agencies could charge. In any case, some of the European agencies did not relish what the AP offered; the Swiss agency dismissed the AP services as "insufficient," while the head of the Fabra agency in Spain wrote that "no American service with such an American psychology could challenge the news content of the Havas and Reuter services." [5] Costs mushroomed. Covering the recurrent crises and conflicts of the 1930s was an expensive business; the AP's direct cable link between New York and London alone cost it $150,000 a year.

But financial matters did not greatly worry the American agencies. Latin America, where the AP had some one hundred customers at the end of the 1930s, provided revenue that helped to offset the soggy financial picture in Europe. When all was said and done, what really mattered was the domestic U.S. market; the significance of the rest of the world to the AP was primarily a function of its struggle to get the better of UP. The transposition of this domestic struggle onto the international stage after 1934 ensured that the world agencies would never get their finances straightened out. The AP and UP were guided more by outdoing each other than by rational calculations of how to cover the costs of world reporting and distribution; Reuters and Havas were, more than ever, dependent on income from sources other than their general news services.

In Paris, the French government had become Havas's paymaster. The Foreign Ministry had met the agency's cable costs to Latin America since 1924, and in 1931 the government agreed to contribute 800,000 francs a month to enable Havas to strengthen its overseas operations. In 1938, the Foreign Ministry took the logical final step and underwrote the agency's operations for the next ten years. The resulting effect on the news service was inevitable; the agency's chairman, Leon Renier, acknowledged that Havas "could not live for one hour if it fell out with the government."

As its financial fortunes declined, the Havas news service became increasingly subservient not just to the government but also to the company's advertising branch. Stories were initiated on behalf of advertising clients. Reports were inflated or suppressed for financial reasons. Havas became a symbol of the widespread decay of French press ethics. "Of all the poisons which demoralized French public opinion," a leading editor, Pierre Lazareff, wrote, "the Havas agency was one of the most dangerous."

Reuters took somewhat longer than Havas to turn to its government. Its finances were bolstered by substantial revenue from India and by news it sold to commodity gamblers in Shanghai. Its news service to the British press, on the other hand, was losing £33,000 a year by 1938. International rivalry was aggravated by free news services offered by the agencies of Germany, Italy, and other expansionist states. Jones ordered campaigns of "rigorous retrenchment," which only threatened the agency's competitiveness both against foreign rivals and against BUP, which now had seventy clients. Jones turned to the AP for help, proposing that the two agencies pool resources overseas. Kent Cooper turned him down.

After that rebuff, Jones went to Whitehall. In 1938 the British government granted Reuters the use of official radio facilities to send out two daily news services, which the agency was paid state money to produce. Jones insisted that, since Reuters wrote the services, there was no threat to the company's independence. He also reminded his board that Reuters had "always taken into account the official point of view." Financially, the agency had every reason to do so. After the outbreak of World War II, the government arrangement brought in £65,000 a year, which kept Reuters in profit despite the loss of European markets and the costs of reporting the fighting.

Jones showed no concern about the increasingly close official links he negotiated in 1939–40.[6] His whole background and outlook ensured he would have little hesitation about involvement with authority, particularly in wartime. In World War I, in addition to holding a high position in the Ministry of Information, he had involved Reuters in the transmission of official messages in return for payment. These dispatches were supposedly singled out from the rest of the file by the label "Agence Reuter." The distinction was easily overlooked.

At the outbreak of war in 1939, a Ministry of Information note commented on the possibility of the government's taking over Reuters to turn it into a more effective carrier of British news (though precautions would be taken to maintain an appearance of independence). After the fall of France, British government interest in Reuters increased because, with Havas now run by the occupation authorities, Reuters was the only channel for Allied news to Latin America, where German propaganda was highly active. The Ministry of Information proposed the establishment of a committee of representatives from both government and the agency to see that Reuters carried out services for the government. Reuters would be free to distribute news received from its own correspondents, but might be required to add comment or interpretation that the government thought desirable. "The Government would give guidance and would expect Reuters to take it," according to the minutes of a ministerial discussion.[7]

As Hitler grew stronger, the British government became increasingly unhappy with Jones, who did not seem as effective a promoter of British interests as it had hoped. Some of the agency's directors from the British press were also becoming uneasy with their chairman. Their preparations for revolt were extremely discreet. On one occasion, dissident directors met in a first-class railway carriage traveling between Yorkshire and London to avoid being spotted. Jones continued to dominate the agency. Directors were not allowed to speak at board meetings except when he bid them to do so. "We just sat there, and it was terrible to hear him telling lies to us," one director recalled. "He still ran Reuters like a family business."

In 1941, the government gave the rebel directors the ammunition they needed. Jones had told the board about the radio transmission agreement with the government. But he did not reveal a secret agreement made in 1938 with Sir Horace Wilson, an adviser to Prime Minister Neville Chamberlain. Nor did Jones tell his board he had accepted a letter from the Foreign Office providing for the agency "at all times [to] bear in mind any suggestions made to them on behalf of His Majesty's Government as to the development or orientation of their news service or as to the topics or events which from time to time may require particular attention." The letter also insisted on the creation of a new executive post, that of direct deputy to Jones. A handwritten addition at the end of the letter informed Jones that his choice for the new post, Reuters manager Christopher Chancellor, "will be acceptable to His Majesty's Government."

Jones did not, however, establish the post. The government, foreseeing that it might never get any improvement from Reuters unless it acted, tipped off one of the directors, William John Haley of the *Manchester Evening News*, about its secret agreement with Jones. Haley told other board members. Jones was asked about the matter. The Reuters chairman, described by one director as still "acting like

God," asked if any member of the board believed he had withheld information in order to mislead them. "I do," Haley replied. "That being the case, either I must resign or Mr. Haley must," Jones said. There was silence around the table. Jones got up and left the boardroom. From his office on the other side of the corridor, he sent the directors a letter of resignation.

The board respected Jones's request that the reason for his resignation should not be made public. The agency's history, written a decade later, was remarkably discreet on the subject.[8] But there was no doubt about the sense of relief Jones's departure brought. The government was content, since Christopher Chancellor soon became the agency's chief executive, although any expectations in Whitehall that he would prove an acquiescent head of the agency immediately proved unfounded.

After a bitter argument over the ownership of the agency, the British national press took a half share in Reuters through its joint organization, the Newspaper Proprietors Association. This not only provided additional financial backing but also ensured that the country's biggest newspapers were directly involved in Reuters' well-being. A trust was established to safeguard the agency's independence, and the owners agreed to plow any profits back into the news service. By 1943, the government entanglements had been unraveled.

William Haley, who had shocked some of his colleagues by installing a teleprinter in the boardroom to remind them what Reuters was all about, traveled to New York to reestablish good relations with the AP. The two organizations agreed on the virtues of worldwide competition. Kent Cooper recognized Reuters as a born-again organization, and the acrimony that had characterized his relations with Jones evaporated. To signal his approval of the new direction being taken in London, Cooper laid on a lavish banquet for Haley at the end of their talks. After the meal, the AP general manager treated his guest to the greatest honor he could imagine paying anybody: he picked up his violin and played a lengthy recital of his own compositions.

American Supremacy . . . .

World War II established the two American agencies as the major forces in international reporting and news distribution. Despite its wider ownership, Reuters remained financially strapped. Havas had been disbanded as a news organization after the German victory over

France, and replaced by "L'Office Français de l'Information," a puppet organization in which the Germans held a 47 percent share, the French authorities 20 percent, and the former owners 33 percent.[9]

The U.S. services, on the other hand, had the resources to respond fully to the thirst for war news. They put more reporters in the field than any other news organizations—a total of 179 for the AP alone. In addition to its traditional textual news services, the AP had built up a strong news-picture operation during the 1930s, and its photographers produced some of the most dramatic images of the fighting. The war made events abroad of compelling interest to Americans who might previously have taken only passing notice of foreign developments. The fast-breaking style of news-agency coverage that the U.S. agencies developed to a fine art was particularly well suited to providing the first dramatic account of a battle, an air raid, or a naval engagement. The human-interest approach to reporting pioneered by UP brought the war alive in personal terms, while the experience gained from prewar expansion overseas gave the AP and UP a valuable fund of practical knowledge about how the rest of the world worked.

At home, the two agencies were at each other's throats even more fiercely than in the past. A 1943 Supreme Court decision made the AP and UP services available to any newspaper or radio station that wanted them. No longer could existing AP members prevent reception of the service by competitors, nor could the AP insist that its members not get any other news service. Newspapers that had felt protected under the old system did not relish the change, but the effect was beneficial for the AP, for its domestic base grew, bringing increased resources. Head-on competition with UP sharpened the association's reporting and editing.

On its side, UP gained from being able to sell its service to AP members. The private agency no longer enjoyed its previous captive market among newspapers and radio stations that had been forced to take UP because the AP franchise was already held by a competitor, but this presented no immediate problems, given the appetite for news in the 1940s. It would contribute to the private agency's problems in later, more stringent times.

The growing American predominance as World War II progressed ensured that the U.S. agencies would be well-placed to increase their world audience once the fighting stopped. The news philosophy that Kent Cooper had articulated so forcefully, and that UP had been putting into practice ever since its foundation, fitted neatly with the idealistic vision of building a new world safe for democracy. The spread of "Americanism," which European news-agency directors had worried about in the 1930s, proved unstoppable after 1945.

Unlike Reuters and the old Havas service, the U.S. agencies went into domestic as well as foreign reporting abroad when the war ended. They set up editing and translation desks in Europe to provide tailored local services, giving them a major edge over Reuters and the weak product of the French liberation, Agence France-Presse. The AP management received a special budgetary increase of $500,000 a year from its members at the end of World War II to expand overseas. In addition, as one of his close colleagues recalled, Kent Cooper had another means of putting money into the world operation. He believed there was no point in the association's showing surpluses, which would only be returned to the membership through lowering the charges levied on them. Much better to spend the surplus overseas in combating UP and, to a lesser extent, Reuters around the world.

UP enjoyed no such subsidy from U.S. subscribers for its international activities. It depended on selling its service wherever it could, and its representatives frequently combined journalism and business in a way that would become much more common among news agencies in later years. "After 1945, some of the UP correspondents went into the newly liberated countries with contracts in their pockets," a former executive of the agency recalled. "In Belgium, one UP man couldn't find any newspapers to sell the service to, so he signed up a butcher after convincing him that he would do better business if he was in touch with what was going on in the world."

Local staff came cheap in postwar Europe, and UP was able to run its translated local services profitably. "There was a tremendous vacuum in the world after 1945," Roger Tatarian, former UP correspondent and editorial vice president, remembered. "The press needed news, and people rushed in to supply it. UP was more interested in living off the land in Europe, in paying its way, and even making a profit. The AP was less interested in this."

Despite the spread of services, the agencies' revenues came mainly from a few large contracts and countries. West Germany and Japan soon emerged as the most lucrative markets for postwar international news services. The environment provided by the American occupation undoubtedly helped the AP and UP in both countries. In both, it proved possible to work out an appropriate rate structure for agency sales. "Elsewhere, it was largely a matter of getting what you could," noted former AP president Wes Gallagher, who had been in Europe when the AP was selling its service for $100 a month to some clients. "The agencies undercut one another. International rates were too low, and this made it very difficult to run a profitable world service on a lasting basis."

For the AP, the foreign operation was only a small part of the business. At the end of the 1950s, $4.8 million of the agency's $35 million annual costs were incurred overseas. Members agreed in 1958 to cover an annual deficit of $1 million on worldwide operations. At that point, each of the U.S. agencies was claiming approximately 8000 recipients of its services at home and abroad.

UP's scope was further increased in 1958 when it took over the Hearst organization's International News Service (INS), which had concentrated on feature reporting and a florid approach to the news since its foundation in 1909. Dogged in its early days by what one of its editors called a reputation for "reliable unreliability" in its reporting, INS had been kept alive by Hearst's insistence that his newspapers use its service. A merger with UP had been considered as long ago as 1926 but had fallen through, apparently because Roy Howard had inadvertently insulted William Randolph Hearst. By the end of World War II, INS had become so worried about money that one of its star reporters was told not to cable more than two hundred words of any story from the European battlefront. In the 1950s, according to testimony given before the Senate Foreign Relations Committee by one of its former employees, INS had taken to issuing, as news copy, material gathered for public relations clients. It had an accumulated deficit of $30 million and annual losses of around $1.5 million.

"Both agencies operated under low profit margins for many years," a UP executive told *Editor & Publisher*. "The merger will give the enlarged agency the opportunity to do more. It is a business enterprise competing against a cooperative and it is tough." The merged agency, taking one word from INS's name, became United Press International. Sounding the noncooperative ideology, UPI chairman Frank Bartholemew proclaimed that "private enterprise with a profit incentive is the best guarantee of objective coverage of world news."

While INS was dying, the ghost of Havas was reviving in Paris. The foundation of AFP in 1944 had aroused hopes in the press and among ex–Havas journalist members of the Resistance that France would eventually get a cooperative agency along AP lines. But the first decade of AFP's history proved disappointing, as the agency functioned under varying degrees of government control and depended on official subsidies. In 1949, a junior minister, François Mitterrand, declared that the agency met neither "the principle of the freedom of information, which our democratic regime is obliged to respect, [nor] the international requirements which demand that France should be endowed with an agency of worldwide influence whose independence with regard to all state bodies and private interests cannot be contested."

Helped by low subscription rates, which the government subsidy enabled it to charge overseas, AFP was able to sell its service in Europe, Japan, and Latin America. Reuters was moved to react against an agency that general manager Christopher Chancellor characterized as a "most dangerous and ruthless competitor." Reuters began what Chancellor described to his board as a "smear campaign," circulating figures about the AFP subsidy as well as reports of its government links to key contacts in domestic agencies around the world. By 1957, Chancellor reported, this campaign had been instrumental in sabotaging AFP contracts in many places. By then, however, the French agency had gained a new lease on life.

The initiative originated with François Mitterrand under the government of Pierre Mendés-France in 1954. Mitterrand appointed a former journalist, Jean Marin, as head of the agency. "I told them they were appointing somebody who would break with what had gone before and who would ask parliament to give the agency its independence," Marin recalled. "Mendés-France replied, 'All right, try to do it.' " In 1956, a parliamentary vote turned AFP into a legally autonomous enterprise to be run on commercial lines, with a statute guaranteeing its independence and the press enjoying a majority on the board. To mark the change, Marin sent a colleague in Washington to brief the State Department, which in the past had classified AFP as a state organization whose news could not be guaranteed to be accurate or independent. After the briefing, the French agency was shifted out of the company of TASS and installed beside the AP, UPI, and Reuters as an independent agency. It was a moment Marin savored.

The change in status was accompanied by a fresh professionalism at AFP. Its service became increasingly competitive in quality, and offered an original French voice and outlook. To sell overseas, however, it had to begin at the bottom of the market. The Dutch national agency paid AFP £1500 a year compared with £16,000 to Reuters. In Sweden, where Reuters' annual charge to the national service was £14,000, the AFP received only £2500, out of which it had to meet its communications costs. The prospect of achieving commercial independence in international operations was nonexistent, whatever the AFP statutes might say about the agency's autonomy. From its earliest days, the reformed agency depended on subscriptions from the French state to balance its books. The theory was that this need not compromise the AFP's independence, since state subscriptions were organized on a commercial basis, but ultimate control of the agency's budget, and of its survival, lay with the government in Paris. The press might have a majority on the board, but the 1956 arrangement ensured that state representatives could always block a candidate of whom the government did not approve from the chairmanship. Internationally, the AFP's presence would always depend on the importance that politicians attached to French membership of the restricted club of major international news agencies.

The competitive renaissance of AFP, and the depressing effect this had on international agency subscription rates, came at a time when Reuters was finding the battle with the American agencies particularly difficult. The London-based agency's services had been revitalized during and after the war. Its ownership had been broadened to take in the press associations of Australia and New Zealand, though further development into an enterprise owned by the British Commonwealth was thwarted by the strength of American influence in Canada, political problems with South Africa, and the unworkability of a short-lived participation in the agency by the Press Trust of India. After 1945, Reuters built a strong network of relationships with national agencies in Western Europe, selling its service to them for editing and translation rather than following the U.S. pattern of producing independent local services. The agency's editor, Walton Cole, stepped up links with major U.S. newspapers. As decolonization gathered pace, Reuters moved ahead of the American agencies in Africa and parts of Asia and its business news service contributed gross revenues that trebled between the late 1940s and the end of the 1950s to around £300,000 a year.

Despite these manifestations of growth, Reuters was eternally short of money. "We could not match AP for financial resources," Christopher Chancellor recalled. "It was like David and Goliath—a great struggle." In 1953, Reuters had a single staff correspondent covering a crisis in Trieste; the AP had eight. At the same time, Reuters did not have a single full-time correspondent in Latin America. Chancellor estimated that the AP outnumbered Reuters three to one in reporting the Suez conflict of 1956. Revenue failed to keep pace with reporting costs; in 1956, Moscow cost £30,000 to cover, an amount equivalent to 70 percent of the total amount paid to Reuters that year by its Australian co-owners. British press subscriptions were too small to support a substantial part of a world news operation, in striking contrast to the huge domestic market behind the AP and UPI. Three-quarters of Reuters' 1955 revenue of £1.75 million came from abroad. Board minutes record Chancellor as warning in 1957 that editorially Reuters was "down to bedrock—perhaps below." If a big news story came along, Reuters would inevitably have to go into the red. The editorial staff could not be reduced any further, Chancellor told the board. "In fact, it is dangerously low now."

Financial pressure forced Reuters to stop distributing in Latin America, and the agency handed much of its Middle Eastern operation to a British-government-backed regional service to save money. An early possibility of diversifying into newsfilm for television had to be passed up for lack of funds. The further development of the business news services that had lain at the foundation of the agency offered a possible escape route. But neither Chancellor nor his successor Walton Cole was willing to jeopardize the supremacy of the general news service by such a step. Reuters entered the 1960s swinging between loss and small profits; without the backing of either rich media or the state, the agency demonstrated the problems that worldwide competition posed. Not surprisingly, Chancellor showed keen interest in a postwar proposal by Kent Cooper for "an offensive and defensive alliance" between Reuters and the AP. Equally unsurprisingly, nothing came of this paradoxical suggestion. The major agencies were all locked into a competitive mold; the question now was whether they would maintain international services on a worldwide basis, and, if so, in what form.

CHAPTER **4** ....

Uniformity
and Diversity:
1960–80

Competition has produced a remarkable uniformity in what the major news agencies offer their international subscribers.

In the days of the cartel, when they were operating in protected markets, the services could adopt individual approaches—even if this amounted to no more than reflecting national viewpoints. After 1945, although the non-Communist world was wide open, the major agencies concentrated on those regions that produced most of the important international news and also provided the main markets for their services. Dedicated to a single, neutral reporting style and aiming at the same recipients, the four major agencies thought and operated increasingly alike in covering the world. The words each used might be different—United Press International might pay more attention than the others to human-interest stories; Reuters might stick to traditional British phraseology; one agency might be faster or more comprehensive than the others on a given story—but overall there was broad similarity in what the agencies produced and how they produced it.

Uniformity was further encouraged by the agencies' efforts to provide subscribers with complete services of available foreign news. In practice, there were many things the agencies were prevented from doing, for internal or external reasons. But the basic aim of each was to give recipients a continuous account of newsworthy events wherever they happened as soon as possible after they took place. This left little room for specialization. Each agency complemented its report of major events with news of specific interest to clients in different areas of the world. Subscribers in West Germany received coverage of the travels of German ministers, performances of German athletes, and accidents involving German holiday-makers, in addition to accounts of summit conferences, air crashes, and the deaths of film stars. The agencies' reporting bureaus in Paris filed complete daily placings of the Tour de France bicycle race to give Belgian, Portuguese, and Italian clients news of even the most lowly placed riders from their countries. Correspondents at the United Nations provided reports of speeches by African and Asian delegates for those regions as well as general accounts of debates.

When a major subscriber was signed up, or an agency was making a marketing push in a particular area, the effect could be spectacular. After Reuters gained two major Japanese clients in 1953, a special desk was set up in London to meet their needs. When President Eduardo Frei Montalva of Chile toured Europe in the mid–1960s, the American agencies each filed up to 10,000 words a day on the visit, as they strove to outdo one another for Chilean subscribers.

The attention each agency pays to subscribers in different parts of the world is partly a matter of historical inheritance and partly the result of more recent decisions to build up services in certain areas. In neither case does it affect the agencies' basic purpose: to provide as comprehensive a service of world news as possible. To all four, a broad picture of the world news is more important than specialized regional views.

In presenting that picture, the agencies assume that a uniform editorial approach is not only possible but also desirable. A government crisis is covered in the same way whether it happens in Nigeria or Holland. Similar standards are applied whether the story is being sent to Pakistan or Argentina. A single, objectively verifiable account of each event is the bedrock of agency reporting. A common denominator of editorial style, drawn from the mercantilist news tradition rooted in nineteenth-century liberalism, prevails.

Even without the weight of tradition, the agencies would have been forced by the pressure of competition to adopt an editorial approach geared to the Western-model commercial media, for only there could they hope to find the revenues needed to underwrite the costs of reporting and editing world news. Whether cooperative or commercial, the agencies have always conformed to the prevailing needs and psychologies of their major distribution areas. They cannot fall out of step or produce services for their own gratification, since news that is unacceptable to subscribers is unlikely to be used, and if their services are not used the agencies have no reason to exist.

Their uniformity gives rise to the portrayal of the four agencies as a monolithic group, moving en masse across the globe in search of news and profits. One prominent early spokesman for a new world information order, Mustapha Masmoudi of Tunisia, pointed to them as organizations that "monopolize between them the essential share of material and human potential." As president of the information council of the nonaligned nations and his country's delegate to UNESCO, Masmoudi was one of the first to put forward the notion that Western domination of the world was underpinned by "the control of the information flow wrested and wielded by the transnational agencies." [1]

Given the financial fragility of their services for the international media, such accusations of monopoly particularly annoy the major agencies. They do not feel like monopolists. They neither maximize profits nor manipulate markets, and are powerless to prevent subscribers from signing up with competitors. It is evident, however, that, as a group, the four major services do exercise something close to a monopoly over the twenty-four-hour-a-day stream of comprehensive, instant news flowing around the world, but this monopoly is a de facto one, reflecting the absence of viable worldwide alternatives. To accuse the major news agencies of virtual seigniory is akin to leveling the same charge against all the world's automobile manufacturers or all of its copper producers—a self-evident truth made worthy of attention only by the allegation that the group of organizations singled out for such rebuke operates in the interests of the industrialized world and against those of the developing nations.

The validity of this political criticism will be examined later. What is immediately evident is that the agencies could not "de-Westernize" themselves even if they were inclined to do so. Economically, they can survive only as long as money and staff are concentrated in prime news and revenue areas. Even this has proved difficult, as was evident in the postwar situation of Reuters and Agence France-Presse and as will be seen again in this chapter's examination of the agencies' development in the past two decades. Alternate sources of revenue remain essential to the maintenance of international general news operations, and these sources are not conducive to any change in editorial philosophy or geographical concentration. Structurally and practically, the agencies will never be in a position to adopt an

"African" stance or a "nonaligned" viewpoint; they are tied—philosophically, financially, and operationally—to the concept of a single editorial standard acceptable to as many subscribers as possible. Their evolution in the past two decades has done nothing but strengthen this constant, at the very time its effects have come under growing criticism.

AP and UPI: America First. . . . .

At the start of the 1960s, both American agencies were much stronger than their European counterparts. The following two decades, however, saw a steady decline in UPI's fortunes and a dramatic increase in the activity and financial strength of Reuters. Between these two extremes, the Associated Press maintained its world position but grew somewhat less international, and AFP enjoyed modest overseas growth while becoming increasingly dependent on French state support.

The U.S. agencies pioneered the distribution of news translated into local languages and edited for major national markets. In Latin America, their Spanish-language services covered the continent, and in Europe they built up, after 1945, a network of national services with particular strength in West Germany, France, Italy, Scandinavia, and Holland. The philosophy behind these services was that they would provide subscribers with direct access to AP and UPI news, bypassing any national-agency filter; as a result, the American agencies could supply full, unedited files without risking cutting or distortion along the way. News could be provided wherever there was a demand for it.

Both the AP and UPI established relationships with major foreign newspapers and broadcasters that would have been impossible if national agencies had come between them. These links were further strengthened by the U.S. agencies' monopoly on news-picture services, which enabled them to offer clients a complete textual and visual package. The overall result was to solidify the positions of the AP and UPI, and to enable them to absorb the costs of producing local services and maintaining special editing desks and domestic news reporters.

As time went by, however, the European services became more and more expensive, and media were no longer able (or willing) to pay enough to keep up with inflation and rising labor costs. The U.S. agencies' national services no longer supported the underlying financial rationale that, since the AP and UPI were in any case going to report the world's news for the U.S. media, they could distribute it abroad at only marginal additional cost. By the 1970s, the costs of operating a desk in Paris to serve French clients, or of running an Italian-language service in competition with the Italian national agency, were far from marginal. The effect of this was felt at the AP, which shut down both its editing desk in London and its Italian service, but it was UPI that found it most difficult to maintain the post–1945 pattern. "The theory for many years was that every bureau should be at least self-sufficient and, if possible, return a profit," UPI senior vice-president Frank Tremaine recalled in 1980. "The realities of news today are that this doesn't work. Bureaus in the Middle East, Europe, or Africa don't create enough revenue to cover their costs. Profit centers were more possible ten to fifteen years ago than they are today."

Overseas offices in unprofitable centers had to be maintained for reporting purposes, but UPI began to dismantle its now-uneconomical foreign-language services in Europe in the late 1960s and early 1970s. In West Germany, it began to sell its service to the national agency, Deutsche Presse-Agentur (DPA), in English. DPA selected the material it wanted and translated it into German. In France, no such outlet was available because the national agency was an international competitor, so UPI could only offer newspapers and broadcasters the generally unattractive alternative of its English-language service in place of the once widely distributed French-language report. By the end of the 1970s, Spanish and Portuguese services, going to 385 newspapers, agencies, broadcasters, and other clients in Latin America, were the only non-English news reports distributed by UPI. Elsewhere, escalating staff costs, social security payments, inflation, and local labor regulations made it impossible to continue in a static media market.

As Western Europe was proving an increasingly difficult area in which to operate, newly independent Africa turned out to be unfertile ground for the two American agencies. The white-owned media of South Africa were useful clients, but elsewhere the AP and UPI made little headway in the 1960s and 1970s. For the AP's former president, Wes Gallagher, "apart from South Africa, it is not worth distributing there." One UPI vice-president noted in 1981: "Whenever the question of Africa comes up, people shudder and remember the bad experience we had before." Initially, UPI had entertained high hopes of the possibility of distributing its news in both French and English to the newly independent African nations, reasoning that Reuters and AFP would suffer from association with the departed colonial powers and that there would be room for a new service. Things did not turn out that way. UPI services were judged too expensive, although in fact revenues barely covered costs. But other agencies sold more cheaply, or virtually gave their services away. The UPI vice-president recalled:

> And there was the problem of getting paid. We hadn't realized how much it would depend on politics. You have a change of regime and the new President won't recognize agreements made by his predecessors. Then there was the problem of finding the man who was meant to pay—once I spent a whole week going from one minister or official to another and I found the man who was meant to pay us only half an hour before I had to leave the country. He said he couldn't pay, pretending he didn't have our invoices to hand. In fact, they were stacked up around him. I made him sign a check and caught my plane. The check bounced.

As a result of such experiences, UPI gave up trying to distribute its services in Africa on anything other than a sporadic basis. The AP, although it made agreements in Nigeria, Kenya, and Ghana in the late 1970s, was also absent from most of black Africa for much of the 1960–80 period. Local news agencies and newspaper editors did not miss either of them; they had found the U.S. services too American in style and content and not sufficiently adapted to African needs.

In the Middle East, the U.S. agencies were generally weak throughout the Arab world, though prominent in Israel. At the end of the 1970s, they began to be used more widely as oil revenues helped boost information services in the area, but they still lagged well behind Reuters and AFP. Unlike their European competitors, neither of the U.S. agencies had an Arabic-language service, so they were generally consigned to the role of supplementary news sources that might be used for major world stories but could not offer the full range of immediately accessible coverage provided by Reuters and AFP.

East Asia, on the other hand, provided a continuing source of strength for the U.S. services (particularly in Japan, Thailand, the Philippines, and South Korea), and their predominance in Latin America was never seriously challenged. Special attention was paid to these markets, but the overall international picture as it developed in the 1960s and 1970s was not conducive to new AP and UPI initiatives abroad. Raising revenue became increasingly difficult, and the costs of reporting and editing overseas rose sharply with inflation. On a personal level, working abroad was no longer the glamorous pursuit it had been after World War II. The dollar no longer assured an easy life overseas, and wives were less willing to follow correspondent husbands wherever they were sent. Prizes and reputations were more likely to be won at home, especially after the Vietnam War ended. On top of everything else, U.S. citizens abroad lost their tax exemptions for several years. A sizable number of American agency journalists began to wonder whether it was really worth being on call twenty-four hours a day when the routine run of foreign news seemed to be making less and less impact at home.

By the beginning of the 1980s, there were distinct signs that both the AP and UPI were questioning, consciously or unconsciously, the assumptions of the preceding decades about the role they should play in the world. The change was most notable at UPI, where new owners who took over the agency in 1982 sold off UPI's news-picture and newsfilm interests outside the United States. This did not, in itself, diminish the role of international textual coverage and distribution in the four-sided operations run by both American agencies consisting of coverage of the United States for the U.S. media, coverage of the rest of the world for U.S. media, coverage of the United States for the rest of the world, and coverage of the rest of the world for the rest of the world. But however strong their commitments overseas are, the first concern of the AP and UPI is their home market.

The recent trend has been to concentrate attention even more closely on domestic services and away from international distribution. The services that the two American agencies issue within the United States are markedly different from those sent abroad. The radio and television stations and small-circulation American newspapers that make up the bulk of UPI's clients and the AP's members have little room for foreign news. For such recipients, the AP and UPI are predominantly suppliers of domestic news, on a state as well as a national level. At higher-circulation U.S. newspapers, the foreign news supplied by the two services comes into its own, but in terms of volume and importance it still takes second place to domestic coverage. No American newspaper devotes more space to foreign news than to domestic events, and a U.S. news agency that put the emphasis on foreign coverage to the detriment of home coverage would not last long.

The tilt toward domestic operations that characterizes both U.S.

agencies was sharpened in the 1970s by the post-Vietnam mood of national introspection and changes in content and style in the U.S. media. The traditional agency style had been built on short, sharp, easily understandable, simply presented accounts of events. But international news was growing more complex. The old simplifications—good versus bad, cold and hot wars, us versus them—gave way to a shifting, elusive pattern of news. Vietnam produced few clear-cut victories. The escalation of oil prices required analysis and understanding beyond what the agencies had been used to providing. At the same time, television outdid the agencies in descriptive and programmatic reporting of events; one minute of film of President Nixon arriving in Peking rendered superfluous the wire services' step-by-step accounts of the airport reception party, the clothes worn by the president and First Lady, the smiles and handshakes, the motorcade driving off toward the city.

Nor could the agencies afford to remain indifferent to changes in the approach adopted by American newspapers. New features catering to the particular interests of different sections of the public blossomed. Readers and broadcast audiences were provided with description, analysis, and explanation by journalists specializing in economics, politics, foreign affairs, health, consumerism, fashion, and leisure. The AP and UPI had to try to adapt while retaining their prime role as suppliers of fast "spot" news.

The message was underscored by agency polls taken in the late 1970s. One, for UPI, showed that newspaper editors wanted "increased emphasis on consumerism, business and economics, lifestyle and leisure, farm news, state news and personalities." Another, carried out by the AP among broadcasting stations, which far outnumber newspapers in the association's membership, reported: "The single largest trend . . . was a desire for more, faster and better regional coverage. Coupled with this were comments such as 'run less international stuff,' 'less emphasis on Washington,' and 'more relevance to what people are interested in.' " When radio members were asked if they would use a regular feature script on world affairs, 67 percent said no. In the newspaper sphere, the head of a members' committee assessing the foreign news the AP sent to smaller-circulation dailies pronounced it "too wordy." A member of one of UPI's editorial advisory boards reflected that, when the agency "has to choose between Africa and West Virginia, West Virginia's bound to win."

Media owners and editors might themselves have a keen interest in world affairs, but by 1980 they were convinced that this interest was not shared by their readers and broadcast audiences. Some polls indicated that this conviction might, in fact, be mistaken, but it was a conviction that had taken hold of the media as a whole. "Our readers' interests differ from our own," the president of the AP Managing Editors Association told his colleagues in 1978, "and we must meet those interests." [2]

It was not just that foreign news no longer commanded an automatic priority in the U.S. media's scheme of things. The kind of coverage the agencies were feeling impelled to supply was, increasingly, not the kind that could easily be provided from most of their overseas reporting centers. "In the overall scheme, we are expected to do more, to explain more and to give more background—and to provide information people can use in their daily lives," UPI editor-in-chief H. L. Stevenson commented in 1980. Or, as Louis Boccardi, then the AP executive editor, told a meeting of the cooperative's managing editors: "It seems to me that one of the many things we have to do in today's circumstances is to help the newspaper [to be] a 'use paper.' " In January 1985, Boccardi became AP's president.

The place this leaves for foreign news is a restricted one. Accounts of European economic developments or pan-African summit meetings might be expanded with informative, explanatory background, although the replies to the AP radio poll left doubts about whether such stories are wanted by the bulk of its members in the first place. But there is little that agency correspondents can do on a daily basis to meet the "use" needs of newspapers. Often working alone and having to cover spot news events as they arise, agency men and women rarely have time to develop features that might be of direct interest to the readers in American suburbs who were the prime targets of newspaper marketing drives and editorial rethinking. The verdict of a 1979 study for the American Society of Newspaper Editors—that readers wanted their dailies to be "more attentive to their personal needs, more caring, more warmly human and less anonymous"— had scant relevance to agency coverage from Brussels, Djakarta, or Cairo. There were attempts, particularly by the AP, to step up analytical and feature coverage from abroad by appointing a few special correspondents who were freed from attending to the hourly flow of news, but their impact appears to have been distinctly limited, in part because of lack of interest among recipients and in part because of the restrictions on agency style. "It may have looked good. It may have let the AP management say they were adding something to the service," one of these correspondents commented. "But you never had the feeling that people at the top in New York were really interested, and we heard that some of the big AP directors were actively opposed to what we were doing. They thought the AP should be providing more statehouse news, not feature interpretations on European politics."

American concerns and attitudes hung over everything the AP and UPI did. "We like to think of ourselves as being international—we have the word in our name, after all," Roderick Beaton, then president of UPI, remarked in 1980. "But obviously when you get so much of your revenue from one country, that country is very important to you." When the new AP president, Keith Fuller, outlined plans for foreign reporting in 1976, he talked of producing "a three-dimensional coverage that makes the world understandable in terms of American precepts." Europe and the Middle East would be covered in "much the way we cover the United States . . . as geographical entities where news would no longer be Swiss, German, Italian, Israeli, Syrian and so forth. If we succeed in adding the dimension of perspective, our concept will, of course, be used worldwide." [3]

While suffering from rising costs and stagnant real revenues overseas, the two U.S. agencies were hit at home by the growth in the number of morning or evening dailies enjoying local circulation monopolies and by the rise of supplemental services offered by major U.S. papers. The drop in the number of directly competing papers in the 1960s and 1970s reduced the need of the survivors for two wire services. In times of local circulation battles, newspapers had been obliged to take both agencies' services, for offensive as well as defensive reasons. A big news break might come in on either of the two services, and a newspaper or broadcasting station that subscribed to only one would find itself being beaten regularly by a rival taking both.

Within the rich and homogeneous U.S. market, press competition had worked to the benefit of the agencies for two decades after the Supreme Court opened up access to the AP service to all who wanted it. But when rivalry in the press slackened, so did newspapers' need for both agencies. As UPI's former editor-in-chief Roger Tatarian put it, subscribing to both is now "a matter for the conscience of publishers." A monopoly daily can receive just one service secure in the knowledge that, even if the chosen service is behind with a news break, there is no competing newspaper to exploit the situation. Nor are readers going to miss the diversity of agency reports if they have no choice of daily newspaper.

The spread of monopoly newspapers hit UPI harder than the AP. The association's cooperative structure gave it a measure of protection; newspapers were more likely to stay within the membership "family" if faced with a choice between the two services. The AP was financially stronger, and the supply of news by its members gave it a greater ability than UPI to satisfy the demand for local-interest stories. By opening up the U.S. market, the 1943 Supreme Court decision had deprived UPI of its previous captive market among non-AP members. "So long as direct competition between newspapers in the same cycle, morning or afternoon, existed, this ruling had no particular effect on UPI," Tatarian noted. "But . . . as city after city was left with only one newspaper, [editors] no longer felt the same need for dual protection and, as they began to cut back to one service, the AP more often was the one retained."

The challenges facing the U.S. agencies, particularly UPI, were magnified by the growth of news services run by the *New York Times,* the *Los Angeles Times,* and the *Washington Post* and several of the major newspaper chains. The *New York Times* service has almost as long a history as UPI, having been started in World War I, when the newspaper defrayed the costs of communications from Europe by selling a "war wire" to half a dozen other papers. It was not until the early 1960s, however, that such supplemental services emerged significantly onto the scene in the United States and abroad.

Although there are areas of overlap, the supplementals do not compete head-on with the news agencies in terms of coverage, and this difference is the essence of their appeal. They provide a single story on an event, as opposed to hour-by-hour agency coverage. Speed is not their concern, but exclusivity may well be. The number of stories they offer is limited; their copy is written for the issuing newspaper, not to appeal to a broad range of subscribers, although it has in fact proved attractive to hundreds of dailies and weeklies both at home and abroad. What the supplementals offer is access to the reporting resources of some of the biggest U.S. newspapers. Smaller dailies can run coverage that would otherwise be far beyond their means, while the originating newspapers can offset part of their reporting costs.

For medium-sized and smaller newspapers the attractions are self-evident. Instead of receiving two wire services providing much the same copy, an editor can publish star reporters from the *New York Times,* the *Los Angeles Times,* or the *Washington Post* by dropping one of the news agencies and keeping the other as the minute-by-minute source of instant news. When a newspaper is in a monopoly position, the attraction of substituting a supplemental for either the AP or UPI is practically irresistible (unless of course the newspaper decides that all it needs is a single wire service and no supplemental at all). Use of supplementals was strongest in the United States, but also grew abroad, particularly in Western Europe, Latin America, and Japan, and provided competition for the news agencies in the allocation of newspapers' foreign department budgets.

In 1960, the *New York Times* News Service listed fifty clients. At the end of the 1970s, the total was 500, 150 of them outside the United States. The services run by the *Los Angeles Times* and the *Washington Post* reached 363 subscribers at the same point—164 of them abroad. "We came along at the right time," according to Rob Roy Buckingham, who built up the *New York Times* service.

> We offered serious, in-depth stories. The AP and UPI were not doing this kind of thing, but readers and editors were demanding it. What started happening in the United States was that papers found they could get more for their editorial dollar by taking a supplementary service, so they were ready to drop either the AP or UPI. And as smaller papers grew, instead of taking a second wire service as in the past, they found they could do well by taking a supplementary service in its place.

Once a newspaper takes a supplementary service, the natural tendency is to capitalize on it and to use its material whenever possible. This produces a further squeeze on the amount of news-agency copy printed. It becomes even more difficult for the agencies to get their more thoughtful, analytical reports used, since newspapers generally prefer similar material received from a supplemental service. The net results have been a reduction in the number of newspapers taking two U.S. wire services and a tendency to limit the agencies to their primary role as suppliers of basic breaking news, both domestic and foreign.

Despite their wide international spread and their continuing commitment to international news distribution, the AP and UPI are overwhelmingly American. Financially, as will be seen, the home market dominates their activities. Editorially, their sights are fixed on the U.S. press and broadcasting organizations. Their staffs are mainly Americans who think first of U.S. requirements whether they are in Peoria or Peking. But their essentially American nature has been disguised by their worldwide organization and reach. Regarded by admirers as well as critics as international organizations, they are really U.S. enterprises that operate on an international scale. The nature of the two agencies is such that this situation is unlikely to change. Without their domestic base, the AP and UPI could not operate as international agencies. With it, they must be American organizations, subject to American pressures and requirements.

Reuters:
Growth Outside the Media . . . .

The situation at Reuters in the 1960s and 1970s was of a very different order. Although its ownership was predominantly British, the agency was forced to be more international in outlook than its U.S. counterparts, since it did not have a domestic news service. Both in Britain and abroad, Reuters provided only foreign news as it ran into growing financial difficulties in the late 1950s and early 1960s.

By 1963, when its general manager, Walton Cole, died at his desk in Fleet Street, Reuters was in a precarious state. Its lack of resources threatened to become chronic. It had no money to develop reporting or distribution. For years, it had lagged behind the AP and UPI in communications technology, and its traditional field of activity—international media markets—offered little hope of any substantial increase in income. While the agency had made considerable headway in newly independent Africa, it did not distribute in Latin America, and its reporting from there was fitful. Its U.S. operations were constrained by an agreement with the AP under which Reuters received the cooperative's domestic news report and saved itself the cost of reporting outside Washington and New York.

Cole's successor, Gerald Long, considered three sources of funds when he became Reuters' general manager. "There were the owners, who had been very good and had gone along with an inflation of costs and had gone on supporting Reuters. There was the British government, and there were commercial operations," Long recalled seventeen years later.

> The first of these I regarded as impossible, and I think that would have been the general view among the owners at that time—there was no more money available if our costs went up, as they inevitably would. There were those who thought Reuters would have to have a British Broadcasting Corporation type of charter, accepting some form of subsidy. I could not and would not consider it, nor was it ever suggested

to me except occasionally in conversation by those who honestly felt that it was the only way. So I was left with number three [commercial operations]; it was the only chance we had.

For Long and Reuters, commercial operations meant developing services to be sold profitably in a way that was proving impossible in the media. The target was the world business community: banks, brokers, foreign exchange dealers, and companies that would pay well for fast information services that enabled them to make money. Before Long took charge, Reuters had developed Western European economic news services, but the emphasis had remained strongly on general news operations. After 1963, however, building up economic news activities went hand in hand with a fundamental change in the agency's operating philosophy. "I gradually changed the old idea that you should break even into the aim of making a working profit," Long recalled. Reuters returned to its roots, and Long spoke often of reverting to the philosophy established by its founding baron.[4] The process involved turning a news agency into a capital-intensive, high-technology company whose main activity was increasingly removed from the everyday pressures and problems of running a general news service.

Reuters faced a fundamental dilemma in applying the commercial approach: if the aim was to make a working profit, and if international general news services were unprofitable, how long should these services be continued at the level the world had come to expect? What is striking is the way in which Reuters not only built up its economic news services but also expanded its international general news operations. The most important instance of this occurred in the United States, where Long was intent on gaining freedom of action in reporting and distribution for both general and economic news services.

The story of how Reuters broke away from its previous, limiting agreement with the AP in the United States—a story that involves all four agencies in one way or another—provides a good example of how the major agencies' interests overlap but rarely converge. The point at issue arose from a long-standing arrangement under which the AP office in London received British news from the Press Association domestic news agency, while Reuters got the AP domestic service in the United States. In the mid–1960s, the Press Association proposed to supply its service to UPI as well. The AP objected that this would reduce the value of the service, since Press Association news would now be available to its main competitor. At the same time, the AP asked Reuters for an annual payment of $200,000 to take account of the differing importance of British and U.S. domestic news. It was, as Long later noted, a very large sum in those days. Some AP executives say the amount was purposely pitched high in order to provoke a break, which the cooperative assumed would work to its advantage as Reuters became bogged down in the costs of covering North America independently.

A similar request went from the AP to the French agency. AFP and Reuters discussed the possibility of joint coverage of the United States. They got nowhere because of the English-French language problem and because AFP decided that independent operations would prove too expensive. So AFP met the AP's asking price and subsequently had the unusual experience of seeing the rate decline—helped along by the French agency's occasional suggestions that it might sign up with UPI if the AP's charges proved too onerous.

The attitude at Reuters was very different. While the London-based agency argued for a reduction in the AP's price, Long was hoping that the cooperative would not yield, for he and his executives were eager to get into the world's biggest news market on a completely free basis. Their development of business news services was already bearing fruit, and Reuters had also embarked on an activity then unique for a news agency: selling financial information delivered by electronic retrieval terminals. For any service dealing in business news, the United States was the prime target, but the AP agreement was linked to one with the Dow Jones financial service, which prevented Reuters from marketing its financial news across the Atlantic as it wished.

The aggressive and expansionist mood at Reuters did not prevent an approach from UPI. Cooperation between the two services appeared logical, since they were complementary in many ways. UPI had U.S. domestic cover, photographs, and a strong position in Latin America. Reuters was well placed in areas where UPI was weak, and had a rapidly growing range of business news services that both U.S. agencies lacked.

Preliminary talks were held in a Washington hotel, where the possibility of cutting reporting costs by cooperating in major centers such as Moscow was raised. Then the chief executives of the two agencies met in the English resort of Brighton during a congress of international news organizations. The fundamental incompatibility between the agencies soon became evident. UPI was still strong and confident enough to insist on being the dominant partner. Reuters was intent on maximizing its freedom of action and wanted to keep the expected gold mine from its economic services to itself. At the end of the Brighton talks, UPI president Mims Thomason gathered his working papers into a ball and threw them into a wastebasket. When the UPI group had left, a Reuters executive went back to the meeting room and retrieved Thomason's crumpled papers, which showed UPI to be considerably stronger than Reuters believed it to be. The conclusion drawn in London was that Thomason, anticipating that his papers would be retrieved, had laid on an elaborate bluff. The incident made Reuters all the more determined to go its own way.

The start of Reuters' independent operations in the United States in 1967 was not only important in itself, it also increased the scope of competition between the world agencies and provided a precedent for similar Reuters moves elsewhere. The agency's newfound spirit of growth had already taken it back into Latin America. General news operations were now organized on a profit-seeking basis; a network of regional reporting, editing, and distribution centers was established to produce services tailored for different geographical markets. A Middle East operation was set up in Beirut, replacing a long-standing arrangement with a regional news organization financed in part by the British Foreign Office. In 1971, Reuters founded a German-language operation of its own, based in Bonn, instead of selling its news to the national agency, DPA. In France, Reuters ended a domestic news-exchange agreement with AFP and signed a profit-sharing distribution agreement for the provinces with a smaller French agency, Agence Centrale de Presse (ACP).

Despite media-market difficulties, Reuters was moving into independent operations just when UPI was pulling back from them. New reporting offices were opened and fresh services were produced wherever there appeared to be a possibility of earning a profit. But the bottom line remained disappointing. While the economic news services won steadily increasing profits, the company's general news division could not get out of the red. This was due in part to the generally poor state of the world media market and in part to the long tradition of low rates paid for agency services. The situation was exacerbated in Reuters' case by a decision to freeze the amounts paid by its owners in the British, Australian, and New Zealand media. There were solid reasons for doing this, reasons that will be discussed in a later examination of the agencies' finances, but the immediate effect was to deprive the general news division of revenue increases from the important ownership areas.

At the same time, the company's lack of capital meant that funds available for technological development were channeled toward the expanding economic news sector, where they would bring the biggest returns. The general news division made powerful use of a major innovation in news-agency communications: the introduction of a computer system to receive, store, switch, and transmit messages. But after this breakthrough in 1967, the investment funds Reuters raised from its profits went to the service that produced those profits.

In 1974, a new philosophy was adopted. General news would no longer be judged on its ability to make a profit; it would instead be recognized as the agency's central activity, conducted for the benefit of Reuters as a whole.[5] But with the economic services needing ever-increasing amounts of capital for new computer projects, and with profits flattening out after 1976, the sums subsequently lost on general news operations inevitably came to be seen as a dangerous drag on growth. By the late 1970s, the gap between what media services cost and the revenue they earned had again begun to arouse concern at the very top of the organization. In stages, the agency brought general and economic news reporting together under unified control. The company no longer spoke of "general news" and "economic news," but simply of "news," which meant everything from the murder of John Lennon to the movement of pork-belly futures.

Some sources recall chief executive Gerald Long predicting in the 1960s that services purely based on the media were doomed, sooner or later. Despite its successive reorganizations, however, Reuters kept paying the price of maintaining loss-making reports for the world's newspapers and broadcasters. Its editorial sights changed in the four years before Long left the agency in 1981. The trend was away from human-interest news, secondary items, and detailed coverage for unremunerative regions. Instead, Reuters wanted to "increase the economic copy and concentrate on major stories," according to editor Manfred Pagel. General news journalists were told that their most important single client was Reuters' economic service. A lengthy study of the agency's markets concluded that it should scale down the attention paid to subscribers outside North America, Western Europe, and Japan, and produce a single news service that would be distributed around the globe. The editorial criteria for this service would, naturally, be those of Reuters' richer markets.

At the same time, the agency's management pronounced the uniformity of agency coverage to be company doctrine. Reuters, they said, was in the business of producing a single report of events that could then be split up and sold to different groups of recipients. "There is a differentiation in markets, but not in reporting," Gerald Long declared.

Long's successor as managing director, Glen Renfrew, declared in 1981 that "our central purpose is to maintain and raise the quality of our news services," and the agency subsequently broadened its editorial sights again. Sports coverage was expanded. An ambitious decentralization program, transferring authority to regional centers for Europe, North America, Asia, Africa, the Middle East, and Latin America, breathed fresh life into the journalistic set-up. The Hong Kong editorial team took control of the world news file for eight-hour stretches. Regional desks produced locally distributed services. But this did not mean any variations in the way Reuters approached its job. One-track editorial standards remain the order of the day, from Bahrain to Buenos Aires.

For the economic services dominating Reuters' activities, there was no question of diversity in reporting. A currency quotation or commodity price had an unchallengeable validity wherever it was reported or distributed. Figures were neutral. Many of the computer services that brought in Reuters' biggest profits did not even involve editorial intervention by the agency. The decentralization of 1982 ensured that producing services for the rich markets would be even further emphasized. In the past, news costs had been allocated to a central budget; now they were charged separately to each region, so that differences in profitability between Western Europe and Africa, or North and South America, would be clear. In such circumstances, there was no way in which Reuters would change its outlook on the way the world's news should be reported.

AFP: No Change. . . . .

Agence France-Presse, unlike Reuters and the American services, appeared to some observers in the early 1980s to be capable of breaking away from the common pattern of major agency services. AFP's linguistic difference from the other three and France's tradition of a more discursive, individualistic approach to reporting were cited as setting AFP, at least potentially, apart from Reuters, the AP, and UPI. But what such suggestions really rested on was the fact that the French agency was much less dependent on the international sub-scriber market than the other three.

In the quarter of a century after its reformation in 1957, AFP established itself firmly as a member of the major agency group. It built up its position in Latin America and Asia, dominated news distribution in French-speaking Africa, and worked closely with European national agencies. In the Middle East, it collaborated with Egypt's Middle East News Agency in running an Arabic service. Desks in Paris produced news files in Spanish, German, and English as well as French. The agency's overseas operations were more important, in terms of staff and money, than its domestic news operations, which did not always please the French provincial newspapers represented on the AFP board.

The period in which General Charles de Gaulle staked out France's position of highly vocal independence in world affairs was particularly beneficial for the agency's expansion. Countries that appreciated the general's stance assumed France's news agency would have a particular, independent view of the world to offer. It was not an impression AFP sought to dispel, although it was based on the belief that the agency was committed to the French government's attitude in international affairs.

Despite its growth in the past two decades, AFP remains restricted in important respects. Its Latin American presence is small compared with that of the AP and UPI. Its attempts to expand in English-speaking Africa have run up against Reuters' entrenched position there. In some parts of the world, it suffers from the legacy of extremely low subscription rates charged in its earlier days. Its English service is limited by its small audience in Britain and, most importantly, in the United States, where it is distributed mainly through the *Los Angeles Times–Washington Post* news service, which has access to the AFP world file. This arrangement means that the French agency can say its news reaches the 200 U.S. clients of the supplementary service, but senior managers report that very little AFP copy is actually used.[6]

In a negative sense, therefore, AFP may seem freer to alter its focus than are the other agencies. But it is unlikely that this will happen. The French government, which pays well over half of the agency's bills, has shown no sign of wanting it to become part of a new world information order with its sights set on the Third World, as some outside commentators have suggested might happen. AFP's internal development plans drawn up in 1983 are aimed primarily at increasing revenue, which inevitably means looking to the richer international media areas. Market researchers commissioned by the agency's newly appointed business manager in 1984 were more interested in analyzing the reasons for Reuters' financial success than in finding out how services might be adapted to meet African needs more closely. At the same time, AFP's paymasters in the Mitterrand administration, attempting to hold down the budget deficit and cut taxes at the same time, have put their early expansionary language aside and are pressing state enterprises to cut losses as fast as possible.

Apart from such attitudes, there was a good reason why AFP should not break off from the ranks of the Big Four to become an agency catering specifically to the Third World. If such a change took place, AFP's international revenue would probably fall as it found itself at a competitive disadvantage in the richer markets, without gaining balancing revenue from subscribers in poor nations. This would make the agency even more dependent on French state support—not an appealing prospect either to the men running AFP or to the framers of the government information budget, who have shown concern in recent years at the escalating costs of keeping the agency going. AFP and the other major news services will not change so long as their international operations are based on commercial competition and their main markets remain within the industrialized world. The status quo of the agencies' outlook is here to stay.

CHAPTER **5** ....

Operations

In the early 1980s, Reuters and Agence France-Presse each distributed news services in 150 countries or territories. The Associated Press's news reached 110, and the United Press International's 92.

Statistics on the exact number of clients receiving the services of the Big Four are all too easily confused, incomplete, and at times clearly wrong. One set of figures appearing in a recent analysis credited UPI with a domestic U.S. press clientele three times the total number of American newspapers. Confusion is compounded by the dual nature of the AP, UPI, and AFP as suppliers of both domestic and foreign news. For AFP, with its relatively small home market in France, this factor is not of great significance, but the inclusion of the very large number of U.S. recipients of AP and UPI in their international totals can be highly misleading, implying that they have more clients spread more widely across the globe than is actually the case.

The four agencies themselves do not know exactly how many newspapers, broadcasters, and other recipients make use of their news. This is because many of their international clients are national news agencies that edit and pass on a selection of their material. A national agency may be included in subscriber figures in two ways: as a single client or as the total of its own subscribers. The difference between the two can be enormous; the Chinese national agency, for instance, can be regarded as a single recipient or as the representative of the hundreds of news organizations that receive its service.

This means that the total of 16,050 subscribers reported by the AP at the end of 1983 must be regarded as a general indication rather than a precise count of how many newspapers, broadcasting stations, and other organizations around the world get the association's news, by one means or another. Within the AP total, one set of figures is finite, the 1500 newspapers and 5700 broadcasting stations that receive the service in the United States. The foreign recipients' total of 8850, however, includes some indirect subscribers that get their news through one of the 42 agencies that subscribe to the AP service. It does not, the AP is quick to point out, include the 3000 recipients of the Soviet TASS agency, which receives the AP service in Moscow and uses it as it sees fit.

Reuters declined to give precise figures for its media subscribers. Such information was absent from the company's share flotation prospectus in 1984, in contrast to detailed figures for its commercially successful business news services. The overall number of media subscribers can, however, be put at around 5000. This is smaller than the AP or UPI totals because of the respective sizes of the U.S. and British domestic markets. It should also be remembered that the 5700 broadcast members of the AP include a very large number of very small radio stations that pay little money and use a minimal amount of world news. Another reason for the lower Reuters figure is the agency's weak position in Latin America, where both U.S. services have had hundreds of subscribers since before World War II. Excluding the Americas, Reuters is, internationally, on a par with the AP in its presence in the world's media.[1]

UPI traditionally liked to claim that it was running just behind the AP in subscriber numbers. In recent years, the distance between the two agencies has lengthened, both at home and abroad. UPI figures for 1977 gave it 7079 clients, of which 2246 were outside the United States. Unpublished figures at the turn of the past decade showed the number of subscribers down to 6000. This has declined further since then. By 1985, UPI's domestic clients were estimated at 4100, 3300 of them broadcasting stations which often pay low rates.

AFP, like Reuters, is affected by its relatively small domestic base. In 1984, its general news services reached only 432 clients in France. Of these, just 89 were newspapers, and 39 were broadcasting stations. Abroad, AFP counted 1297 subscribers to its general media service, making a total of 1729 clients at home and abroad. Among the foreign subscribers, 353 were newspapers, 203 broadcasting stations, and 99 news agencies. French ministries, embassies, official missions, and other state organizations account for much of the difference between the total number of recipients of the AFP service and the agency's restricted presence in the world media. By any measure, the French agency remains much the smallest of the Big Four on a global scale, to the extent that Reuters did not even mention it as a principal competitor in its 1984 share prospectus.

While maintaining a uniform editorial standard for all subscribers, each of the major agencies organizes its worldwide distribution on a regional basis to try to cater to the news requirements of different areas of the globe. This division of general-news services by regions means that none of the agencies issues a single world-news report; rather, each puts out a series of services that contain a substantial amount of common coverage but differ in the material targeted for specific regions. Coverage of a British general election would be included in all services, while a report of a speech by a Zambian minister to a food conference in Rome would go only to Africa. The common-content copy could be said to constitute the agencies' basic world report, but this is a theoretical concept that has little bearing upon the way services actually operate, for even common-content stories may be sent at different lengths in different services. It is therefore necessary to look at the range of individual services and how they are constituted to get an idea of just how the agencies go about supplying news to subscribers at home and abroad. This examination will underscore one of the most salient features of news-agency operations: the major factors affecting what the Big Four issue to subscribers are the international importance of stories, regional interests, the accessibility of news, and the proximity of region of origin to region of use—*not* a desire to tilt the balance of world-news reporting in favor of the West.

The Big Four: Structure of Services. . . . .

For the AP and UPI, and to a lesser extent AFP, the biggest and most varied services are those distributed at home. The AP report for U.S. newspapers, issued through the agency's general desk at its New York headquarters, consists of high-speed and slow-speed services tailored to either large-circulation or smaller publications. The contents of these four services vary according to the needs of different recipients. Studies over the twenty-five-year history of the service to large-circulation newspapers show that foreign news makes up anywhere from 22 to 33 percent of the total amount of copy. The proportion of foreign news falls in the services sent out on an "Interbureau" wire to smaller AP members, to which reporting centers in ten major areas of the country add state and local news. In addition to these basic services for U.S. newspapers, the AP operates a news-feature service, a sports wire, a business-news file, high-speed stock price listings, and a service of news highlights for a thousand private nonmedia clients.

The AP's radio and television members get two services: a special news wire edited and written for broadcasters and an audio service of voice reports and sound recordings. The Broadcast News Wire is claimed to be the longest single news circuit in the world, stretching 180,000 miles across 48 states and serving 33,500 AP members representing 5000 broadcasting stations. While this service makes substantial use of foreign news from AP correspondents, it operates in a market in which domestic considerations are foremost. "There is a feeling in broadcasting circles," one of its editors remarked, "that international news is not of great importance."

UPI's services in the United States, organized on a similar basis, also differentiate between large- and small-to-medium-circulation newspapers. The agency's state bureaus insert local news for local consumption; coverage of sports, business, and the stock markets, as well as special features, are also offered. "Rip and read" news services for radio stations, written in broadcasting style so that newscasters can read them on the air as received, were pioneered by UPI in the 1930s. The agency was also first into the audio business, and supplies voice reports from its correspondents, live relays of major press conferences, and recordings of everything from the sound of gunfire in battle zones to interviews with beauty-contest winners. UPI currently issues some 150 audio items a day. As at the AP's similar service, the emphasis is overwhelmingly domestic; some 80 percent of the service deals with U.S. events.

The impact of changing news requirements in the United States is clearly reflected in the inclusion by both U.S. agencies of coverage of domestic items previously absent from regular wire-service offerings. In its daily file to newspapers, UPI runs features dealing with gardening, home repair, health, and Hollywood gossip, as well as a "Backstairs at the White House" column. The AP's regular items include columns on consumer affairs and citizens' band radio, weekly features by some of the agency's top writers traveling the country, and the results of polls on matters of domestic concern.

All this is now available on 1200-words-per-minute delivery that can be fed straight into a newspaper's printing process. The speed not only answers the basic agency requirement to be as fast as possible, it also increases the amount of material that can be transmitted in each news cycle. The agencies now issue all the features and columns they can produce, meet the early deadlines adopted by U.S. afternoon newspapers in recent years, and still avoid the backlogs of copy that characterized the old sixty-words-per-minute teleprinter circuits. When correcting an error or adding a new element to a story, the AP and UPI simply run a complete new version of the report. Recipients, no longer slowed down by the laborious process of modifying the original story, can quickly and easily replace it with the new version received on the high-speed wire.

In the United States, the agencies have kept up with technological developments, but the application of such technology to international services has been slower. Much of the world's press is not ready to make use of high-speed wires or services fed from an agency's computer into an electronically controlled composing room; in some instances, the agencies serve subscribers whose journalists still write in ink. Some news services distributed to the international media are still delivered by slow-speed circuit teleprinters. In some parts of the world, transmission by radio, with all its attendant snags of interference, meteorological problems, and faulty reception equipment, can still be found.

Newspaper and broadcast subscribers cannot choose what information they receive; each gets everything issued for its region in the same order and at the same length as the others. Newspapers using only one or two foreign items a day receive as much material as publications devoting several pages to covering the world. This lack of subscriber choice puts a premium on the role played by editing desks, which are located differently by each of the major agencies. At AFP they are centralized in Paris, ranged in a row along the editorial floor at the agency's headquarters. The AP operates its European-language services locally; otherwise, it concentrates world news editing and production in New York. Reuters works on a much more decentralized basis, allowing regional offices to file local news to subscribers in their areas. Pushing decentralization to its limits, Reuters gave its regional centers operational autonomy from London in 1982, with its major editing desk in Hong Kong taking control of the main news flow during the European night time. UPI was formerly highly decentralized, but has recently reduced the role of regional editing.

Wherever it is located, the editing desk determines the shape and content of an agency's services. Desks rewrite, cut, or expand copy received from correspondents, making reporters' complaints about mutilation of their work a constant feature of agency life. Since only one story at a time can be transmitted to a teleprinter subscriber, the sequence in which copy is issued is critical. Desks determine the order in which stories are issued, and indeed whether they are issued at all. A news-agency file is constantly changing; it cannot be frozen in the way that a newspaper is when printed. Effective control thus lies in the hands of the men and women who determine the makeup of a service from minute to minute. Their power has been reduced at some agencies by the technical ability of correspondents to ''inject'' copy direct to subscribers, but desks remain dominant in deciding what reaches clients.

The pressure of speed and the sheer volume of copy handled mean that the chief editorial executives of an agency, who bear overall responsibility for its news reports, cannot as a rule intervene before copy is dispatched. Sensitive items or problem stories are likely to be referred to them before being issued, but the task of monitoring every service issued by the agency on a twenty-four-hour basis would be impossible. Instead, the chief editors of agencies depend on the editors working in shifts under them to ensure that certain standards are met and that the quality of services is maintained. Delegation of decision making, essential if an agency is to operate effectively, can amount virtually to blind trust. Effective control of a service in Arabic is impossible at an agency's head office if nobody there understands the language. As one U.S. editor commented about his agency's services issued locally in Europe: ''We don't see what they put out. If we did, we wouldn't understand it. We just have to trust the people concerned.''

Despite their power to control services, desk editors cannot originate stories. They lay down requirements for coverage of programmed events, request expansion of items already filed, or ask correspondents to file ''matchers'' to stories the agency missed the first time around, but they cannot witness the events that provide the material for news reports. Nor can they decide which breaking stories to cover—at least not until after they have broken. Correspondents, on the other hand, are unable to shape the news services in which their reports appear, or to evaluate them against stories being filed simultaneously by other offices. The resulting interdependent relationship between correspondents and desks is at the heart of agency editorial operations.

The extent of desk control and the freedom given to correspondents to inject their copy directly into outgoing files to subscribers vary among the four agencies, but the overall pattern is the same. Correspondents make the initial coverage decision based on their own assessments of the news interest of an event. Their stories go to a central point where editors make further decisions based on *their* judgments of what subscribers want. The resulting news files are organized according to the priority of the news items they contain, with the mix between world-interest and regional-target reports decided on by the issuing desks.

The variety of such files is greatest at Reuters, which distributes two dozen services for media clients internationally. In the early 1980s, seven of these emanated from London, all in English. Three were aimed at subscribers in Europe. The service to Africa was issued from an editing desk in Nairobi. Hong Kong issued six Reuters services to Asia, again all in English. Three French-language services went from a desk in Paris to clients in North Africa, West/Central Africa, and French-speaking Europe. Bonn put out a German service, Cairo an Arabic service, and New York a general-news file for North America, while Lisbon undertook a limited translation and editing operation in Portuguese. In Buenos Aires, the collapse of a regional agency Reuters had backed left it editing, translating, and distributing a Spanish-language service in Latin America.

AFP, despite its centralized editing in Paris, is second only to Reuters in the number of international services it issues. In France itself, the agency supplies separate files for the Paris media and provincial subscribers, and runs a much-used horse-racing wire. Abroad, AFP distributes thirteen different general news services. One, in Arabic, is put out from Cairo after being edited and translated by Egypt's Middle East News Agency (MENA). The other dozen, originating in Paris, consist of French, German, and English services for Europe; French and English files for Africa; a French service for the Middle East; Spanish and Portuguese services for Latin America; and different French and English files for Asia, North America, and the Caribbean.

The American agencies offer less variety in the total number of their different services abroad, but this is balanced, at least in part, by the strength of the services they issue in Latin America, and by the AP's continuing local language services in Germany, France, Holland, and Sweden. In South America, the early strong expansion of the U.S. services prompted them to set up local national editing and translating operations. This system was later revised, as both agencies established centralized Latin American desks at their New York headquarters. The AP ran five separate services, going to Venezuela and the Caribbean, Mexico and Central America, Brazil, Argentina and Uruguay, and the west coast of Latin America. UPI's distribution routes from New York went to Puerto Rico, Mexico, Colombia, Brazil, Argentina, Paraguay, Bolivia, Peru, and Chile, where it ran a domestic news operation in addition to distributing foreign copy. In volume terms, these AP and UPI services contain among the highest proportions of regional copy to be found in any agency files. Up to half the material sent to Latin America originates from correspondents there who dispatch it to New York for retransmission in the appropriate Latin American services. The volume of their reporting makes the AP and UPI the prime suppliers of Latin American news within the region.

In Europe, apart from its local language services, the AP distributes a single English file, formerly edited in London but now issued from New York. In Asia, the association puts out a main "trunk" wire, to which material is added for particularly important countries like Japan. The agency's limited African service goes to Kenya and Nigeria by radio, and South Africa receives its service via permanent cable circuit. The AP distributes its French-language service to North African as well as European clients, with some modifications to take account of their particular requirements. Another service, transmitted by radio, goes to the Middle East and India, while satellites transmit an AP file to Australia and the South Pacific.

UPI issues a basically similar service throughout its Europe/Middle East/Africa division, with stories being added or deleted according to local interests. A similar type of trunk file, with local additions, is distributed in Asia. UPI also sent news files to the Caribbean, to ships at sea, and to the ARAMCO oil company for its staff in Saudi Arabia. Alone among the agencies, UPI ran a news distribution operation in Canada, in conjunction with two Canadian companies, before pulling back for financial reasons. From London, UPI offered subscribers a special sports wire.

In addition to supplying news files, the agencies offer subscribers a wide variety of other services, including photographic services, discussed in the next chapter. They extend help and professional hospitality to traveling correspondents and—sometimes more importantly—to media owners and managers visiting in foreign lands. They transmit clients' copy on their own circuits, a process made easy and profitable by the introduction of computers that switch incoming messages from agency headquarters to a subscriber's office. They provide advice and expertise to national news agencies for a fee.

"Technology and communications have become as much a market-able property as news," a UPI vice-president remarked in 1980.

Flow and Use of News-Agency Copy. . . . .

Despite the selectivity of correspondents in picking which events to cover—and despite all the editing done by desks around the world—news agencies issue far more words than any single subscriber can use. This is a result of trying to meet the requirements of a variety of clients within each region. Reuters' subscribers in Italy, for example, get items targeted for Spain (and vice versa) because the service for continental Europe covers both countries. The volume of copy moved on the wires is also a product of the continuous coverage techniques practiced by the agencies to ensure that subscribers who are going to press or on the air have the latest significant news.

In covering an international conference, an agency might begin with a forward-looking report forecasting likely developments during the meeting. This would be followed by a story reporting the opening of the conference. A bit later, a third story might be sent following a major speech, and a fourth to round up developments at midafternoon for the benefit of early editions of the next day's morning papers. In the evening session, a delegation walkout might produce a fifth story, topped by a report of a final vote at midnight. The successive stories would be written, as much as possible, to avoid repetition; they would dovetail into each other, with ever-newer and more important elements succeeding each other as lead paragraphs.

In such a case, radio stations might use several of the different reports in successive hourly news bulletins. No newspaper, on the other hand, would be likely to print more than one of the stream of agency stories. Morning papers would be interested only in copy sent from midafternoon onward, by which time the afternoon papers that used the early copy would have stopped publishing for the day.

The huge difference between the volume of copy issued by an agency in any twenty-four-hour period and the amount that any one subscriber is likely to use should be borne in mind when confronting the awesome statistics frequently quoted for the daily volume of words issued by the big agencies. So, too, should two other considerations: first, much of the copy carried by the major services is not international general news at all, as is often implied, but domestic reporting, business services, and material transmitted for clients; second, much of the agencies' general-news wordage is made up of identical stories sent out in many different services. The same reports are counted over and over again, resulting in the impression that the agencies issue even more stories than they really do. For example, a reporting office files 1000 words on the death of a leading statesman. Aware of the wide general interest of the story, it sends the item to decentralized editing desks as well as to headquarters. The head office, if it judges the story acceptable without changes, sends it out untouched to all its subscriber services, and the regional editing desks do the same. The computers through which the story is transmitted on its various passages from correspondent to desks to subscribers register each word on each incoming and outgoing circuit separately, with the result that the 1000-word story creates a communications statistic of 20,000 words or more.

These technicalities must be spelled out to account for the astonishing wordage figures collected by UNESCO at the end of the 1970s and subsequently reproduced uncritically by a number of writers. According to these totals, the AP issued 17 million words a day, UPI, 11 million, AFP, 3.5 million, and Reuters—with the greatest range of international services—1.1 million. Such statistics are meaningless as a basis for comparison and analysis. They say nothing about either what subscribers actually receive or the amount of agency material actually used.

The daily wordage issued by the major agencies in their various services differs considerably. At the lower end of the scale, services sent to Africa by radio run to 25,000 or 30,000 words a day, while the report furnished to subscribers in Western Europe and other developed areas approaches 80,000 words per day. The actual amount of this copy reaching newspapers and broadcasters in most countries is much smaller because of the filtering performed by national agencies. Copy from the major services often makes up all the foreign coverage a national service offers its subscribers, but the actual wordage used is far smaller than that received. Where a national agency has foreign correspondents of its own, the proportion of material used drops even further. In Japan, the Kyodo agency, which maintains a 44-person foreign reporting staff of its own, receives 600,000 words of foreign coverage a day from 50 agencies. Of these, it gets more than 69,000 words a day from UPI, 64,000 from Reuters, and 52,000 from AP, as well as 20,000 words from its own correspondents. But Kyodo's general file to Japanese subscribers contains a daily average of only 12,000 words of foreign news, according to the agency's statistics, and two-thirds of this is from Kyodo's own correspondents. Receiving three major services, Kyodo gets coverage of many events in triplicate, and thus must discard most of the coverage from Reuters, UPI, or the AP. The amount actually used is strikingly small; considering only the least voluminous of the international services, Kyodo uses no more than 8 percent of the AP file even if it decides to ignore the other two services completely.

Such calculations need to be hedged somewhat in recognition of the many uses made of agency copy—for information, planning, background, and alerting the recipient's own correspondents. Kyodo obviously represents an extreme case because of its extensive foreign reporting network. But the example shows how essential it is to draw a clear distinction between the volume of words issued by the agencies and the volume of material that actually reaches the public. Data from national agencies with much smaller foreign staffs than Kyodo indicate that the use of international copy may normally run at around 20 percent of the amount received from the major services. When this selection reaches the press and broadcasting stations, the proportion used falls further, and a final reduction takes place when the end users—the public—decide what to listen to, read, or watch.

This is not to belittle the importance of the major agencies in the world information process. However much of their copy ends up unused, they remain the major international collectors and distributors of news. What distinguishes them from other news organizations is their global reach and their application of a single editorial standard around the world. The 32.6 million words a day counted by UNESCO are not, in themselves, significant.[2] Rather, the importance of Reuters, the AP, UPI, and AFP lies in the fact that their news is used so widely. Among them, the four major services have proved more acceptable as sources of international news than any alternatives that have emerged. As a result, the news choices they make have a major bearing on the way the world views itself.

What Gets Reported and Why. . . . .

Within each agency, news decisions are made on a story-by-story basis. The physical appearance of a roll of teleprinter paper on which a service is received by clients fosters the illusion that an agency file forms a unity, constructed as a whole by editing desks. In fact, it is a series of individual items that run in chronological order for technical reasons and share only the prospect of being of interest to the same group of subscribers. The mortar of the teleprinter roll is ephemeral, as has been shown by video-screen retrieval services that enable clients to pick and choose the stories they want. There is no whole, only a collection of parts.

Each event is evaluated on its own merits. No relationship between them is assumed by correspondents or editors, except where there is an obvious connection or similarity. Stories are not lumped together under subject headings, or according to geographical origin. Political stories from Zaire and Tokyo are not regarded as having anything in common. A crime story and a crop report, both from Kansas City, are treated in complete isolation from each other.

Similarly, there is no attempt by correspondents or editors to achieve a balance among different subjects or regions. A correspondent who has sent ten political stories during a week and only one economic item will not elect to cover an unimportant Finance Ministry press conference and ignore a cabinet appointment in order to get a better balance in the file. If a plane crashes or a ship sinks, the desk does not reflect on the number of accident stories it has issued that month before putting out the news. Each story stands on its own and is judged individually as regards its likely interest to subscribers.

This interest can be evaluated in a number of ways. A story may be issued simply because it is unusual or evocative. It may fall into the category of disaster news: accidents, earthquakes, or floods. It may have a special regional appeal or be of worldwide interest. Overwhelmingly, as will be seen, agency news is about obviously important people and events. It deals with power, wherever it may be exercised, and reflects the existing balance of strength in the world.

This balance may be unpalatable to some recipients, but the realities of the world, unjust though they may be, are not the invention of the news agencies. News services claiming to operate on principles of neutrality and accuracy cannot impose a more equal pattern on an unequal world. Much of their reporting from rich and powerful nations is, in any case, of great interest to poor ones. What the president of the United States or the Soviet Union says and does is of prime concern to developing countries as well as to Western Europe and Japan. As worldwide services, the agencies naturally concentrate on events of global importance. This is not to deny that there may be a place for another kind of international news service, based on different approaches and values, but it is unrealistic to expect the Big Four to do other than to order their priorities in direct relation to the balance of the world as they, and most of their clients, see it.

Their view is a decidedly serious one. Politics and economics dominate their reporting. The agencies pay relatively little attention to human-interest stories, entertaining items called "brights," or the more trivial news that is so prominently featured by so many of their subscriber newspapers, radio stations, and television stations. Agencies like big numbers. A demonstration of 1000 people would not get onto the wire. A demonstration of 10,000 might merit a paragraph or two, if the protest were about something interesting internationally. A demonstration of 100,000 would merit a full story, whatever the cause of their protest.

Because stories are judged on their individual merits, statistics on how many agency items fall into one or another subject category have little or no bearing on the decision making that goes into making up the daily file. But they do show how, without a conscious design, agency copy conforms to certain patterns. Averaging data from seventeen studies of international agencies for the media since 1974 shows that 45 percent of items dealt with international or domestic politics.[3] Three-quarters of these were about foreign affairs in one form or another. After politics, economics concerned the agencies most, accounting for an average of 14.7 percent of the general-news files. While politics has always been the agencies' staple, economic coverage has increased considerably in recent years; a survey taken in 1952–53 had shown that only 4.8 percent of foreign news distributed in the United States concerned economic events.

After politics and economics, sports coverage accounted for an average 11.5 percent of agency files. But the percentage of sports news in individual services varies widely, from 23 percent in some Latin American files to none at all in a Reuters service to the Middle East. While figuring in third place in the surveys overall, sports tends to be more regional than other categories of news, with a premium placed on the performances of local athletes. The passionate interest in cricket coverage in South Africa or Australia is matched by a corresponding degree of indifference in Japan or Saudi Arabia.

Other subjects maintain a low profile on the agencies' world files. Eleven studies in 1979 and 1980 showed that military clashes and domestic or international violence took up an average 8.5 percent of agency files, while 5.6 percent concerned crime and legal matters and 4.4 percent accidents and disasters. Human-interest items, brights, and reports about celebrities made up 2.2 percent of the total—a huge drop from the figure of 12.7 percent reported in the 1952–53 survey. Coverage of arts, culture, entertainment, science, and religion all tallied under 2 percent.

Many agency journalists and executives dislike such totaling up of the output of their services. "Dividing up what we do into so many percent of this and so many percent of that is a sociological exercise which has nothing to do with the way we operate," Reuters' chief executive Gerald Long said shortly before he left the agency in 1981. But while journalists invariably evince at least a measure of distrust of statistical and academic researchers, the figures quoted above confirm what no agency reporter or editor would deny: political, diplomatic, and economic news is their overwhelming concern. There is little room for lightheartedness in their outlook.

The geographical origin of agency copy is heavily influenced by the balance of international strength. It would be amazing if the major powers did not provide the bulk of agency datelines. But it is too facile to conclude that, because a country appears frequently on an agency's file, it is regarded as being more important than countries mentioned less often.

The amount of space given to a nation depends not only on its interest to recipients, but also on the availability of information about its affairs. Democracies are reported at a greater length than dictatorships. Countries where a wide range of opinions is expressed, where government policies have to be explained, and where media operate on an independent commercial basis breed the news that agencies want to carry. Closed societies, by their nature, are difficult to report. Their leaders would be worried if it were otherwise.

In some countries whose rulers take a less restrictive view of what should be made known, the technical backwardness of the media acts as a brake on the flow of information, both internally and to the international agencies. Correspondents depend on the national media as sources of information. Where these media are skeletal in their coverage of national news, the stream of information flowing out through the international agencies is unlikely to rise above a trickle.

These political and technical restrictions apply to news moving in the other direction as well. Authoritarian governments regulate the flow of foreign news in their societies as part of their general control of information. Nations with few newspapers, limited broadcasting facilities, and technologically backward national news agencies will be ill-informed about international events on the popular level, although their leadership may enjoy full access to the incoming files of the world agencies.

The flow of information is thus conditioned by national information systems—or nonsystems. It is impossible to give equal coverage of U.S. and Soviet crop figures when the American statistics are regularly announced and the Soviet ones treated as state secrets. There is no way that an agency can get its news distributed to the public if the media channels are closed or nonexistent. Even if the subjects of most concern to them were not to be found primarily in the industrialized world, the agencies would be pushed by the practical problems of reporting and distribution toward a concentration on Western Europe, North America, Japan, and other industrialized regions.

The geographical spread of coverage in any particular agency service is also affected by the pull of proximity. As a general rule, people are more interested in an event if it happens in a neighboring country than if it occurs on the other side of the world. One study of the Asian press reported that 53.3 percent of foreign news in sixteen newspapers came from Asia. A similar survey of nine Arab countries showed 45.7 percent of foreign items originating from the Arab world. Figures collected for sixteen newspapers in Africa, Asia, and Latin America attributed 46 percent of 2000 foreign news items published to the newspapers' "home" regions, while Europe accounted for 40 percent of foreign items in eleven leading U.K. newspapers.[4]

The agencies that supply much of the copy evaluated in such surveys use geographical proximity as one of their guidelines in determining where to send stories. Reuters has always attempted to ensure that 50 percent of the material it sends to Africa is from the continent or directly concerns it because it believes its African subscribers value this kind of copy. In Latin America, agency files studied in 1979 contained up to 48 percent of regional stories, while Asia, the Middle East, and Africa together provided only 5.6 percent.[5] If African clients suddenly expressed an overwhelming interest in Latin American news, and Latin American clients developed an absorbing concern for Africa, the agencies would consider switching their priorities. But there has been no sign that the media, as distinct from politicians and ideologues, have any strong interest in events outside their geographical areas, except when those events are of worldwide significance.

Such events of general significance, occurring mainly in the United

Operations. . . . .

States and Western Europe, spread across all agency services. Coverage of a Paraguayan minister's visit to Spain would be sent only to Latin America, but a U.S. presidential press conference is reported to all parts of the world. On top of that, the amount of Western European news run by the agencies in international services is boosted by the importance of the files they issue to European subscribers. Up to 40 percent of the material sent to Europe, for instance, consists of news from within the continent.

As a result, the United States and Western Europe dominate statistics on the geographical origins of agency coverage. In the seventeen services studied since 1974, stories from the two areas accounted for half the total output. But this aggregate conceals huge differences; in one service to Latin America, for instance, Western European coverage amounted to 13 percent of the total, while in another file sent to South Africa, the proportion was 40 percent.

A difference is also apparent between the services put out by each agency. Eight separate AP and UPI files sent to Latin America,

Table 1   Percentage Treatment of Subjects in Five Agency Services
to Europe, Africa, and the Middle East, May 8, 9, and 10, 1980*

Subject	Items	Wordage
International politics/relations	31.9	33.0
Economics	13.7	10.0
Domestic politics	12.7	15.2
Sports	11.9	9.2
Political violence/unrest	4.9	4.0
International violence	4.3	6.4
Accidents	3.8	2.8
Crime	3.1	2.5
Religion	3.0	3.5
Brights/human interest	2.5	2.2
Miscellaneous	2.2	1.8
Social	2.2	3.6
Art/culture	0.9	1.2
Science	0.8	1.0
Disaster	0.8	1.1
Tito funeral	1.2	2.3

*Because percentages are rounded to nearest decimal point, totals do not add up to 100 percent.

97

Table 2   Origin of Coverage Carried by Five Agency Services to Europe, Africa, and the Middle East, May 8, 9, and 10, 1980

	North America Items	Words	Latin America Items	Words	Western Europe Items	Words	Eastern Europe Items	Words	Africa Items	Words
International politics/relations	215	61,295	41	9,085	165	41,585	119	24,790	36	7,320
Domestic politics	59	15,610	19	5,035	61	17,865	26	6,405	44	11,200
Economics	101	16,975	3	865	105	14,110	5	340	29	4,545
Sports	124	21,260	4	1,090	138	26,465	14	1,640	4	920
International violence	0	0	0	0	39	16,435	0	0	14	3,950
Accidents	48	10,425	4	555	15	2,250	5	420	1	120
Political violence/unrest	3	620	8	1,790	35	7,000	10	1,990	23	3,630
Crime	32	6,610	3	950	26	3,875	0	0	3	310
Disasters	2	520	2	560	0	0	0	0	11	4,200
Religion	1	250	0	0	7	1,280	2	300	62	18,390
Science	16	4,600	0	0	0	0	2	320	0	0
Social	14	4,500	0	0	20	8,640	1	580	9	2,330
Miscellaneous	19	4,900	0	0	6	950	1	380	2	350
Brights	15	3,770	3	710	30	6,225	0	0	7	1,640
Art/culture	7	2,520	0	0	15	4,520	1	120	0	0
Tito funeral	0	0	0	0	0	0	27	12,630	0	0
Total	656	153,855	87	20,640	662	151,200	213	49,915	245	58,905

	Middle East		Central Asia		Australasia		Far East		No Dateline		United Nations		Total	
	Items	Words	Items	Words	Items	Words	Items	Words	Items	Words	Items	Words	Items	Words
International politics/relations	71	18,840	38	5,525	12	2,150	59	12,765	0	0	29	6,255	785	189,610
Domestic politics	23	4,205	62	21,280	0	0	18	5,695	0	0	0	0	312	87,295
Economics	38	13,860	6	1,180	0	0	41	5,290	6	260	2	335	336	57,760
Sports	1	130	4	500	2	240	2	540	0	0	0	0	293	52,785
International violence	34	10,780	20	5,695	0	0	0	0	0	0	0	0	107	36,860
Accidents	9	1,380	9	640	0	0	3	390	0	0	0	0	94	16,180
Political violence/unrest	16	2,970	18	3,255	0	0	6	1,445	0	0	1	190	120	22,890
Crime	2	220	6	990	0	0	5	1,520	0	0	0	0	77	14,475
Disasters	0	0	1	660	1	140	2	400	0	0	0	0	19	6,480
Religion	0	0	0	0	0	0	1	150	0	0	0	0	73	20,370
Science	0	0	0	0	0	0	2	700	0	0	0	0	20	5,620
Social	3	900	1	700	0	0	7	2,930	0	0	0	0	55	20,580
Miscellaneous	1	70	7	720	0	0	13	1,670	5	1,340	0	0	54	10,380
Brights	2	100	0	0	0	0	4	500	0	0	0	0	61	12,945
Art/culture	0	0	0	0	0	0	0	0	0	0	0	0	23	7,160
Tito funeral	0	0	0	0	2	210	0	0	1	300	0	0	30	13,140
Total	200	53,455	172	41,145	17	2,740	163	33,995	12	1,900	32	6,780	2,459	574,530

Europe, and Africa contained 32 percent of U.S. news, while nine Reuters and AFP services recorded an average of 14 percent of items from North America. The high figure for the AP and UPI reflects not only the importance they place on U.S. news but also the easy availability of a great deal of information from their domestic services. A similar pattern, in reverse, is evident among the agencies in the volume of copy they carry from Western Europe, which makes up an average of 30 percent of Reuters and AFP services. Throughout, the agencies react primarily to external factors—the interests of their subscribers, even if these are not always clearly formulated, and the freedom with which they can gather information within their limited resources. They are not out to change the world, nor are their news services framed to further Western hegemony or distort international understanding.

Tables 1 and 2 give details of the subject matter and origin of 2459 news items totaling 574,530 words counted in five agency services on May 8, 9, and 10, 1980. The services were *Reuters Europe North (EUN),* which went to subscribers in the north, center, and east of the continent and to the *International Herald Tribune* in Paris (Reuters now runs a single service for all continental Europe); *Reuters West Africa* (English only); *AP Europe; AP Middle East/Africa;* and *UPI Europe.* News schedules, advisory notes, and information about photographic services were not included. Corrections and substitutions were counted as part of the item to which they referred.

Each completed individual news dispatch was counted as a separate item. There was thus multiple counting of a story covered in a number of successive leads, developing or rounding up previous information. These leads accounted for 288 items and 91,065 words.

There were a number of items that fell into two subject categories. In these cases, the item was counted once in each category and the wordage split between the two. Because of this the total number of items by subject matter and by geographical area may differ slightly.

Wordage figures were rounded to the nearest ten, and percentages to one decimal place.

For purposes of geographical classification, the Middle East extends eastward to the Iraq-Iran border and includes Egypt, and Central Asia runs from the Iraq-Iran border eastward to Burma's eastern frontier. The term "undated" applies to stories run without an identifiable dateline. Stories based on radio monitoring or newspaper reports were attributed to the area where the information originated; a story from Moscow reporting a Soviet press dispatch on conditions in Afghanistan, for example, was classed under Central Asia.

Under the subject classifications heading, "international politics" includes neither economic nor violent events, each of which is given a separate category. "Political violence/unrest" includes hunger strikes. The category labeled "brights/human interest" includes news of celebrities. A separate category contains reports from Belgrade on the funeral of President Tito, or stories from elsewhere directly connected to that funeral, but not reports of meetings between international leaders before or after the funeral, which appear under "international politics."

The figures under "religion" are inflated by a papal visit to Africa, which also affects the African geographical column.

Business News,
Photographs,
and Television

In addition to supplying general-interest news to the media of the world, the major agencies have become involved in three other information services: business news, photographs, and television newsfilm. Of the three, business news has grown in the past two decades into a major activity that has made Reuters a highly profitable business and has been of increasing importance to the Associated Press internationally. News-agency involvement in television is indirect—Reuters has, and United Press International had for 17 years, substantial shareholdings in newsfilm agencies—but news pictures are a direct activity and have long been regarded by the American agencies as an essential part of their operations. These services are rarely discussed in the debate about world information and the agencies' place in it, but to ignore their important role—especially that of business news operations—would be to take an incomplete view of the Big Four and would make a full evaluation of their present and future roles difficult.

The debate about news-agency reporting and distribution in the developing world has been conducted entirely in terms of general news for the media. If it were not for its economic news services, however, Reuters would be in no position to operate on its current scale as the major supplier of foreign news to Africa, India, and the Middle East. Computerized money-market operations may appear to have little to do with the daily news file received by the Zambian news agency, but the second depends on the financial cushion provided by revenue from the first—and the Zambian central bank is

102

well aware of the value of being kept abreast of dollar, mark, or sterling fluctuations. Photographs edited by computer in New York or television newsfilm transmitted by satellite are rarely cited in complaints about hostile Western reporting of bad news from the Third World, but how many Americans carry in their minds images of the developing countries that are primarily visual—refugees fleeing in oxcarts, mothers and children fording flooded rivers, earthquake victims huddled in makeshift shelters? The agencies need to be seen as a whole if they are to be seen in proper perspective.

News Pictures . . . .

Picture services cover far fewer events than do textual news files. The AP's picture service contains 60 to 70 items a day, while the agency's high-speed news wire can transmit as many stories as that in an hour. In the early 1980s, UPI reported putting out 200 pictures a day on its various services, but a count on the average day in Europe in 1980 showed that only 16 pictures moved on the UPI network between 1:00 and 9:00 A.M., and a mere 12 in the following ten hours.

Pictorial reporting techniques and values are also different in important respects from those used in textual coverage. To produce a picture, a photographer has to be present at an event, whereas textual news can be gathered by telephone or from secondary sources. Then, too, a picture may be run by an agency and used by newspapers even though it has no intrinsic importance. Visual appeal or emotional effect can compensate for its lack of significance. Newspapers might run a picture of a naked holiday-maker standing on his head on the beach at Cannes, or a photograph of a weeping mother whose child has just been run over by a truck, but would ignore a textual story on either subject. News stories about the chief of South Vietnamese police shooting a prisoner during the Tet offensive of 1968 were widely printed, but it took an AP photograph to make the event enter the public consciousness around the world.

The permanent photographic staffs maintained by agencies outside their home territories are subject to the same kinds of manpower limitations as their textual reporting. In the early 1980s, UPI maintained a photographic staff of 50 outside the United States, compared with 148 in the United States. In addition, agencies employ part-time photographers on an ad hoc basis. Part of the journalistic topography of Vietnam was the presence of young amateur photographers sitting in base camps scattered around the country waiting for something to happen so that they could take pictures to sell to the agencies.

After a news photograph has been taken and supplied to an agency reporting office, technology takes over. Editing is minimal, a fact that perhaps makes photographs appear simple in comparison with textual news. The agency's main concerns are speed and reproduction quality. A picture may be rejected on grounds of taste, but if it is eye-catching it will not be cut out of the service simply because it lacks balance or gives an inaccurate impression. The news photographer's quest for drama, emotion, and the spectacular could make picture services a natural target for critics who object to the agencies' selective, commercially oriented news approach, but picture services are largely ignored in the debate about information. It is almost as if the critics agreed with the agencies that the camera never lies.

Agency news-picture services date back to 1927, when the AP began to distribute photographs by mail, messenger, road, and rail, or occasionally transmitted them by the telephone system in the United States. In 1935, Kent Cooper organized direct transmission of photographs by leased wires to the cooperative's members in twenty-five U.S. cities. A quarter of a century later, recipients of the AP's wire-photo service in the United States totaled 500, well under half its press membership. Smaller newspapers still made do with mailed pictures. UP's photographic clients in the 1950s totaled around 600, many of them gained by taking over a U.S. picture agency, ACME.

Foreign distribution of pictures by radio began in the early 1950s, to Latin America. The U.S. agencies then moved into Europe and the Far East, setting up permanent picture networks that, in the AP's case, reached fifteen European countries including the Soviet Union by 1964. In the 1980s, the agencies use satellites for photographic transmissions, and have developed laser technology and computerized editing. At the start of the decade, each of the U.S. agencies counted some 1500 direct recipients of its pictures, half in the United States and half abroad.

Photographs delivered by the agencies, like their textual news, are widely redistributed by recipients. This was particularly true of UPI, which reached a series of agreements with European national agencies as it pulled back from independent overseas distribution. In West Germany, UPI sold its photographs, together with its textual news, to the Deutsche Presse-Agentur. In France, it joined forces with AFP on a national basis. By the end of the 1970s, UPI reported that it reached 350 European cities through picture deals with national agencies. The AP, on the other hand, remained independent where this was feasible. While abandoning direct textual distribution in Italy, for instance, it held on to its picture business, which had a $1.5 million annual turnover.

AFP had been interested in getting into pictures ever since it was reorganized in 1957. For a time, the French agency pinned its hopes on a regional grouping, the European Picture Union, but this yielded disappointing results. Several approaches to Reuters received frigid responses. Up to the early 1960s, the London agency was too financially pressed to embark on anything new. After 1963, Reuters had better uses for its money in other areas. AFP first contented itself with distributing American agency photographs in France. It then entered into lengthy negotiations with UPI's owners in the late 1970s. Finally, the French agency decided to try to build a picture network of its own, based on centers in France, the United States, and Japan. The project, which enjoyed financial backing from the French government, aimed to fill a market gap by concentrating on regional requirements, in contrast to the heavily American-angled AP and UPI services. Before the launching of the new AFP service in early 1985, Reuters had also stepped into news pictures—changing a pattern that had existed since World War II.

Until 1984, news pictures had been essentially the province of the two American agencies and of specialized photographic services. This gave the AP and UPI a competitive edge. They could offer clients packages of text and pictures.[1] Reuters had only words to offer, so its newspaper customers had to turn to one of the American agencies for photographs. Reuters had considered going into photographs in the early 1970s, but dropped the idea on the grounds that the chances of making money were slim: evidence from the U.S. agencies suggests that, as a rule, photographs are hardly any more remunerative than textual news internationally. The absence of a photographic service was an undoubted weakness, but since general-news competition was proving unprofitable in any case, Reuters decided to limit itself to textual news and put up with the disadvantage.

By 1984, however, Reuters' outlook had changed. With its profits mounting, the agency could afford to branch out in new directions. Adding a photographic service, it was thought in London, would make Reuters into a complete news agency and could help it exploit openings in new media markets. A joint venture agreement with the

American Gannett newspaper chain covering photographs was close to being signed, but fell through in the face of counteraction by the AP. On June 25, 1984, Reuters and UPI announced a deal by which Reuters took over UPI's news-picture operation outside the United States, for $3.3 million. This enabled Reuters to launch an international photographic service, to which UPI had U.S. rights, in January 1985.

The new service got its U.S. news pictures from UPI's domestic operation, for which Reuters agreed to pay $2.46 million over five years. Reuters also intended to invest in advanced picture transmission technology, which the agency's managers hoped would enable it to leapfrog ahead of the AP, in both reproduction quality and transmission speeds. Though there were some worries expressed within Reuters about the amount of management effort that a potentially marginally profitable new venture would require, the London-based agency felt confident that it could carve out a new market and buttress its position in the press.[2] Its pictures soon became a familiar feature of European and Asian newspapers, and one was used for the cover of *Newsweek* magazine two months after the launching of the service. What remained to be seen was whether the onset of triangular international news-picture competition would lead to unremunerative rate-cutting and whether AFP, which had been busy hiring staff from UPI before the Reuters deal, would be able to steal a march on its rivals by producing a picture service catering to regional rather than global needs.

Television Newsfilm . . . .

Although absent from news pictures until 1985, Reuters had been involved in television newsfilm, as an owner rather than an operator, since 1960, when it took a share in the British Commonwealth International Film Agency. Four years later, this organization underwent a change of name and ownership; it became Visnews, with Reuters and the British Broadcasting Corporation each taking a 33 percent stake. Smaller shareholdings went to the broadcasting networks of Australia, Canada, and New Zealand.

Reuters and Visnews have similarly worded trust documents, and one of Visnews' founders expressed his desire to see "a British agency which would hold in the newsfilm world the same position that Reuters does in the world of words." This emphasis on the British nature of the two organizations became outmoded during the 1960s and 1970s. The Visnews managing director in the late 1970s, Sir Charles Curran, made public his belief that the time had come to reflect the service's international character in its shareholding pattern. Nevertheless, the link between Reuters and Visnews remains a close one; Reuter chief executive Gerald Long was chairman of Visnews from 1968 to 1979, and two of the text agency's senior managers also sat on the board. Currently, Reuters' deputy managing director, finance director, and one other executive are Visnews directors. Visnews executives speak of the value of being joined to a larger worldwide organization for both practical and policy reasons. In 1984, Reuters tried to make the relationship an even closer one by seeking a controlling stake in Visnews. The BBC opposed the idea, and the smaller shareholders rallied to its side, partly because they liked the status quo and partly because they had been alienated by the bluntness of the Reuter bid for control. Reuters dropped the attempt and, within a couple of months, expanded on another front by signing its news-picture deal with UPI.

A second British television news service, Independent Television News (ITN), joined with UPI in 1967 to form a newsfilm operation, UPITN. The American agency had been involved in newsfilm since the early years after World War II, when it worked first with Fox Movietone and then with the British Movietone company. But development in the United States had been held back by the strength of the networks, which had their own news-gathering operations. UPITN's shares were originally split between Paramount Pictures, which owned half, and UPI and ITN, with 25 percent each. In 1975, American publisher John McGoff bought Paramount's stake. According to a South African judicial commission investigating attempts by that country's Department of Information to buy media influence abroad, McGoff received funds from Pretoria. One South African official testified that McGoff had told him, "My understanding is that I represent you in that company." McGoff became joint chairman of UPITN, and one of his American directors was appointed the organization's president in London.

Whatever the South Africans may have expected, they were disappointed. The newsfilm agency's editorial operations were insulated from the board by an editorial committee on which UPI and ITN controlled two-thirds of the seats. It was, however, an embarrassing episode for UPITN, and after the disclosure of the South African connection, ITN bought McGoff's shares to increase its holding to 75 percent. In 1981, a further change brought the American ABC network in as a 30 percent shareholder under an agreement aimed at modernizing and expanding the agency's operations. A bigger change was in the offing: new owners who took over UPI in 1982 decided to get out of the newsfilm agency because of the low financial return it was bringing them. UPI continued to supply its news service, but diversification into newsfilm no longer looked attractive.

During the 1960s and 1970s, Visnews and UPITN came to dominate the flow of film coverage of foreign events to television stations outside the United States. Visnews supplied 200 subscribers in 98 countries in the early 1980s, while UPITN had 120 subscribers in 70 nations. Each provides regular feeds of film delivered increasingly by satellite and electronic circuits instead of by the original method of air freight. In Western Europe, 40 to 50 percent of material in the regional film exchange system, Eurovision, originates from the two agencies. The majority of television stations elsewhere in the world depend on one or both of the services for international coverage, and each agency has exchange agreements with major U.S. networks. In addition to supplying newsfilm on a daily basis, Visnews and UPITN run a range of subsidiary operations, including film archives, the provision of technical advice, and the production of films for companies and governments.

In 1984, Visnews drew up plans to go into the expanding world of cable television with a pilot thirty-minute package of news and features that would be continuously updated and transmitted by satellite to cable systems in Britain and continental Europe. The service, called World News Network, did without news presenters and used radio sound tracks and still pictures where newsfilm was not available, together with computer graphics for financial and weather news. Paralleling the growth of video retrieval systems for textual news, the Visnews project was aimed at giving cable television users news when they wanted it, rather than when broadcasters decided to transmit fixed-time news programs.

Each of the newsfilm agencies makes considerable use of its corresponding text agency's facilities. Visnews gets news services from Reuters, uses its communications system for messages, and gets assistance for its cameramen from Reuters offices, all for an annual fee. Without the news and infrastructure provided by Reuters or UPI, Visnews and UPITN would have found it difficult and very expensive to organize their world coverage.

Business-News Services . . . .

Services offering economic news for the business world have been the most spectacular area of growth for news agencies in the past two decades. Reuters, which spearheaded the development of these highly specialized and highly lucrative services, dominates the market. Both U.S. agencies moved to jump on the bandwagon after Reuters with varying results. AFP also made a stab at the business-news market, but met with little success, even in France.

Economic services fall into two categories, distinguished not by content but by the way in which they are distributed. Traditional teleprinter delivery, transmitting news to clients in an order determined by the issuing desk, is still widely used. Increasingly, however, business news is available via video-screen retrieval services that give subscribers direct access to an agency's data base of constantly updated information, enabling each client to choose the news it wants. If there is one stock price or one corporate announcement in which it is particularly interested, the subscriber can get that news immediately without having to wait while other, less important items run out on a teleprinter roll.

Both types of service have proved successful because they give subscribers information from which money can be made. Knowing about an interest rate shift, a devaluation, or a company's profits or losses a few minutes before the rest of the market helps financial operators, foreign exchange dealers, and stockbrokers to realize substantial profits. Receiving a news service that relays such information at high speed becomes essential for them, if only as a defensive measure.

Business-news services concentrate on ''market-moving'' items, some of which may come from general-news files. These services are designed for specialists who are able to capitalize on their information by getting into the market before it moves. The explanation, background material, and adjectives that characterize general-news services for the media are superfluous in business services; worse, they retard the flow of news items. A guidance note to journalists on how to write for Reuters Economic Services (RES) described the typical subscriber as

> a specialist who reads the RES news report, not out of general interest, but because he needs to know. He relies on the RES service to provide him with accurate and fast information on events affecting the business

world. The RES news is the raw data he draws on to make the business decisions he hopes will keep him competitive in the market places and in the business communities of the world.

For "competitive," one could just as well read "profitable." A service that can achieve such an aim for its clients is bound to be popular, and can charge higher subscription rates than are possible in stagnant media markets.

Meeting the needs of businessmen had been the goal of Paul Julius Reuter's original operation in Aachen and later in London, but the importance of its economic services declined as his agency developed. After World War II, Reuters sold much of its business news to national agencies for translation and redistribution, along the same lines as it distributed its general news. In the 1950s, however, Alfred Geiringer, head of Reuters' commercial-news department (which operated under the name of Comtel), began to build up a communications network that could be used to deliver business news directly to clients. At the same time, he hired a group of bright young managers and tried to instill in them an esprit de corps so that his staff would no longer think of themselves as the poor relations of the general-news journalists, relegated to clerical copying of prices while their colleagues reported wars, summit conferences, and coronations.

Geiringer's ambitions for his economic services brought him into conflict with the reigning orthodoxy at Reuters, and he ultimately left the agency to establish his own service of information about companies. Soon after his departure, "markets opened up and communications costs stabilized, so that you could run an instantaneous, centrally-edited economic news service," noted Michael Nelson, one of Geiringer's bright young men, after becoming general manager of Reuters a decade and a half later.

Reuters took its first step in Belgium, where Belga, the national agency, had traditionally distributed Reuters' economic news. Reuters decided to investigate the possibility of selling an independently distributed teleprinter service of financial news directly to clients from an editing desk in Brussels. A market survey by another Geiringer recruit, Glen Renfrew, was encouraging enough for top management in London to give the project the go-ahead in 1962, although the general-news ethos was still as dominant as ever at the agency's Fleet Street headquarters. Renfrew and a colleague, Desmond Maberley, arriving in Brussels to set up the service, found their task complicated by the lack of authorization from London to rent an office. Unsure whether this reflected a lack of enthusiasm for the project or a simple planning slipup, the two men worked out of a hotel room for several weeks until the authorization finally came through. It covered rent, but not the purchase of furniture, so Renfrew and Maberley sat on the floor as they went through the telephone books looking for prospective subscribers.

Their International Financial Printer (IFP) service began in 1963. Its financial news was assembled from national-agency information, material from Reuters offices, and telephone calls to stock markets. "It wasn't a roaring success, but it formed a basis," Renfrew recalled shortly before he became the agency's managing director and chief executive in 1981. Above all, the IFP gave Reuters the taste for delivering its economic news directly to clients. By doing so through its own communications links, Reuters could ensure that all subscribers received the same material at the same time. Guaranteed equality of access to the news as it was transmitted was an important marketing attraction, as the first Baron Reuter had realized when he locked his Aachen clients in his office to give them his stock market information more than a century earlier.

As international teleprinter delivery of economic news was getting under way in Europe, the second business-news format—information retrieval—was emerging in the United States. Video screens were still in the future; the first retrieval system, which Reuters sold internationally under an agreement with the Ultronics company of the United States, had a rectangular terminal with banks of typewriterlike keys and three display windows. By pressing the appropriate key codes, a subscriber could view the latest prices of selected stocks displayed electronically on the windows. No longer did stockbrokers have to wade through hundreds of prices to get the ones they wanted. "For the first time," as Michael Nelson noted, "the user could select the information he required. The movement to retrieval was an absolute landmark in the handling of news."

The year was 1964, and Reuters was still financially pressed. The landmark would have been impossible for the agency without some financial help from Ultronics. In addition to granting Reuters the right to use its system outside the United States on a profit-sharing basis, Ultronics agreed to put up the necessary capital. "If Ultronics had not done that," Nelson remarked, "I don't think we would have gone ahead."

Once launched, use of the retrieval service, known as Stockmaster, spread quickly through Europe and then to Asia, Australia, and South

Africa. As Stockmaster grew, Reuters built up a data base of prices from financial markets around the world. It established computer centers in Paris, Geneva, Frankfurt, and Amsterdam, and developed storage and processing capacity in London as well. Meanwhile, in the traditional teleprinter field, Reuters was building up its commodity- and company-news services, absorbing a private economic news agency in Switzerland, beginning a joint business service in France with a local agency, and launching a new international service to report world money markets in 1970.

Then retrieval services leaped ahead with a new delivery format, Videomaster, that enabled clients to receive stock prices on a television screen. By the end of 1970, economic services, operating either independently or in association with General Telephone and Electronics Information Systems (GTEIS), as Ultronics had become, were firmly established as Reuters' principal source of revenue. They were opening the way to the commercial profitability for which the company had been aiming since 1963. They also attracted competition.

In 1967, the AP and the Dow Jones business news company joined forces to launch an economic news service outside the United States. This was direct retaliation for Reuters' decision to embark on independent distribution in the United States following its break with the two U.S. organizations. Sources at the AP recall that Dow Jones was particularly enraged by reports that Reuters had been prospecting for clients while still formally prohibited from doing so by the old agreement between them. Dow Jones and the AP were complementary; Dow Jones had the lion's share of U.S. financial information at its disposal from its domestic services and was looking for openings abroad, while the AP had an international organization. The AP did not expect media operations overseas to grow much, and thought that moving into business news could produce what one executive described as "more bang for the buck."

The venture began badly with an attempt to make the new service a wire version of Dow Jones's *Wall Street Journal,* aimed at upper-level managers in U.S. companies abroad. It was, in the words of one of those involved, "a complete and total flop." Executives did not need the AP–Dow Jones service. Costs were high, and the delivery mechanism hardly fitted into executives' office suites. "Teleprinters were still huge black hulking monsters that dripped oil, made so much noise nobody could speak, ran on paper that jammed, and provided a convenient source of heat in winter," an AP–Dow Jones manager recalled. "They were a source of horror for businessmen. Take-off had to wait for new machines with low noise levels, smaller size, and acceptable esthetics.''

It also had to wait for the AP and Dow Jones to find the right service and the right market. To begin with, they went after newspaper business pages and American executives. Some newspapers welcomed the service because it was easier to put into print than the more specialized Reuters copy; a contract with the Kyodo agency in Japan helped to finance the service's international expansion. But the more important newspapers and general-news agencies became for AP–Dow Jones, the less the service suited the real market for business information.

This changed in the early 1970s with the breakdown of the postwar Bretton Woods system of fixed currency rates. It was a watershed for both Reuters and the AP. The new uncertainty generated by fluctuating rates bred a huge appetite among banks, foreign-exchange dealers, and companies for fast, specialized news about currencies. Large amounts of money could be made or lost due to knowledge or ignorance of money-market movements and of developments likely to affect currencies. Supplying such information could only be a gold mine.

From 1971 to 1975, AP–Dow Jones concentrated on selling banks and foreign-exchange dealers news that was still too broad in scope to satisfy the specialist requirements of the market. But eventually, in the words of one AP–Dow Jones manager, ''we took an axe to the banking wire and produced the Foreign Exchange Report targeted very specifically for foreign exchange dealers—and it was a tremendous success.'' Reports on the progress of AP–Dow Jones became a regular feature of AP board meetings. In 1976, the service reached 33 countries. AP president Keith Fuller described it the following year as ''the fastest growing division of AP's large overseas operation.'' In 1977, board minutes recorded a rise in net income of nearly 70 percent.

At AP–Dow Jones, reporting and editing were the keys to growth. At Reuters, the way ahead lay through technology. As AP–Dow Jones was picking its way from executive office services and newspapers to the sharp-end traders, Reuters had taken another major step forward. The international money markets, which were the obvious field of activity for as commercially minded an enterprise as Reuters, had a peculiar feature: unlike stocks or commodities, they were not located in central places where deals were made. Foreign-exchange operators worked on a person-to-person basis by telephone or telex. In the early

1970s, Reuters decided to evolve a system called Monitor, which—instead of involving the agency in reporting in the conventional sense—put its communications and computers at the disposal of clients. Subscribers with foreign currencies to sell announced the amounts and the rates they wanted on the video screens of the Monitor system; potential purchasers reviewed these offers and closed deals by telephone or telex. Later, the system was further refined to enable transactions to be consummated within the Reuter computers, at subscribers' instructions. Michael Nelson reflected that

> this was the first major development of an original concept—that you get the originators of the information to contribute that information to the system without the physical intervention of a reporting organization, and you get them to pay for the privilege of doing that because of the contribution it makes to their business.

At the start, Monitor was a technical instrument, a communications facility that Reuters rented out to clients. "Reuters was an electronic post office," one of the men who developed the system commented. "It added nothing to the information conveyed. The only Reuters control was a technical quality check."

This changed as the system grew. A news service was fed in, enabling subscribers to call up the latest information from Reuters of interest to them. Clients' interests were not confined to events that moved money markets. There was heavy demand for the latest scores during Wimbledon and the world soccer cup. When Reuters decided to expand its sports service in the early 1980s, one motive was to satisfy the demands of desk-bound business executives and foreign-exchange dealers who wanted the latest sports news. Video pages giving background economic data on money supply, interest rates, trade balances, and other figures were added to the service. By the end of 1983, Monitor foreign exchange and money market services were going into 8300 subscriber offices.

Reuters' massive success in money markets spawned a crop of other retrieval services. In each case, the Monitor pattern of taking data contributed by subscribers was applied. Reuters' long-standing commodity services were expanded to include contributed material from clients in 1977. By 1984, commodities video retrieval services were being supplied to 2000 subscriber locations. (As with the other Reuters business services, one subscriber might have video terminals in several different locations, as, for instance, in the case of a bank, stockbroker, or commodity dealer. Reuters counted its presence in terms of subscriber locations rather than individual clients.)

After commodities, contributed data were introduced in 1978 into the equity retrieval services that had been first introduced in 1964. By 1984, the service supplied the prices of 37,500 equity securities and options from fifty-six world exchanges and markets to 1600 subscriber locations. In both the commodity and equity services, around 125 subscribers were contributing about 650 pages of their own prices, quotations, and recommendations to the system. Another contributed data and retrieval service, for bonds, grew from its launch in 1975 to 2200 subscriber locations by 1984, while more recent video retrieval services for shipping, energy, and coins and precious metals each numbered 400 subscriber locations by the time Reuters went public in mid–1984.

The growth of services based on information received directly from exchanges or from subscribers' contributed data changed the nature of Reuters. News gathered by reporters could still be of great importance, but the emphasis in the company as it went public was inevitably on those activities that made the most money.[3] The introduction to the company's description of its business in its flotation prospectus put its sources of information in a significant position.

> Reuters' primary business is the collection and distribution of news and other information. This information is obtained from the world's major security and commodities exchanges; from subscribers to Reuters who contribute information about the markets in which they deal; and from Reuters journalists.

The relegation of journalists to last place should have surprised only those who still viewed Reuters through its credits on newspaper pages.[4] In 1983, financial and business services yielded £215 million in revenues, 89 percent of Reuters' sales. Media news contributed 6 percent. By the spring of 1985, Reuters' business news contracts totaled 19,500. The number of video screens on which Reuter services could be retrieved reached 47,000.

Monitor produced initial apprehension among foreign-exchange dealers that it might make them redundant but this soon proved unfounded, and they adopted it as a necessary tool of their trade. At the AP the attitude toward letting clients contribute information to business services was hostile, and President Wes Gallagher ruled out allowing other organizations access to the AP system. For a while,

AP–Dow Jones tried to exploit the absence of news on Monitor to win subscribers, but when Reuters put news on its booming service, AP–Dow Jones had to rethink. So far, it had stuck to teleprinter delivery. Now, as a senior AP executive recalled, "we had to have an alternative to Monitor."

To be in economic news at all, an agency had to be in computerized services, and the alternative to Monitor that AP–Dow Jones chose was an international link with a U.S. financial news retrieval service, Telerate. "You could say we got into this as a defensive measure," the AP executive conceded. "We weren't opening up a new market as Reuters had with Monitor." The AP–Dow Jones Telerate Service did not enjoy anything like Monitor's success in the world market. On the other hand, Telerate, with 8000 terminals installed in the offices of clients in the United States, easily outdistanced Reuters as a supplier of electronic financial information in America. Telerate's position was bolstered by a major advantage it held over Reuters. The U.S. service had direct access to one of the big Wall Street brokers who act as market-making intermediaries for American government securities. This enabled it to provide subscribers with information on bond price movements faster than Reuters could. Reuters was negotiating in early 1985 for similar information from another of the major bond brokers.

As Reuters' business news services grew, and became dominated by computerized systems, so the pattern of the agency's growth began to alter. Major services were still developed within Reuters, but the agency also began to buy companies to help its growth. In April 1985, it bought a Chicago-based designer of communications systems for the dealing and trading rooms of financial institutions, Rich, Inc., for $67 million in shares and cash. The following month, Reuters disclosed plans to link up with a U.S. supplier of computerized share-trading systems, Instinet. The agreement was seen as a possible first step toward developing a worldwide computerized share-dealing service as a new weapon in Reuters' competitive armory. Not to be outdone, Telerate announced, also in March 1985, that it was close to reaching an agreement to provide its information to a new system being launched by International Business Machines (IBM) and the Merrill Lynch brokerage company under the name of Imnet. At the same time, another U.S. financial information service, Quotron, which was associated with AP–Dow Jones outside North America, expanded its European distribution and added real-time quotations from major European stock exchanges to its New York equity prices. Increasingly, the competing services battled not only to provide more prices and more news, but also to offer clients video terminals which could handle as many functions as possible. What a terminal could do, as well as what it could receive, became a vital element in selling to the business world.

AP executives express admiration for the way Reuters found a path to financial success, but there has been a distinct desire at the co-operative not to change the balance of general to business news in the way that happened in London. At AP, the consensus is that general-news and photographic operations should remain very much the top priorities.

UPI, too, was attracted into the business-news market by the revenue Reuters was earning. Since AP–Dow Jones had gone into financial news, UPI moved into commodity reporting in association with the Knight-Ridder press chain's subsidiary, Commodity News Service (CNS). Again, it was a logical tie-up. CNS was the largest commodity service in the United States but did not distribute abroad; UPI offered an international infrastructure, communications, and reporting offices. In 1977, a joint international service was launched under the name of UNICOM.

The new service, which soon signed up the important Japanese economic news organization (Jiji), began slowly in Europe, but eventually a breakthrough occurred when Reuters ended an agreement it had had with the West German national economic news service, VWD. UNICOM subsequently won clients in Britain, France, Switzerland, and Scandinavia, and moved into Latin America and Southeast Asia. It counted on the fluctuations of commodity markets to attract clients, just as the ups and downs of currencies brought subscribers to Reuters and AP–Dow Jones. "Speculators now see more room in commodities than in stock markets," UNICOM president Terry Andrews commented hopefully in 1980. The agency's sales remained limited; at the start of 1980, UPI estimated that UNICOM, directly or indirectly, reached 7000 recipients, but only 240 of those were direct-paying clients. New owners who took over UPI in 1982 found the UNICOM involvement unattractive financially. They believed that the contract with CNS unduly limited UPI's revenue potential from the joint venture and, accordingly, pulled out.

Reuters thus remains dominant in supplying specialized news services to the business world. By 1984, it had 32,500 video terminals in subscribers' offices in 81 countries. Teleprinter services went to 112 countries, but were declining as part of the company's overall business as clients switched to Monitor screens. The agency's role in international business was perhaps best symbolized by the extent to which subscribers were ready not simply to receive and exchange information through the Monitor system, but to use it to negotiate and conclude trading deals in foreign exchange and bullion. When the Monitor Dealing service was introduced in 1981, the average number of daily contracts made between subscribers through the system was 3000. By December 1983, the daily average reached 20,000. In early 1985, the service had 710 subscribers. A dealing service for bonds, started in September 1984, attracted 120 clients in its first six months. The next step was the deal with Instinet and an examination of a dealing service enabling equities to be bought and sold through Reuters terminals. The investment for developing a full-fledged service would, it was estimated, run into tens of millions of pounds. Another project being prepared in 1985 involved launching a historical data-base service, which was reckoned to have a market potential of $300 million a year, rising to $500 million by the end of the decade.

The success of teleprinter business services from 1964 onward, and of the later retrieval services, has changed the overall face of the news-agency world. It has increased awareness of commercial forces and has led the agencies into new fields. In making substantial profits internationally, and in developing a direct relationship with the end users, business-news services contrast to the traditional services of general news for the media, raising the question of why these traditional activities have become caught in a loss-making spiral and why the Big Four continue to defy commercial logic by operating them on such a wide scale.

Finances

The major news agencies are easily portrayed as rich and powerful giants, assimilated into the ranks of profit-seeking transnational companies exploiting helpless developing countries from their Western headquarters. They are criticized for treating news as a marketable commodity and for monopolizing markets that, it is assumed from the mere fact that the agencies are trading there, must be profitable. When the question of funding the development of media in poor nations came up in UNESCO discussions around 1980, one suggestion put forward was that a special tax be levied on the major news agencies because of the alleged profits they were making out of their world-news operations.

Given the ground they cover and the multiplicity of their services, the big agencies are, in fact, remarkably thinly stretched. The combined staffs of the four organizations totaled 10,000 people in the early 1980s: 3600 at Reuters, 2600 at the Associated Press, 2000 at Agence France-Presse, and 1800 at United Press International. Drawing a distinction between those employed at home and those working abroad is vitiated by the fact that the agencies' headquarters staffs produce services distributed overseas. Even so, the preponderance of home-based employees at three of the agencies was still striking: the AP housed 75 percent of its staff in the United States, two-thirds of UPI employees were home-based, and at AFP 62 percent of the staff was located in France. Only Reuters, with no domestic general-news service and a policy of extensive decentralization, had more people abroad than at home, roughly in a 70 to 30 percent ratio.

The limited number of agency employees working abroad is not immediately apparent from the numbers of overseas offices they maintain: 100 for Reuters, 87 for AFP, 81 for UPI, and 63 for the AP. A few of these offices are staffed by 50 or more employees, many of whom are commercial, administrative, or technical staff. Most bureaus of this size are found in Western Europe, the United States,

119

and the countries chosen by the agencies to house their Asian and Latin American headquarters. The vast majority of agency offices, in contrast, are staffed by only one or two "international" correspondents, expatriates posted abroad for a set period of time who are assisted by one or two local employees and an array of part-time stringers.

In Africa, Asia, and Latin America, bureaus with only one full international staff correspondent are common. UPI figures for 1979 showed that the very areas in which that agency was most thinly staffed were those having the greatest number of offices; Asia, with 24 offices, contained only 120 staff, while Latin America's 20 bureaus employed 140. The Europe/Middle East/Africa division, with 18 offices (mainly in Western Europe), accounted for 200 employees, the largest number of staff outside the United States. At Reuters, the dominance of Western Europe was reflected in the 35 offices the agency maintained there at the start of the 1980s—as many as in the whole of Africa, the Middle East, and the rest of Asia combined. The balance at AFP was more even—the agency's network of offices in West Africa meant that it counted the same number of bureaus in Europe and in Africa—but its 17 offices in Europe were considerably more heavily staffed than the corresponding number in Africa.

The distribution of offices and staff is based mainly on the agencies' assessments of the importance, interest to subscribers, and accessibility of news of different countries. Some are covered only in the most superficial manner, and this tends to have a self-perpetuating effect: because a country is not reported by any of the agencies, nobody remarks the lack of news from it. This neglect is not always of the agencies' own doing, for some countries actively bar them or place such restrictions on their correspondents that reporting is impossible. In others, the absence of a regular flow of internal information makes an agency's presence both expensive and unproductive. Where such external factors do not apply, the gaps in news coverage are the product of the precarious financial position of the agencies' international services rather than the result of any mutually contrived decision to ignore the poor nations of the world.

Because different activities overlap, agency finances are complex, making the allocation of costs to one department rather than another a hazardous undertaking. At Reuters, for instance, general-news reporting clearly contributes to the agency's economic services, since some general news is of a market-moving nature.[1] At the AP and UPI, stories gathered within the United States for domestic recipients may also be used on international services, and these agencies' photographic services require textual news files to inform them of what is going on in the world. Investment in communications links or computer equipment is likely to benefit several sectors of an agency.

Plain figures, therefore, are of limited utility in any attempt to evaluate the financial position of the agencies' international general-news services. In addition, the rivalry among the agencies makes them reticent about financial disclosure, a tradition dating back to the past century, when the chairman of Reuters told the company's 1890 annual general meeting that "in a business like ours, it is always unwise to disclose our affairs too minutely for the advantage of active competitors whom we have to face in many quarters." Reuters and the AP publish annual reports with some balance-sheet figures; neither UPI nor AFP does even this. In conversation, agency managers and editors tend to draw a veil when financial questions arise. UPI, for instance, has traditionally made it clear that, as a private company, it intends to keep to itself everything except a broad outline of its overall gross revenue. The rare figures that the agencies release about specific areas of their operations are usually couched in percentage terms rather than actual amounts—as when Stanley Swinton, the executive in charge of AP's world service, estimated in the late 1970s that his agency's expenditure in the Third World was fifteen times greater than its revenue there.

Reuters' share flotation in 1984 obliged it to publish figures that lifted the financial curtain somewhat as far as that agency was concerned.[2] But, understandably, the bulk of Reuters' share document was devoted to its money-making business-news services, and only overall revenue totals were given for media-news services. The merging of business and media services under a single editorial umbrella means that it is impossible to calculate the profit or loss incurred by media services, since Reuters gives its production and communications costs as a single, companywide figure. Equally, it lumps together its different sources of revenue region by region so that one cannot work out how much services for the media make or lose in each geographical area.

Whatever its commercial logic, the lack of financial information given by the major agencies has opened the way for assumptions that, apart from being frequently inaccurate, work to their disadvantage. In the absence of precise figures, suspicions that the agencies are commercially exploitative, particularly of the poor nations, are easily nurtured. In fact, an examination of agency finances makes it clear that running international general-news services is a loss-producing proposition, particularly in the developing world.

A calculation of the overall financial position of the agencies, taking into account all their different activities, showed revenue and costs in almost exact balance at the start of the 1980s. This equilibrium masks extremes of profit and loss. Maximizing net revenue was not the agencies' prime concern. When the figures are adjusted to reflect only general-news services distributed outside the agencies' home countries, the very great difficulty of avoiding often substantial losses becomes all too evident.

Between them, the four agencies finished the 1970s with a combined annual gross revenue of $377 million in 1978 and $436 million in 1979. The 1980 figure is estimated to have barely topped $500 million. Reuters ended the decade with the largest turnover of the Big Four: £76.3 million ($161.8 million) in 1979, ahead of the AP's $121.6 million, UPI's estimated $79 million, and AFP's Fr 312.8 million ($73.5 million). Over the six years from 1974 to 1979, the four agencies' total sales or membership revenues amounted to $1907.6 million, of which 39 percent came from sales outside their home countries. In 1979, the proportion of foreign revenue rose to 43.5 percent, but more than half of this came from Reuters' sales of business services. After deducting the income from economic services and photographs, the gross revenue earned annually by the four agencies from foreign sales can be put at $60–$70 million at the start of the 1980s. At least 75 percent of this is estimated to have come from Western Europe, Japan, and Latin America (see table 3).

This was not a lot of money with which to run four world news operations on the scale of the major agencies. All of the services have given up the idea of balancing general news costs and revenues in individual countries (except for the United States). It is clearly unrealistic to expect nations that produce a lot of news to be equally productive of revenues. This may be due to the local media situation— no agency, for example, could have expected to draw as much revenue from the South Vietnamese press and radio as it spent reporting the war there. It may also be because of official constraints imposed on agency distribution; the agencies, for instance, maintain expensive reporting offices in Moscow, but their only Soviet client is the officially monopolistic TASS.

Combined agency operating costs for all services ran to $376.9 million in 1978 and $436.3 million in 1979. Reuters' accounts showed operating expenses of £64.3 million ($122.8 million) and £72.6 mil-

Table 3   News Agencies' Revenue and Profit Figures, 1974–79
(in thousands of $U.S.)[a]

	1974	1975	1976	1977	1978	1979
Gross Revenue						
Reuters	52,500	66,125	75,457	93,067	129,330	161,775
AP	83,782	90,891	97,392	101,624	112,097	121,570
UPI	58,083	62,372	63,405	67,372	74,307	78,858 [b]
AFP	35,301	45,811	46,462	50,575	60,774	73,520 [c]
Foreign Revenue						
Reuters	42,523	55,546	62,629	78,356	107,344	134,273
AP	16,503	17,706	19,318	19,879	22,657	25,574
UPI	12,910	13,901	14,185	15,190	17,829	18,926 [b]
AFP	5,968	7,091	7,238	8,080	9,619	11,038 [c]
Operating Profit						
Reuters	2,076	2,161	4,863	5,077	6,540	7,819
AP	[d]	[d]	1,435	1,496	[132]	[3,128]
UPI	[4,103]	[2,586]	[3,804]	[5,086]	[5,549]	[4,804][b]
AFP	728	1,633	920	1,791	[1,300]	[100][c]
Net Profit						
Reuters	1,326	2,267	5,317	5,044	6,071	6,572
AP	[339]	[2]	1,295	1,067	[173]	[1,835]
UPI	[1,920]	[845]	[1,404]	[1,091]	[2,538]	[2,436][b]
AFP	nil	nil	nil	nil	nil	nil

Sources: Reuters annual accounts; AP consolidated financial statements; UPI limited partnership prospectus; AFP accounts and budget figures submitted to National Assembly.

a. Figures rounded to nearest thousand. Conversions from sterling and francs at Organization for Economic Cooperation and Development (OECD) annual rates for relevant years. Figures in brackets denote losses.
b. Based on projection of half-year figures.
c. Based on budget figures.
d. Unavailable due to then-current accounting procedures.

lion ($154.0 million) for these years, while the AP's costs for the same period were $112.2 million and $124.7 million. After incurring expenses of $79.8 million in 1978, UPI's costs rose to an estimated $84 million in 1979, and AFP's jumped from Fr 280 million ($62.1 million) in 1978 to Fr 313 million ($73.6 million) in the following year.

While staff and communications are the main sources of expenses for all four agencies, the relationship between the two kinds of expenditures varies. Reuters, with a heavy investment in computer and communications development, already spent a relatively small 31.7 percent of its operating costs on staff at the end of the 1970s, but nearly half of UPI's 1978 expenditures went into salaries. At AFP, where there was the greatest concentration of staff relative to equipment, personnel accounted for 65 percent of costs.

Were it not for the profits of Reuters' economic services and, to a lesser extent, the AP–Dow Jones operation, the agencies' annual combined losses would have run to an estimated $15 million by the start of the 1980s. And without the U.S. basing of the AP and UPI and French state payments to AFP, their overall financial position would have been even more catastrophic. As monopolistic exploiters of world-media markets, the agencies cut a sorry figure.

Subscription Rates. . . . .

The basic financial problem from which the agencies suffer in their general-news services is that they do not charge enough to international subscribers. There are exceptions: in West Germany, Reuters and the AP both operate on a set scale of fees linked to the circulations of newspapers and the potential audiences of radio and television stations, and in Japan there is a general correspondence between the fees charged by each agency and the size of its clientele. But elsewhere, well-established anarchy reigns, with charges depending mainly on history, personal salesmanship, proprietorial pride, and the agencies' long-standing desire to maximize the number of subscribers they serve. There is little attempt to gauge either the value of the services being offered or the cost of producing them. As a result, an agency service offering an around-the-clock reporting of the world may cost a newspaper less then a single journalist's salary.

In some cases, rates are so low that they barely cover the technical costs of delivering the service. Allegations of price dumping are often heard—particularly in Latin America, where competition is intensified by the presence of the Spanish, Italian, and West German agencies. It almost seems more accurate to speak of the rates the agencies are willing to accept than of the fees they charge. They operate in a buyer's market largely of their own creation, and find it difficult to conceive of any other state of affairs. ''We all charge ridiculous prices overseas,'' AP president Keith Fuller admitted in 1980. Reuters' managing director Gerald Long, reporting to his board in 1975 that the two American agencies were close to dumping in their international rates, labeled this "the largest single influence in depressing rates in media markets throughout the world." AFP executives admit privately that the agency sells its news in some parts of the world for little more than the cost of delivering it, considering presence to be more important than revenue. "People will talk about having a rate structure but they'll always sell the service for whatever they can get," one former UPI executive with experience on four continents noted.

This widespread acceptance of low subscription rates stems from the agencies' attempts to outdo one another in the number of subscribers they signed up before and just after World War II. UP used low pricing as a means of breaking into countries previously dominated by the cartel. When the AP began to distribute internationally, it was ready to accept the rate levels set by its U.S. competitor. Without the cartel to protect it, Reuters cut rates in some areas, while throughout the 1930s the Havas management bemoaned the impossibility of increasing subscriptions to the break-even point, or indeed of collecting revenues at all from some national agencies.

After 1945, the same pattern applied. The U.S. agencies, in particular, sold for what they could get, and (apart from West Germany and Japan) the going rate was often uneconomical. Two factors made this state of affairs acceptable: first, the U.S. agencies were locked into an institutional contest in which the one with the greatest number of subscribers would consider itself the victor; second, world reporting was underwritten by such a large number of recipients in the United States that the need to charge more overseas if international operations were to break even was obscured.

With the U.S. agencies setting the pace in the postwar years, Reuters and AFP had to accommodate themselves to the rates the AP and UP charged. The strains this caused for both European agencies have already been noted. The situation was made more difficult for all four major services by a development that became evident in the 1960s: media markets, which had been reasonably buoyant since 1945, began to contract in many parts of the world. Newspapers and broadcasters previously taking two or three agencies' services cut back to one or two for economy reasons, and often used the threat of cancellation to hold down increases in subscription levels. Since the newly independent nations of Africa and Asia could, as a rule, afford only low subscription rates, increases in the numbers of clients there did not necessarily result in increases in the agencies' net revenues.

At the same time, rising inflation sharply boosted the agencies' costs just as revenues were becoming stagnant. Winning new clients became increasingly difficult: as a UPI document put it in 1979, "There is limited opportunity for profitable increases in market penetration." [3] Keeping revenues in balance with inflation was the best any international agency could hope to do in its general-news operations as a whole.

The financial picture was further darkened by the emergence of the Spanish, West German, and Italian national agencies onto the international scene, particularly in the developing world and the already highly competitive Latin American market. These three agencies—Agencia Efe of Spain, Deutsche Presse-Agentur of West Germany, and Agenzia Nazionale Stampa Associata (ANSA) of Italy—took few clients away from the Big Four. A senior ANSA executive acknowledged in 1980 that "this activity would not be worth doing except for the prestige involved," while Efe admitted that the part played by foreign income in its activities was unimportant. DPA likewise earned only a tiny part of its revenue overseas. But the willingness of these services to sell at rates well below those of the Big Four acted as a further depressant on the market and gave clients another bargaining weapon in their efforts to prevent subscription levels from increasing in real terms.

As a result, radio stations in Latin America were buying world news services for a mere $100 to $200 a month in the early 1980s. In Pakistan at the same time, one local agency paid a total of only $300 a month for its foreign news. At the other end of the scale, the annual rates charged to major Japanese media organizations for news, pictures, and communications were as high as $500,000. UPI's largest foreign client paid $867,805 for a package of services in 1978; its four biggest foreign subscribers together contributed $2,655,201, or 3.6 percent of the agency's total turnover that year. [4]

There are often wide variations in the amounts that one client pays to different agencies. This may be due to (real or perceived) differences in the quality of what is delivered; the Tanzanian national agency, for example, paid Reuters 33 percent more than it paid AFP in the late 1970s, because Reuters has traditionally given more attention than the French agency to East Africa. But the huge variations existing among some countries owe as much to history as to what is being delivered. In the past, when an agency established itself as the main news supplier to a given country, this had two effects: the dominant service was in a relatively strong position in contract negotiations, and the other agencies were obliged to offer artificially low rates to get into the market. In India, for instance, Reuters commanded three times as much revenue as UPI in 1978, a disparity only partly accounted for by the London agency's coverage of cricket matches and traveling Indian politicians. In South Korea, figures from a survey carried out by one of the agencies in 1978 showed that Reuters received 22 percent more than the AP and 52 percent more than UPI from the national agency. In France, in the 1970s, the main broadcasting network paid as much for one foreign agency as for the two other non-French services combined.

The competition in Latin America, and the entrenched position of the U.S. agencies there, provides an even more striking example of just how inequitable agency rates can be. Major Latin American newspapers can pay considerably more in agency fees than their counterparts in Europe, while small radio stations pay next to nothing. In 1978, AP rates in Mexico were ten times as great as what AFP earned from individual clients, and five times larger than the highest subscription amount paid to the regional agency (Latin), which distributed Reuters news in the area. In Venezuela, the AP's top subscription price was double Latin's largest fee, while in Argentina AP sold for five or six times as much as either AFP or Latin. In Chile, on the other hand, Latin was able to command as much as the U.S. agencies combined from the major Santiago newspaper, whose publisher was the leading figure behind the regional agency's foundation.

While the agencies have generally been ready to accept whatever their clients were willing to pay them, they have been unable to apply corresponding limitations on their costs because of the need to remain competitive. Being a world agency entails offering coverage of the whole range of accessible events likely to interest clients. An agency has to offer the same level of basic coverage whether it has 2000 or 5000 recipients. Reporting costs do not vary with revenues; a desk operation costs the same whether its files go to 1 client or 1000. The equation on which the commercial agencies were originally based has been reversed: instead of building up profitable revenues above a fixed-cost base, the agencies have seen their earnings fall inexorably below the expenditures required to report the world's news for the media. Nonproductive competition has affected both what they charge and what they spend, and the two cannot be brought into line.

Agency managers are all too aware of the bind in which they find themselves. "You could not run an independent, unsubsidized international general news service on a profit basis and survive today," the AP president in 1980, Keith Fuller, said. At Reuters, Glen Renfrew expounded a basic truth shortly before becoming the agency's chief executive in 1981: "We couldn't afford to stay in general news if we weren't in the expanding markets that are serviced by [computer] technology."

The Associated Press: A Cooperative Cushion . . . .

The financial problems of running general-news services have plagued all four agencies since the mid-1960s. Because of its cooperative structure, the AP might have been expected to have escaped much of the pressure—AP members are assessed annually with fees that cover the cooperative's costs, so theoretically no pinch should develop—but there is a limit to what the members are willing to pay, and the costs of reporting rose steadily in the late 1960s. The expense of covering Vietnam ($750,000 in 1966 alone), the development of new reporting techniques, and the price of modernizing the cooperative's technical equipment all exacerbated the tug-of-war between costs and membership revenues. In 1970, the AP's management implemented economy schemes that proved temporarily effective, but in 1975 the board ordered $3 million cut from the agency's draft budget. Assessments, meanwhile, rose by up to 1 percent a year— a far cry from the late 1950s, when a 7 percent hike had been enough to cover three years of expenditure increases.

Some 30 percent of the AP's textual news costs are incurred outside the United States, but the AP World Services bring in only 20 percent of the cooperative's total revenue. In 1979, the AP earned $25.574 million abroad and announced it had spent $23.558 million on foreign news reporting and distribution, but the two figures are not directly comparable because of the AP's internal allocations of costs and revenues. The expenditure figure does not include photo-service costs, but the earnings figure does incorporate this service's profits; 40 percent of overseas revenue came from news pictures. AP president Keith Fuller estimated in 1980 that 60 percent of what the AP spent on world reporting would still have to be expended even if the World Services did not exist, in order to report international news for the United States (see table 4).

Year	Gross Revenue[b]	World Service Revenue	News Costs Domestic	News Costs Foreign	Supple-mental Service Costs[c]	Gross Costs[d]
1970	67,219	11,403	31,408	10,689	15,963	66,622
1974	83,782	16,503	38,234	14,192	20,357	84,122
1975	90,891	17,706	38,824	16,674	22,782	90,894
1976	97,392	19,318	41,870	16,984	23,995	96,096
1977	101,624	19,879	43,003	17,894	24,792	100,128
1978	112,097	22,657	47,623	20,661	28,150	112,229
1979	121,570	25,574	52,006	23,558	31,999	124,698

Table 4 — AP Revenue and Costs, 1970 and 1974–79 (in thousands of $U.S.)[a]

Sources: AP consolidated financial statements and World Service revenue as supplied by president's office.

a. Figures rounded to nearest thousand.
b. Includes deduction for equipment renewal as per AP accounts.
c. Includes photographs, sports, radio, audio, books, Press Association.
d. Includes nonoperational costs such as administrative expenses, legal fees, and—up to 1977—state and federal taxes.

According to AP executives, the World Services were running at a profit of around $5 million a year at the start of the 1980s. This figure, however, must be qualified in two ways. For one thing, it includes the cooperative's share of the growing profits of AP–Dow Jones. Although details of net earnings from this source have not been revealed, they could be large enough to account for the whole of the World Services' profits. In addition, the AP's international files get their coverage of the United States free of charge from the cooperative's domestic copy. While setting a dollar value on this would be purely arbitrary, it could well be enough to equal the reported World Services' profit figure.

However variable its use of foreign news, the AP membership has always expressed a commitment to international reporting and distribution and has provided the essential financial mattress for the agency's worldwide operations. As a result, the AP has been less affected by the problems of low rates and high coverage costs than the other three major agencies. The pressures have still been there, but the cooperative agency model has undoubtedly helped the AP to sustain uneconomical activities, an effect not always welcomed by the other three services. The net result has been to prevent the flow of one agency's world news from diminishing to any significant extent.

Agence France-Presse: State Support . . . .

AFP's continued presence as a major supplier of international news is entirely the consequence of the financial support the agency receives from the French government.[5] The 1957 reorganization of the agency changed the way these state payments were calculated; henceforth they were charged on a subscription basis instead of being paid in a lump sum as a subsidy.

Today AFP maintains set subscription rates for domestic French newspapers, and each government department or official organization receiving the service is regarded as being equivalent to a daily newspaper with a circulation of 180,000. In theory, therefore, what takes place is a strictly commercial transaction between the agency and the recipients of its services in ministries, embassies, and local government offices. In fact, the total amount to be paid each year by the state to AFP is fixed in advance. The number of official recipients is adjusted annually to produce the required amount, determined in negotiations between the agency and the framers of the government's annual information budget. AFP's financial dependence on the government is heightened by its need to get ministerial approval for subscription rate increases under the French policy of officially administered price controls. Ministers can be benevolent. After the agency had run up a two-year deficit of Fr 44 million in 1981–82, the government approved subscription rises large enough to produce a surplus of Fr 11.3 million in 1983.

This gives the government a strong hold over the agency—if it chooses to exercise it. With state payments accounting for some 60 percent of AFP's revenues, a hostile administration could throttle the agency, although no such threat has ever been made. Financial dependence on the state is an inescapable fact of AFP's continued existence, something that successive rapporteurs of the information budget have not exactly welcomed. In his report on the 1981 budget, Gaullist Louis Salle concluded that "the situation of the Agence France-Presse appears worrying from certain points of view," and urged the agency to develop nonstate revenues through economic news services and expansion of its foreign activities.

Table 5	Sources of AFP Revenue, 1969–78 (in percentages)			
	1969	1974	1975	1978
State[a]	55.98	59.37	61.46	60.70
French press[b]	14.81	13.92	13.91	14.56
State broadcasting network	5.25	5.21	4.58	4.53
Private broadcasting stations	1.03	0.98	1.17	1.77
Foreign clients	18.79	16.88	15.48	15.49
Private nonmedia French clients	4.14	3.64	3.40	2.95

Source: National Assembly report on information budget for 1980.

a. Includes payment designated as being for French diplomatic missions overseas.
b. Includes newspaper clients in French overseas departments and territories.

This was easy enough for a politician to say, but the pattern of the past decade suggests that AFP will have a very hard time developing revenues in this way. Its attempt to build up an economic news service has met with little success and is restricted almost entirely to France. About 3 percent of AFP's revenue comes from nonmedia, nonstate subscribers.

Foreign sales had appeared to be a bright hope when the agency got its new statute in 1957. An energetic sales campaign in selected areas, together with low subscription rates, boosted foreign sales to 19 percent of the agency's gross earnings by the end of the 1960s. In the following decade, however, foreign earnings grew more slowly than domestic revenues; by 1978, foreign sales were down to 15.5 percent of the total. In 1978–79, foreign revenues rose by 9.7 percent, but this figure must be compared with a 13.1 percent jump in domestic earnings. In 1969, AFP's foreign income had comfortably outdistanced its domestic press revenues, but by 1978 the two were comparable. Media revenues as a whole rose more slowly than either costs or the state payment needed to balance the books—and foreign sales increased most slowly of all (see table 5).

To try to get the agency onto a more independent financial basis, AFP management drafted a 250-million-franc development plan in late 1982, designed to boost revenues by 50 percent over ten years and to reduce the state contribution to 40 percent of the total budget. The main source of funds was to be the government. But President Mitterrand's Socialist administration was busy switching from its early free-spending ways to policies designed to restrain state expenditure. When the plan was finally signed by the agency and the government in June 1984, it was for Fr 115 million spread over two years. At the end of 1984, the finance ministry complicated AFP's life by ordering the agency to hold down its subscription rate increase for 1985 to 4.9 percent, that year's inflation target. AFP had hoped for 6 percent.

Despite the very real desire of AFP's management to develop its commercial independence, one thing remains plain: most of the capital needed to establish new services and more than half the revenue required to operate the agency on a week-to-week basis are going to continue to come from the French state for the foreseeable future. As long as the government goes on contributing the necessary sums, the French agency can escape from the full effects of low media rates and generally depressed markets. The government payments ensure an international presence for what politicians refer to as "the voice of France," and AFP subscribers around the world get a cheap ride.

Reuters: Profitable Business . . . .

While the French state kept AFP alive as a world agency, Reuters found its financial salvation in-house. The growth of the London-based agency since the mid-1960s singles it out as the one news service that has found a path to mounting commercial success. In 1963, Reuters' turnover stood at £3.1 million and its net profits at £26,789. Ten years later, expansion of its economic services and a much more modest increase in media revenues had raised the agency's turnover to £17.5 million and its profits to £1 million. Subsequently, the spectacular development of retrieval services in the 1970s sharply boosted turnover to £76.3 million by the end of the decade, but even faster growth was in store.

In 1981, Reuters recorded profits of £16.3 million on turnover of £138.8 million, and paid a dividend to its press owners for the first time since 1941. In 1982, pretax profits jumped to £36 million on turnover of £180 million. The following year, as Reuters prepared to issue shares to the public, the profit before tax rose by 50 percent to £55 million on turnover of £242 million. In 1984, the pre-tax profit rose another 34 percent to £74.3 million on revenue of £313 million.

Geographically, Europe provided 50 percent of Reuters' revenue in 1983 with sales of £122 million. High as this was, Europe's contribution was down from 64 percent in 1979. Just over half the

European earnings came from Britain and Switzerland. North America, where Reuters had hoped for major expansion in the 1970s, turned in between 17 and 18 percent of total earnings in 1981–83. Africa and Latin America, which were combined in a single operating division by the Reuters management, contributed a steady 7 to 8 percent of total sales, the bulk of it coming from South Africa, Argentina, Brazil, Mexico, Venezuela, and Israel (which Reuters, for political reasons, lumps in with Africa rather than the Middle East). The big growth was in the Middle East and East Asia, which contributed 26 percent of the company's revenue in 1983 compared with 15 percent in 1979, reflecting the extension of the Monitor system and an upsurge in international financial trading by banks and institutions in Hong Kong, Tokyo, and Singapore.

The growth in Reuters' earnings was not entirely due to Monitor and its offshoots. General news revenue from sales to the media rose by 66 percent between 1979 and 1983, from £9.4 million to £15.6 million. This compared with a 260 percent jump in earnings from financial and business information to £215 million. A 20 percent rise in revenue between 1982 and 1983 would have looked healthy enough in most circumstances, but it was dwarfed by the 35 percent increase in business-news earnings in the same period from a base twelve times as big. In 1983, worldwide media accounted for 6 percent of Reuters' overall revenue. This was slightly more than the company as a whole earned from West Germany alone.

Reuters' profits and its concentration on capital-intensive computer projects for its business services have taken it out of the traditional news-agency league. In 1976, chief executive Gerald Long had told his board, "Reuters has no single competitor for all its services throughout the world, not even for the greater part of them." The commercial criteria that Reuters applied to its retrieval services and the requirements for ever-growing amounts of capital were far removed from the traditionally unremunerative, labor-intensive world of general news. With only a small equity base, Reuters needed to make ever-increasing profits to finance the investments needed for future growth in the years leading up to the 1984 flotation. Its spending on new equipment jumped from £3 million in 1974 to £7 million in 1977, then mushroomed to £10.8 million in 1980 and £27.6 million in 1981. "Reuters is now in an essentially communications business," one of the developers of the Monitor service noted. "The biggest competition is from companies that are not news agencies but are run by people who know about electronics."

Year	Turnover	Operating Profit	Fixed Assets Investment per Annum	Overseas Revenue as Percentage of Total Revenue

Table 6   Reuters Turnover, Profit, Investment, and Overseas Revenue (in thousands of £U.K.)

Year	Turnover	Operating Profit	Fixed Assets Investment per Annum	Overseas Revenue as Percentage of Total Revenue
1968	6,428	21	742	75
1969	8,827	214	1,185	76
1972	13,846	400	1,234	79
1973	17,495	820	1,600	80
1974	22,532	891	3,031	81
1977	53,487	2,911	7,050	84
1978	67,712	3,424	5,958	83
1979	76,309	3,688	5,989	83
1980	90,095	4,136	10,871	82
1981	138,804	16,371	27,629	82
1982	179,910	36,530	44,631	83
1983	242,630	55,253	36,302	84

Source: Reuters Annual Reports share prospectus, 1984.

Financial success perpetuated the international outlook the London agency had always taken. Reuters' business emphatically does not begin at home. In 1967, three-quarters of the agency's revenues came from outside Britain; ten years later, the proportion was up to 84 percent. The 1983 result showed the U.K. share of revenue remaining at 16 percent, or £39 million. (See table 6.)

The growth of economic services has enabled Reuters to maintain its international general-news service. In theory, the agency could close down large sections of the general-news operation without seriously affecting the economic services. In practice, however, it has seen itself as an organization that should serve the media as well as the business world, however elusive general-news profitability proves. Reuters' entry into news pictures in 1985 was the latest illustration of this. The exact amount lost on media services is currently obscured by the uncoupling of general-news costs from media revenues and the merger of all editorial activities under a single-management structure. But from 1968 to 1973, Reuters ran its general-news operations on a clearly delineated profit-seeking basis. The experience provides an apt illustration of the internal and external financial problems that surround international news-agency services for the media.

Reuters' establishment of a separate General News Division (GND) and Reuters' Economic Services (RES) in 1968 was motivated by a desire to identify costs and revenues, to give the economic services an identity of their own, and to boost net earnings from the media. The general-news operation benefited financially from cost cutting in its head office following the introduction of computerized message-switching, an innovation enabling journalists to be concentrated at a single editing desk instead of being scattered among a string of regional service units. The GND staff in London fell from 285 in 1968 to 213 in 1973, while the service improved markedly.

To accompany such economies, the GND management set about seeking new sources of income. German and Arabic services were launched. A joint regional agency was established with Latin American publishers. An audio service was set up for radio clients. Feature services were expanded, and "special traffic" copy for clients was moved on Reuters' wires to mutual financial advantage.

This all cost money, and it was soon apparent that Reuters was not earning commensurate revenues. The United States, where the agency had entertained high hopes of a media breakthrough, proved slow going. At home, chief executive Gerald Long decided not to try to impose what would have been normal annual rate increases for the general-news service on the agency's owners in the press. The savings that the owners made thereby could be seen as the equivalent of the dividend that the agency was still unable to pay them as shareholders. This decision could also be seen as appropriate in view of the agency's increasing concentration on economic services that had nothing to do with its owners' prime field of activity and did not directly benefit the news service they received.

The overall effect on Reuters' finances was small, but the impact on general-news revenues of not being able to charge the British, Australian, and New Zealand media owners even straight inflationary increases was evident. An estimate in 1972 showed that £311,000 would have been added to general-news revenues if the owners' payments had simply kept pace with British inflation. By then, the British Broadcasting Corporation was paying Reuters £320,000 for its services, compared with £273,000 from the whole of the British London-based national press.

In addition to suffering from a frozen home press market, the general-news division was also affected by a decision to limit the amount that the economic services paid for the use of Reuters' general news to 3 percent of the gross revenue earned by the RES teleprinter business. GND managers thought this rate could easily have been increased to 5 percent, which would have solved their financial problems. This view, naturally, was not shared by those more immediately concerned with competitive pricing of business services and the maximizing of the economic news division's profits.

Reuters' media revenue did not, of course, stand still, but the rate of increase was slow. The company's restricted capital resources were channeled toward profit-making economic services, and as a result media services were unable to benefit from the substantial economies and operational benefits Reuters would have gained from investment in electronic editing on video screens. In 1972, GND showed an overall loss of £215,000. The amount was not huge, but it was big enough to suggest a basic question: could a commercially oriented company seeking to maximize profits from a successful product afford to keep a loss-producing division alive?

Under the GND structure, Reuters had tried everything possible to make international general-news operations profitable. Internal factors—the freezing of the owners' payments and the size of the economic-services payment—certainly contributed to the general-news department's financial problems. But its difficulties were more basic than that. The international recipients to whom general-news services were sold were simply unwilling to pay for the costs involved. So in 1974, Reuters decided that its search for profits from the media should be abandoned; the agency would henceforth support the net cost of general-news operations from its own resources. If the media would not pay enough, then Reuters would make up the difference from the revenues it earned elsewhere. In a very real sense, Reuters had outgrown the media it served; they now depended on the agency to pay for supplying them with international news, rather than the other way around.

Reuters' profits enabled it to do this without strain from 1981 onward. Profits after tax of £33.39 million in 1982 and a profits-to-earnings level of 20 percent enabled the agency to open 12 new reporting offices that year, considerably more than in the years between 1974 and 1977, when the general-news editorial had been run as a separate unit but with no real growth in spending, before being merged with the economic-services editorial in progressive stages. By 1985, the number of offices opened since 1981 had risen to 30. These new outposts, from West Africa to California, could be justified on financial grounds because of the news they supplied to the money-making business services. But they also gave a big boost to general-news coverage. The motive for setting up a new office in Africa might be that it contributed fresh material to the commodity services which loomed so large in Reuters' U.S. sales. But the correspondent could also add to the agency's non-economic coverage of the developing world in a way that would have been impossible had the existence of his post depended on media earnings. Even if journalists still worried about the company's approved career path leading away from news and into sales managership, they were now far more numerous and better able to cope with covering the world (not to mention far better paid) than had ever been the case before.

Financial success prompted the agency's owners in the British press to look at Reuters in a new light, not just as a supplier of news services but also as an excellent investment—if their shares should be given a value through a flotation on the stock market. This was a particularly alluring prospect to those owners who were running loss-making British national newspapers. For the agency, a share float offered the prospect of being able to raise fresh capital in the equity market to provide the kind of resources appropriate to Reuters' position as a capital-intensive company with annual revenue of more than £300 million.

At the end of 1983, the Reuters board decided to go ahead with a public flotation in London and New York.[6] British newspapers forecast that the company could be worth up to £1.5 billion. Shares of press groups that owned Reuters jumped up on the London stock market. When the owners of the big British publisher Mirror Group Newspapers announced plans to hive off their group, financial analysts said the main attraction for investors would be the chance to get an indirect stake in Reuters.

But there was a snag. If Reuters went public like any normal commercial company, it would be open to a takeover bid or influence from a big shareholder. A determined buyer of Reuters shares would be able to affect the agency's news service. How would that square with the stipulation in the trust document governing Reuters' activities that the agency should "at no time pass into the hands of any one interest, group or faction" and that "its integrity, independence and freedom from bias shall at all times be fully preserved"? Reuters received legal advice that the 1941 trust document could be regarded as a shareholders' agreement that could be undone by agreement of the current owners, rather than as an immutable legal document. Even if this was so, Reuters clearly could not put itself in a position where it might be bought up by a government or some rich group that would use the agency for its own purposes. The nature of Reuters' business sets it apart from the ordinary run of companies. As the agency's editor in chief, Michael Reupke, said in early 1984: "If we were producing baked beans, we'd be able to go public tomorrow."

To protect itself, Reuters and its advisors devised a double scheme to enable the original owners to retain control. Separate classes of shares were created for the existing proprietors and for the public. The owners' shares represented 25 percent of the equity but, by being given four votes per share, 58 percent of the voting power. On top of that, a new company was created, controlled by the trustees of Reuters, which held a single "founders' share" that was given special overriding voting power to enforce the principles of the trust and to prevent any single shareholder or group from owning more than 15 percent of the company's capital.

This double safeguard seemed excessive to some people. Associations representing major British institutional investors advised their members to boycott Reuters shares because of the two-tier voting structure. Investors who paid for shares should get corresponding voting rights, the associations argued. But Reuters went ahead with the flotation in June 1984, issuing 113 million shares in London and New York, the first time such a simultaneous transatlantic float had been staged. The prospects of a takeover receded even further when it emerged that none of the high-voting "A" shares and only 38 percent of the lower-powered "B" shares would be put on the market, and that the newspaper groups would have priority in buying any "A" shares that were subsequently sold by the original owners.

Although Reuters could not have foreseen it, its timing was terrible. The shares were put on the market amid a stock market slump on both sides of the Atlantic. Prospects were hit by a wave of Wall Street skepticism about technology stocks. Nor was Reuters helped when a member of its New York underwriter, Morgan Stanley, told a reporter that the Securities and Exchange Commission (SEC) had reproved Reuters over possible infringements of the regulations covering share offerings and threatened to cancel the offer if there were any more suspected lapses.[7] The American offer did not turn out to be as successful as Reuters had hoped. Nearly a quarter of the shares offered in New York had to be switched to London, where buyers were more enthusiastic. The effect of the boycott call by the institutional investors' associations was easily outweighed by the attractiveness of the shares, however restricted their voting power. One major international investor, the Abu Dhabi Investment Authority, built up a holding of nearly one-third of the shares issued to the public. To anybody who worried that this might mean potential Arab political influence on the agency, Reuters' management pointed to the voting structure.

Reuters has erected enough barriers to an external takeover. Some people wondered, though, whether one of its original owners, such as international publisher Rupert Murdoch, might not be tempted by the idea of increasing his influence from within the Reuters share stockade. Questions could also be raised about the intangible effect of the agency going public on its management and the way Reuters evolved. Under the previous structure, the owners had played little part in the way the company was run. Management had been left largely to make its own equation between the profits from business-news services and the losses incurred in media operations. Now, a shareholder, particularly a big shareholder, has every right to ask why Reuters is spending money on unprofitable activities rather than concentrating on profitable ones. A management that has to be responsive to its shareholders, and to the opinion of stock exchanges on both sides of the Atlantic, could find it difficult to put such questions from its mind. The prospect, therefore, appears to be not the much-touted danger that Reuters could fall into the hands of manipulative shareholders but that the pressures resulting from becoming a public company will push Reuters into an even greater concentration on making money.

In all, the sale of 28.6 percent of Reuters in June 1984 brought £221 million for Reuters and its original owners. One existing shareholder that did not sell any shares was Murdoch's News Corporation, which held 9.5 percent of the "B" shares and 34.9 percent of the powerful "A" shares through its British and Australian newspaper groups. The share price of £1.96 arrived at in the flotation valued the agency at £770 million, or just over $1 billion. This was a long way from the original bullish forecasts. But it was even further from the days when the Reuters board had had to agonize over whether it could afford to appoint a single staff correspondent to cover all Latin America.

The share price soon rose, to reach £3.65 by the time Reuters announced its first year's results as a public company in February 1985. Casual questions to Reuters managers about how the company was doing were as likely to be answered by bullish remarks about the share price as by reference to the latest news beats or Monitor contracts. The Press Association, the domestic British news agency, launched a search for the heirs to its original shareholders, who were entitled to a slice of the Reuters bonanza. British national newspapers used part of their new-found wealth from Reuters shares to fund bingo-game circulation wars. On the other side of the world, the New Zealand Press Association, which held 10,000 Reuters shares, was the target of an unsuccessful $18.2 million take-over bid. Reuters' three senior executives, managing director Glen Renfrew, general manager Michael Nelson, and finance director Nigel Judah, had been voted shares by the board, on which they sat as executive directors, before the flotation was decided. All three became sterling millionaires several times over. Gerald Long, who as chief executive until 1981 had presided over the build-up of Reuters' business services and the pioneering development of electronic retrieval, had no shares and so made nothing out of the flotation. Indeed, Long's past role was obscured by the glow of present profits. A journalist who interviewed Reuters' top brass for a magazine article in 1983 does not recall Long's name having been mentioned once in the accounts of how the company had developed. A story in the London *Observer* in March 1985, headed "Renfrew of Reuter [*sic*]," described the agency's managing director since 1981 as "the man responsible for transforming the news agency into a major force in communications."

Reuters' 1984 results were certainly bright enough to eclipse the long years of development for those with their eyes fixed solely on the share price and Reuters' entry into the take-over market. In the first year after flotation, pretax profits of £74.3 million were 23.7 percent of turnover and earnings per share rose by 28 percent. Because of a deferred tax charge in the 1983 figures, the rise in net profits was even more striking, from £11 million in 1983 to £42.6 million in 1984. Sales rose by 29 percent overall to £313 million. The biggest growth was still in Europe and Asia. In sterling terms, European sales increased by 29 percent and Asian sales by 36 percent.

The United States was proving harder going. Revenue rose by one-fifth in sterling terms during 1984, but this could be attributed almost entirely to the strength of the dollar against the pound. Reuters did not disclose a dollar figure for its North American gross revenue. But it was known that its U.S. performance had been hit by problems among commodity dealers, who made up a significant slice of the agency's clients. There was also the strong competition from Telerate in financial information. The announcement of Reuters' 1984 figures coincided with the disclosure of the agreement to buy the Rich system design company as Reuters' bid to strengthen its North American position.

While Europe and, even more, Asia could be expected to continue to grow healthily as sources of revenue, Reuters' main testing ground appears, increasingly, to be the United States. The battle there is not being fought with traditional news-agency services. Reuters' success in maintaining its steep growth rates does not depend on the success of solo correspondents in Africa or Latin America beating the opposition with the first news of an election result or a peace treaty, a plane crash or a coup d'état. But the agency's ability to go on providing a high level of coverage of good and bad news from the developing world does depend, in not too indirect a fashion, on Reuters' performance in the battle for supremacy in the supply of business information.

UPI: Losses and Changing Owners . . . .

The 1970s, which saw Reuters' financial fortunes boom, witnessed mounting difficulties at the agency that had been founded as a commercial, private-enterprise venture at the start of the century. UPI describes itself as a company "organized for profit as well as to provide a needed service," and it did indeed enjoy modest profits after 1945. It had areas of great strength in the United States, notably in California; Latin American operations made money; West Germany and Japan were useful markets. The early plunge into newsfilm with Fox-Movietone also brought in profits, and UP (as it was before it absorbed INS, Hearst's International News Service) also earned lucrative commissions for handling overseas syndication of the United Features service. In the first decade after World War II, its owners at the E. W. Scripps Company received regular dividends.

But by the 1960s, UPI's position had begun to deteriorate sharply. Its syndication revenue was cut by new arrangements after the INS takeover, and the newsfilm business cost more and more to operate. The AP became an increasingly active competitor in Latin America and cut into some of UPI's traditional domestic fiefs. The rebirth of AFP added to international competition, while inflation and stagnant media markets were making overseas editing and translation desks increasingly unremunerative. In the United States, UPI was hard hit by the growth of monopoly newspapers and the development of supplemental services.

For a while, the agency's pioneering development of audio services for radio clients offered a prospect of salvation, but when the AP came onto the scene with an audio service, competition played havoc with rates as radio stations pitted the two services against each other. The AP could absorb the financial pressure because of its cooperative financing. UPI had to turn to its owners for support. The private agency's operating losses rose to $4.1 million in 1974 on total revenue of $58 million (after tax credits the loss for the year came to $1.9 million). The following year was less unhealthy, with a net deficit of $854,000. Thereafter, costs rose faster than revenue year by year (see table 7).

UPI imposed cost-cutting campaigns. It sought new areas of revenue in the commodity service venture UNICOM, retrieval services for home computer owners, a news service for television delivered by satellite, and sales of equipment. Losses went on rising. The operating deficit increased from $3.8 million in 1976 to $5.5 million in 1978. Telecommunications rates shot up; in 1978 alone, hikes in American Telephone & Telegraph tariffs for leased lines in the United States added $2 million to UPI's bills. At the same time, development of new, high-technology services was requiring capital investment on an unprecedented scale. "In the past, UPI's annual capital requirement hadn't been more than $200,000 to $300,000," president Roderick Beaton noted in 1979. "Now computers put it into the millions and tens of millions."

By the end of the 1970s, a change of ownership was in the wind. The E. W. Scripps family trust, which controlled UPI, would in any event end when the last trustee died. In April 1979, Edward W. Estlow, president of the Scripps company, said at a UPI luncheon that "methods are being explored and studied for the purpose of strengthening UPI and to further its perpetuity." That could only mean altering its ownership.

The possibility of doing this had been broached in the early 1970s when the agency's corporate registration was switched from New York to Delaware to facilitate a possible stock offering. Nothing came of that, but in 1978, Roderick Beaton returned to the question of broadening the agency's ownership. He discussed the matter with the agency's advisory board, made up of newspaper publishers and editors. They agreed that Beaton should talk to Scripps.

The result was an invitation to 200 press and broadcasting organizations in the United States to become partners in UPI. The offer, issued in the autumn of 1979, described such an investment as in-

Table 7		UPI Revenue and Costs (in thousands of $U.S.)			
Year	Gross Revenue	Foreign Revenue	Operating Costs	News Revenue	Picture Revenue
1974	58,083	12,910	62,186	38,999	10,272
1975	62,372	13,901	64,958	42,272	10,995
1976	63,405	14,185	67,209	43,046	11,133
1977	67,372	15,190	72,458	45,490	12,005
1978	74,307	17,829	79,856	49,620	13,518
First half 1979	39,429	a	41,831	a	a

Sources of UPI Revenue
(in percentages)

	1974	1975	1976	1977	1978
Domestic					
Press	45.8	48.3	47.2	49.3	49.4
Broadcast	33.8	35.5	35.4	35.4	35.0
Other	20.4	16.2	17.4	15.3	15.6
Foreign					
Newspaper	51.3	50.0	47.2	44.1	44.2
News agency	16.7	18.6	21.2	22.6	22.3
Broadcast	18.0	15.5	14.3	16.8	15.0
Feature	11.2	13.0	14.2	13.1	14.9
Other	2.8	2.9	3.1	3.4	3.6

Source: UPI limited partnership offer, 1979.

a. Figures not given.

volving a high degree of risk and suitable only for those who did not need liquidity in their investments. Forty-five "limited partnership units" were put on offer, each representing a 2 percent stake in UPI. Scripps would keep the remaining 10 percent. UPI hoped to raise $8.1 million immediately, followed by an additional $13 million between 1980 and 1984. The partners would not only plow cash into UPI; they would also agree to pay higher subscription rates. If everything went according to plan, UPI expected an annual profit of $2 million in 1983.

The offer was a failure. With hindsight, UPI executives felt the approach to the media could have been handled better. Newspapers and broadcasters, for their part, showed little willingness to sink money into the agency. They wanted UPI to continue as a competitor to the AP, but they felt unwilling or unable to invest in it. Some feared they would have no control over how their money was spent, while others saw possible conflicts of interest if part ownership in UPI were combined with their own supplementary news services. Publicly quoted newspapers and broadcasting organizations faced possible trouble from shareholders if they sank money into such a financially uncertain venture. Some U.S. papers were reported to have been antagonized by a proposal, late in the offer period, that major foreign clients of UPI should be brought in. The failure of the offer did nothing to lessen UPI's search for new proprietors.

The agency's pretax loss in 1980 rose to $12 million, 14 percent of gross revenues. The chairman of the UPI advisory board, Joe D. Smith, warned an agency convention in 1980: "Operating results must be improved drastically regardless of who UPI's owners will be, and the improvement must be made immediately." Revenue from overseas had held up better than domestic earnings in the late 1970s, and accounted for 31.5 percent of the total in 1978, but this figure reflected UPI's problems with its home market rather than any dramatic growth overseas. The agency recognized that all it could expect abroad was to keep subscription increases in line with inflation—containing costs rigorously all the while. If UPI were going to be turned around financially, the secret would have to be unearthed in the United States. Uncertainty about its ownership made the quest no easier.

Inquiries about buying the agency came from a number of directions. An oil company looked at it, then decided not to get into the agency business. The U.S. National Public Radio considered an arrangement under which it would marry its communications with those of UPI internally and cooperate with Reuters overseas. There were contacts, of varying degrees of concreteness, with West European agencies and an Arab group. In the spring of 1981, secret negotiations began with another possible purchaser, Reuters.

The two agencies had each changed a good deal since their abortive negotiations following Reuters' break with the AP in the 1960s. Reuters was now well established in the United States, particularly as a supplier of economic news services. The domestic satellite communications network that UPI was building up would enable Reuters to leap ahead in delivery of its electronic retrieval services. UPI would also bring Reuters into the medium- and small-media markets in the United States, which it had never penetrated. Overseas, UPI and

Reuters operations could be amalgamated and run on a more economical basis. UPI would bring Reuters a photographic service and give it a leading position in Latin America, where it had traditionally been weak.

Weighing against such potential advantages for Reuters were the costs of taking on a loss-incurring operation. Reuters would not have paid anything for UPI. Indeed, the U.S. agency's owners would have had to pay Reuters for taking it over, and would have been required to put money into the unfunded UPI pension plan. The problem for Reuters was not only UPI's operating losses—the London-based agency would also find itself tied to media activities that would distract it from the primary aim of building up profits from its economic-news services. At the end of 1981, Reuters formally withdrew from negotiations, only to resume talks in 1984 that led to the news-picture agreement between the two. By then, UPI had acquired a totally unexpected new owner in the shape of Media News Corporation, a company newly formed by the two owners of a Nashville-based cable television enterprise, an Illinois newspaper publisher, and a Chicago lawyer.

The financial arrangements of the ownership change in 1982 were kept secret, immediately arousing controversy. A former UPI official was quoted by the *New York Times* as saying the new owners paid $17.5 million. Other sources, however, reported that Scripps put $10 million into the agency's pension fund as part of the deal, recouping on tax deductions for worthless stock in UPI, which Scripps had built up as it covered the agency's losses in the 1970s. Controversy over the purchase rose as it was disclosed that one of the two Nashville cable television operators, William Geissler, had gone to prison for refusing to serve as a draftee in Vietnam. The other, Douglas Ruhe, had been arrested twice while taking part in civil rights demonstrations in Missouri and Kansas in the 1960s. Both were members of the Baha'i faith, and they made a point during their early months at UPI of denying strenuously that any "funny money" or foreign funding was involved in the purchase of the agency.

As Ruhe tells it, he and Geissler had wanted to build up a new television network. "The primary product of a network is news," he noted in a 1983 interview.

> When we heard UPI was available, we said to ourselves that this is a great news-gathering organization. It has credibility. We felt intelligent management had been lacking at UPI. There had been a "penny wise,

pound foolish'' approach, with management getting into a lot of bad deals and saving money on staff while getting caught in escalating major costs.

Within a year, UPI's new ownership had undergone two further changes. First, the newspaper publisher and the lawyer left. Their combined 30 percent share was taken by a Nashville businessman, lawyer, and unsuccessful gubernatorial candidate, John Jay Hooker, who became chairman of UPI on February 1, 1983. Hooker announced that he had acquired his stake in UPI for ''$1 and other valuable considerations.'' What this meant, Ruhe later explained, was that Hooker was going to raise $150 million for the agency. But things evidently did not work out as planned. Three months after going into UPI, Hooker left, and his shares went to Ruhe and Geissler. The two men, who planned to put a quarter of the agency's shares into an employee stock plan, were twin masters of one of the world's major minute-by-minute sources of news.

The American media establishment did not know quite what to make of the new situation at UPI. The previous obscurity of Ruhe and Geissler, as much as their having been arrested or belonging to the Baha'i faith, made them suspect in a world in which editors, publishers, and broadcasting executives were all part of a well-established professional society with its own hierarchies and traditions. In such a world, two men who owned only a pay-television station simply did not take over the second biggest news agency in the United States.

Ruhe and Geissler were well aware of the problems of what they called ''the legitimacy factor.'' They hired two well-known editorial figures: William Small, formerly president of NBC News, became president of UPI, and Maxwell McCrohon, from the Tribune Company of Chicago, was made editor in chief. A sustained effort was launched to improve the quality of the news service, with particular attention directed at stepping up regional coverage of the United States and making copy easier to handle. In the autumn of 1983, Ruhe reported that 60 percent of editors said the service had improved significantly, and 30 percent said it had held steady, compared with a 70 percent negative rating a year earlier. On the financial side, mid-1983 losses were cut back to $500,000 a month, one-third of the mid-1982 figure. Speeding up installation of antennae around the United States enabled UPI to switch from expensive telephone-line communications to cheaper satellite transmissions.

The agency's new owners insisted that they saw fresh revenue potential in international services, but their priority was overwhelmingly in the domestic market. This was evident not only in the allocations of investment funds, but in the pattern of international disinvestment shown in the sale of UPI's share in UPITN and, even more significantly, the 1984 news-picture agreement with Reuters. Ruhe announced that this agreement would "result in valuable service enhancements for all our subscribers." Showing once more the domestic direction of American agency thinking, he must have meant U.S. subscribers since foreign clients would now have to turn to Reuters. Quite how the UPI service could be enhanced by selling what had been one of its more highly regarded elements was, in any case, obscure. What was evident was that UPI needed all the money it could raise, and quickly. The costs in 1984 of covering the American presidential campaign and the Olympic Games weighed heavily on the agency's operating budget. Improved profits at some newspapers in the United States had brought back clients like the *Philadelphia Inquirer* which had given up the agency a few years earlier. Still, by the summer of 1984, UPI was estimated to be supplying only about half the number of newspapers taking AP.

Discreetly, UPI's owners were offering a stake in the company to a buyer ready to pump in sufficient capital. The 1984 operating deficit was put at $7 million, well below the $23 million racked up in 1982 and 1983 combined. But UPI owed about $9 million to creditors, including domestic U.S. communications companies. Its fragile hopes of showing operating profits on a regular basis from 1985 onward depended on cutting costs, boosting sales, and finding new services with high profit margins. In August 1984, management told staff of "a serious cash crunch." In September, William Small left. He was replaced by Luis Nogales, formerly the vice-president for administration. The appointment was generally seen as a sign that UPI was going to strengthen its financial management.

The wire services guild, representing about half UPI's staff, agreed to pay cuts and job lay-offs. In return, 6.5 percent of the company's stock was handed over to the employees. The cost-saving enabled UPI to report an operating profit in the last three months of 1984. This was its first profitable quarterly statement for two decades. But debts were still rising. Staff began to worry about their paychecks bouncing. In early March 1985, UPI entered a hectic new phase in its long fight for survival.

First, the company announced that Ruhe and Geissler were taking steps to relinquish some of their controlling interest as part of "a program to recapitalize the company and to guarantee its future." Then, on March 7, UPI reported that its president, Luis Nogales, was leaving. A spokesman for the newspaper publisher Rupert Murdoch said Ruhe and Geissler had approached Murdoch about buying the agency. Murdoch refused.

After Murdoch's refusal, Ruhe and Geissler went into a 20-hour negotiating session with the agency's major creditor, the Foothill Financial Corporation of Los Angeles, union representatives, and members of the agency's management, including Nogales. At the end of the negotiations, Nogales was reinstated and Ruhe and Geissler offered most of their stock to UPI's creditors in return for cancelling the agency's debts, which some reports put as high as $12 million. It seemed the only way out, but the offer faced problems. Accepting UPI stock would make the creditors liable for a slice of severance obligations if UPI did not survive. One big creditor was American Telephone & Telegraph (A T & T), which believed that it was barred from ownership of a news service under the terms of the recent disinvestiture of the Bell System. "Everyone would be coming down on our necks if we were to own our own wire service," an A T & T spokesman told the *Wall Street Journal*. And did the American Express Company, another substantial creditor, really want to get into a precarious news agency? The reinstated Nogales, who became chairman and chief executive officer, sounded an optimistic note, telling reporters, "We now have the framework to make financial and organizational stability possible and to provide a vehicle to bring about the future that we all wish to see."

Stability was hardly the word to apply to UPI in the spring and summer of 1985. Some of the bad news was conveyed by the agency itself. In April, UPI put out a story quoting Nogales as saying the agency did not have enough cash to cover paychecks. He asked staff not to deposit their checks for the time being. Then UPI issued a story quoting agency officials as saying that the two principal owners had diverted money to a management firm they owned and used other funds to set up "questionable venture deals." The story also charged that Ruhe and Geissler had not carried out an undertaking to invest $2 million in UPI. Ruhe told the *Washington Post*, "We've made our share of mistakes," but denied any wrongdoing.

On April 28, bowing to the inevitable, UPI filed for protection from its creditors under chapter 11 of the U.S. bankruptcy code. This protected its assets from seizure while the agency worked out a financial rescue package. The filing revealed that UPI's debts had reached $45 million, far more than had previously been estimated. UPI raised domestic subscription rates by 9.9 percent and set up sale-and-leaseback arrangements on some of its equipment to raise cash. The extent of its plight was shown dramatically when the White House requested payment of $30,000 to cover the costs of a UPI reporting team due to accompany President Reagan on a trip to Europe. Two newspaper editors from the *Chicago Tribune* and *Newsday* had to step forward to offer guarantees of $15,000 apiece. Client figures reported at the time gave UPI 800 press subscribers and 3300 broadcasters, compared to 1260 and 5700 respectively for the AP, crediting the cooperative with 70 percent more subscribers than the private agency.

Soon after UPI had sheltered under chapter 11, talks opened again with Reuters. A Miami-based group, the General Federal Savings Association, also began discussions about a possible purchase of the agency. Reuters' managing director told his company's annual general meeting that "any action we take will be done very much with the interests of Reuters' bottom line in mind." The attractiveness of becoming involved in UPI's loss-making activities remained highly problematical for the London-based agency, which was deeply committed to acquisitions and agreements to expand its position in financial information and communications. After inconclusive discussions, Reuters dropped out, saying it had not been given enough information by UPI. The American agency's internal affairs were, meanwhile, going through another stormy phase. Ruhe and Geissler sought a court order to oust Nogales as chairman. Ruhe said this would clear the way for the sale of the UPI holding company, Media News Corporation, "without interference from third parties."

Longtime observers of UPI found it difficult to muster much hope of a speedy change in the agency's plight. If there was to be an improvement, it would have to come from within the United States. The rest of the world, which had watched the UPI saga for a decade, had little part to play in determining whether the number of international agencies was reduced from four to three.

UPI's financial history in the past decade has illustrated most dramatically the commercial vulnerability of the major agencies in their general-news services. It is clear that the other three agencies would be equally exposed in their international operations if they did not have the support of economic services revenue, a domestic membership base, or state financial backing. The four major services have come under attack in recent years for not paying enough attention to the specific news requirements of the poorer areas of the world, the implication being that they could be doing more if they wished and that they are using a monopoly position to avoid allocating the proper resources to covering the developing world. The financial reality is that they have no spare resources, and that reporting and distribution efforts must necessarily follow the pattern of revenue sources. If the four major agencies were the rich organizations they are sometimes portrayed as, they could afford to be more responsive to the requirements of regions where their revenue is low. But because they are insufficiently funded for the job they have taken on, they are tied to those areas where the most money can be earned, and to an editorial approach that seeks to combine maximum acceptability with minimum outlay.

Agencies, Clients,
and Governments

"We are a purely commercial agency," a Reuters executive told a visiting Chinese delegation in 1977. "Our editorial standards are absolute and are not influenced by our subscribers, private or governmental." Such independence is an essential element of the philosophy and operations of the major international news services. Certainly their overall editorial approach is weighted toward North American, West European, and Japanese media (although it is widely acceptable elsewhere), but the international market forces affecting the Big Four are so diverse—and the financial rewards so meager—that the agencies enjoy almost complete autonomy in shaping their day-to-day files of general news.[1]

In the United States, the Associated Press and United Press International have established regular forums in which subscribers and members can make their opinions heard. Foreign news is never high on the agendas of these meetings of newspaper and broadcasting editors, but this is nothing new. Back in 1948, as an observer at an AP convention tells it, a request for suggestions to implement wider coverage of world news by the association was greeted by a long silence, broken finally by one delegate. "Did he ask whether the public could be told more of what goes on inside China beyond the birth of eight children at once?" Zechariah Chaffee wrote in *Neiman Reports*. "Did he regret the drastic reduction of Associated Press correspondents in Europe, or express the wish that we might learn more about the way American soldiers were governing our own zone in Germany? No—he complained because the Associated Press did not carry news of the Irish Sweepstakes."

In the 1970s, discussions of foreign coverage by the AP Managing Editors' Association (APME) were dominated by the editors' desire to present the news of the world in ways that were relevant to their readers' knowledge and concerns—and that gave them something television could not offer. As Carol Sutton of the *Louisville Courier-Journal,* who headed an APME Foreign News Subcommittee in 1976, put it:

> I think we have to realize that television gives many people most of the news they want about a war that may seem remote and unimportant. And television has the advantage of moving pictures in color that talk. . . . I think we need a minimum of bulletin information—just enough to fill in the essential details. Then we should concentrate on explaining what is happening and why it is important in terms of people who live in Louisville, Ky., or Topeka, Kan.

Both U.S. agencies have been trying to meet this requirement in recent years. In the words of one AP editor, "We try to tell American steel workers that they should be interested in the state of the European steel industry because you've got the same problems on both sides of the Atlantic."

But even within the United States, these two agencies face a problem in seeking to satisfy everybody. In addition to pleasing the mass of small- and medium-sized newspapers whose voices dominate their annual conventions, the AP and UPI are trying to get as much copy as they can into newspapers that do not simply want their news presented in terms attractive to ordinary citizens in Kentucky or Kansas. Such newspapers are few in number, but agency journalists find greater satisfaction in landing a story on the front page of the *New York Times,* the *Washington Post,* or the *Los Angeles Times* than in scoring in hundreds of less celebrated dailies. AP correspondents like to say that they are in competition not just with UPI but with reporters working abroad for the major U.S. metropolitan papers as well.

No matter how many meetings they hold to get the views of their clients and members, the AP and UPI are still obliged to remain free, in their editorial decisions, of any single group of recipients. The United States is the country where subscribers' requirements are felt most immediately, but this serves only to underscore the impossibility of satisfying the market as a whole and individual groups of recipients at the same time. Faced with the choice, the U.S. agencies attempt to compromise in ways that—while satisfying nobody completely— are acceptable to both sides: to the foreign editor of a major East Coast daily who wants broader global coverage and to the managing editor of a small-circulation paper who likes foreign stories that "answer some basic questions, such as 'what does it mean to the average person in a mid-West industrial city with 12 percent unemployment and a natural gas shortage.' " The necessity of compromise arises from the nature of the market the agencies serve; the shape it takes is determined by the agencies themselves.

If this is the case in the United States, it is even more so in the rest of the world. Agencies note what major subscribers say (on the rare occasions when they say anything concrete), but the bulk of international clients, paying only a few hundred or a few thousand dollars a month, have little individual influence on services going to so many recipients in so many countries. If a single Paris newspaper complains about a lack of news from Brazil, the agencies are hardly apt to put more Brazilian stories in their French services. Only if the subscriber is a major payer will an agency respond directly to its suggestions—and very few clients, in Paris or elsewhere, put up enough money to be able to command this kind of attention.

Individual subscribers' opinions about what they do *not* want elicit even less of a response. A client may complain about getting too much sports coverage or too much secondary news from the United States, but nothing is likely to change as a result. Another client, receiving the same service, would only complain in turn about the cut in U.S. or sports items. And as already noted, agency desks judge stories on their individual merits rather than on the number of similar reports already transmitted. A client unable to use the copy it receives has only to use the spike or hit an electronic kill button—and consider canceling its subscription when its contract expires.

Contract renewal time marks the one point at which agencies and subscribers can confront one another. In theory, this should be the moment at which the value of an agency's service is weighed against its subscription rate. In fact, such objective judgment appears to be rare, particularly in the agencies' international operations; the anarchic nature of subscription rates militates against rational negotiation. With nothing to gain from removing its teleprinter from a client's office and much to lose, an agency is usually ready to accept minimal annual rate increases, or sometimes none at all. The subscriber knows this—and also knows that another agency will be only too willing to step into the breach if an existing contract is canceled. Even if this were not so, it would be virtually impossible to establish the true worth of an agency's service to a newspaper or broadcasting station. Clients once taking three or four services now get by on two without any effect on their own revenue. Does this mean that the one or two agencies they discarded were worthless?

The financial answer to that question might well be in the affirmative, and decisions on what subscribers can afford to pay agencies are often made by financial managers rather than by the editorial departments that actually use their services. Big news organizations generally regard a multiplicity of news sources as a virtue, and editors tend to be unwilling to take the initiative in canceling an agency contract even if its copy is little used. When pressure to contain editorial budgets becomes strong, however, dropping an agency is a relatively painless way of realizing the required savings. The decision as to which service to drop may be influenced by the amount to be saved as much as by the quality of what is being supplied. When one agency commands as much as two others put together, it is obviously hard for editors to drop two rather than one, however high their opinion of the more expensive service.

On the other hand, it is difficult for an agency to convince a newspaper or broadcasting station that an additional source of international news will bring demonstrable returns. If a foreign editor has additional money at his disposal, he is more inclined to spend it on an additional correspondent than another news agency. An extra correspondent can give a newspaper added impact with on-the-scene reporting or well-promoted feature writing. Exclusive reports from the trouble spots of the world have a readily observable punch that the addition of yet another agency credit line sadly lacks. "When one of our own staff members goes abroad, we give his or her reports the full treatment. Yet when well-known wire service reporters come through with good yarns, we chop them down," one U.S. editor told researchers for a news-flow study carried out by the International Press Institute (IPI) in 1953. Three decades later, the foreign editor of a leading U.S. newspaper noted: "If our man sends x many words, we are likely to use them. If we get the same thing, and just as good, from the wires, the tendency is to cut it down." At a major U.S. daily, the foreign department even found it difficult to get copy from Reuters on the front page during the U.S. embassy hostage drama in Teheran when the agency was the paper's only major news source following the expulsion from Iran of American correspondents. The problem was that too many editors automatically downgraded the Reuters reports as being "only agency copy."

As a result, there is a tendency for the actual merits of an international agency to count for less than might be expected when it comes to the question of subscribing to or dropping a service. Knowledge of each agency's successes and failures, and of the level of its routine daily reporting, is fragmented and confused. Copy editors know how well Reuters or UPI has performed on the story they happen to be handling, but they may be ignorant of the relative strengths and weaknesses of the major services when it comes to other events. Trying to get an overall idea of agency performance from what is printed is often rendered difficult by the tendency of many subscribers to use combined credits, or no credits at all. A survey of leading British dailies in 1977 showed that only 15 percent of foreign stories were credited to agencies, a figure that in no way reflects the amount of wire service copy actually used.[2] National news agencies receiving several wire services often meld stories from different services, then transmit them under a joint credit or the national agency's own name. In broadcasting, attribution is extremely rare, and no lasting record of where a story came from remains.

The wholesale nature of the agency business means that the end user—the newspaper reader, radio listener, or television viewer—has little or no idea of what the agencies actually provide. For the same reasons mentioned above, news retailers are often incapable of delivering an accurate assessment of what they receive. A survey carried out for this book of twenty-nine agency subscribers in twenty-one countries on five continents produced generally consistent judgments on the performance of each agency, but wide differences became apparent when the services of individual agencies from specific countries were discussed.

Some subscribers took it for granted that each agency would be the best source of news from its home country. "We would normally accept [Agence France-Presse] reporting a speech by the French president from Paris," said one broadcasting editor. "If they're not right on that, what can you trust them for?" Other clients, however, judged that the agencies were often not particularly good from their home countries. "As a rule any other agency is better than AFP for coverage of French events and any other agency better than Reuters for British events," one editor commented. Several believed that the AP and UPI provide too much copy from the United States, but one leading West European newspaper editor singled out the AP to praise its U.S. coverage. A newspaper foreign editor unequivocally voted Reuters the best agency from Moscow, while another judged UPI ahead of the field in reporting from the Soviet Union. A national agency in Europe complained about excessive coverage of what was then Rhodesia (now Zimbabwe) by one of the services, but another said it could have done with more Rhodesian copy. A broadcasting editor's high marks for the AP's coverage of the Far East were balanced by another's judgment that AFP was superior in this area.

Many editors voiced a consistent theme: their assessment of an agency's coverage of a particular country or area depends heavily on their confidence in its correspondents there. "We tend to know the names of reliable agency correspondents and to use them," one broadcasting executive said. A U.S. newspaper foreign editor added, "The strength of the agency changes with its people." It is apparent from the disparate comments quoted above that different subscribers often have vastly different opinions of individual agencies and their correspondents.

Given the similarity of much agency reporting and the difficulty of forming a distinct picture of the performance of each of the services, the wide range of opinions expressed by subscribers is striking. The diversity of their appreciations is an essential element in the maintenance of competition among the news services, however contradictory that may sound. If all newspapers and broadcasters reacted in exactly the same way to each agency, there would hardly be a need for four major services. If the standards of the recipients were not so varied, subscribers would use the same agency for a given story instead of spreading their choices across all four. It is precisely because the market for news is so varied that each service can find users for its stories somewhere in the world.

What the Big Four cannot determine is where usage will occur. Quite apart from the merits of the agencies' stories, which will be judged differently by different clients, a number of uncontrollable factors influence what is used and what is discarded. Two stories, for example, may be of equal importance; Reuters sends them out in the order in which they were received, but the AP decides to issue them in the opposite order. One recipient chooses the Reuters material because of its particular interest in the story that Reuters released first, while another acts in the opposite way. If a newspaper approaching deadline suddenly needs a two-paragraph item to fill a hole in its foreign page, it uses an agency story of appropriate length that comes up on the teleprinter at the right moment—even if it is not as significant as other stories discarded earlier. An agency might, entirely by chance, hit a local news nerve—running a story about traffic problems in Cairo, for example, just at the time when authorities in Tokyo are holding a conference on that city's congestion, thus winning good play in the Japanese media. Some time ago, my own analysis of the growing political problems of a French prime minister was held up for several days at Reuters' head office and then issued as a feature. Two hours after the story had moved on the wire, the prime minister resigned. The analysis was much more widely used than it would have been if it had been issued when originally written.

Apart from such unpredictable factors, the agencies are quite powerless to control their stories once they have been issued. Because of the great number of subscribers they cater to and their frequently updated accounts of major events, they know that only a small proportion of their daily copy is going to be used by any one client. Even subscribers with large numbers of foreign news columns publish far less material than the agencies run. The *New York Times,* for instance, prints even less international wordage than the AP includes on its interbureau state wire—where copy from abroad is cut back to essentials. In Britain, studies for the 1977 Royal Commission on the Press showed that seven daily newspapers published an average of twenty-one items a day over a twelve-day period, or only about 10 percent of the stories issued daily by the major agencies. In some cases, the space allotted to foreign events narrowed such reporting down to six or seven items, many of them brief "fillers," sports reports, or news of celebrities or scandals. Averaging figures in this way brings together newspapers of widely varying types, so the application of such figures can be only general. But then, the agencies themselves are trying to appeal to an equally varied audience with a service that will meet their clients' "average" requirements.

National news agencies have more space for foreign news than the press does, but they too use only a fraction of what they receive from the Big Four. "The flow of agency copy is almost certainly too much," the foreign editor of the Swedish national agency commented. "You use only about 10 percent of what is coming in." Figures for Japan's Kyodo agency, whose use of foreign agency copy has already been noted, show that for the entire month of September 1979 only 242 items from Reuters, 233 from the AP, and 210 from UPI were picked up. Each agency issued that number of stories to Kyodo in a couple of days.

Not only are relatively few agency items used by each subscriber, the length of chosen items is also often pruned back. For example, a lengthy agency story recounting the opening of an international conference—complete with details about the major participants, the themes to be discussed, and previous conferences on the same topic—

may end up in many newspapers as only a paragraph or two, and on the air as a single sentence in a broadcast news bulletin. In the face of the flood of daily wordage, brevity can bring its own rewards. "On Rhodesia, Reuters and UPI gave us too much for two or three years," the foreign editor of a major European national agency recalled. "Instead of taking the trouble to cut their stories, we preferred to rely on AFP just because it was shorter and it was easier to use a service that came in compact form rather than cutting and summarizing longer services."

The Big Four:
Agenda Setters to the World?. . . . .

The agencies are thus both powerless and all-powerful. They cannot determine how their news is used; they cannot even ensure that it is credited to them. Their control stops the moment stories are filed down the wire to subscribers. On the other hand, they are free from the influences of direct market forces in their daily editorial operations. Correspondents and editors of course have a general idea of the markets they are serving, but that idea is a synthesis of the many varied requirements formed collectively by each agency's editorial staff. Its composition changes over the years—as can be seen, for instance, in the growing importance of economic news coverage for the media. But the breadth of the market as well as disparities among subscribers leaves the agencies to decide what goes into the daily flow of world news.

This has led to the description, in sociological studies, of the Big Four as "gatekeepers" and "agenda setters" to the world—organizations that control the flow of news and set priorities for their subscribers. To the extent that the agencies decide the contents of their services, they are obviously gatekeepers, although they exercise this function in the positive sense of deciding what should go out rather than in the restrictive spirit the term implies. This process, previously known simply as editing, is akin to the action of any supplier of goods or services that controls output and adapts its products to what it thinks recipients want.

"Agenda setting" is a more nebulous concept. Like "gatekeeping," it has been employed in recent years to foster an impression of the Big Four as monopolistic, manipulative organizations. In order to serve Western interests, it is argued, the agencies determine news priorities and choices of subscribers in ways that work against the interests of the nonaligned, developing nations. The actual content of the news that the Big Four issues to and about the Third World will be examined in chapter 10; what is immediately relevant to the charge of "agenda setting" is the combination of power and power-lessness noted above. The agencies do of course set the news agenda for their subscribers, merely by supplying their services, just as the local butcher sets the meat agenda by deciding on the selection of meats available to his neighborhood. Subscribers are undoubtedly guided by the weight the agencies place on stories; a report marked "urgent" or a story developed at length for morning newspapers has an indisputable impact. But the agencies have no way of imposing their own priorities on subscribers. A newspaper is free to discard stories the agencies consider important, or to print nothing but secondary items from the file.

The fact that this does not often happen, and that the news choices of agencies and their clients are likely to be similar, is not so much a matter of external agenda setting by the agencies as it is the result of shared editorial values. An agency that persisted in dealing at length with events of no interest to its subscribers would not last long. The Big Four have remained so widely used because they work within the common ground existing between them and most of their clients. It is this common ground that determines the news agenda and enables the agencies to remain autonomous.

Owners, Managers, and Editors . . . .

Not only are the agencies largely autonomous of their clients in their day-to-day international reporting and editing, their managers and editors also enjoy a great deal of freedom from direct control by their owners. The nature of agency operations places a premium on fast editorial decisions and managerial expertise in individual areas and services. Given the predominantly national composition of agency boards, and directors' general lack of professional knowledge of the international news-agency business, the distancing of owners from daily operations is inevitable and, one may safely guess, not unwelcome to editorial and management executives.

The result has been the enhancement of the role of management in the agencies' international activities. The postwar growth of the four main services was influenced considerably more by managers than by boards of directors. There was, of course, general board policy approval, and the chairmen of the agencies were more closely

159

involved in operations than other directors. But the scope and complexity of international operations require decision making of a kind with which no group of domestic newspaper executives could be expected to deal in anything but the broadest manner.

This has been less the case for the two U.S. agencies' domestic operations than it has for the run of international services. The American owners of UPI, in particular, were obliged to take a close interest in the agency's domestic operations as losses mounted in the 1970s, and it was naturally the new owners after 1982 who decided the ways in which a turnaround should be attempted. At the AP, the domestic members *are* the owners, and they make their opinions heard both through their board representatives and through a managing editors' association. But—as noted previously—the attention paid to foreign news by the AP's recipients/owners at the association's meetings is limited, and minutes of recent board meetings record few interventions by directors on matters extrinsic to the United States.

The AFP has a special body, the Superior Council, whose task it is to ensure that the agency remains independent both of its major subscriber, the state, and of any other influence. The French government has not hesitated to intervene on occasion, but in general this intervention has been prompted by issues such as the appointment of the head of the agency rather than by the actual content of AFP services. When there has been direct intervention concerning news coverage, it has come straight from political leaders who assume the right to oversee what the agency issues.

The ownership of Reuters up to the 1984 flotation was somewhat less national than that of the other three agencies, since it included the press associations of Australia and New Zealand as well as Britain's two newspaper groupings. But the participation of Australia and New Zealand was strictly limited, accounting for only 12 percent of the company's shares compared with 44 percent each for the London-based Newspaper Publishers' Association and the provincial Press Association. Seven of the agency's nine nonexecutive directors were British; only one came from Australia, and one from New Zealand. Three senior company executives—its managing director, general manager, and finance director—also sat on the Reuters board. Interviews with board members indicate that their attention has historically been concentrated on the agency's financial progress and general development policy rather than on editorial matters. Board decisions may affect the broad shape of editorial activities; it was a board decision, for instance, that gave the final impetus to the wedding of economic and general news under a single management in 1980. But there is no way in which individual directors could influence the daily news service, and comments on how Reuters is meeting the news needs of its British and Commonwealth owners are seldom heard at board meetings. With the appointment of prominent businessmen from Britain and the United States as directors in 1984, the likelihood of editorial intervention by the Reuters board grew even less.

Under the trust agreement drawn up in 1941 and renewed in 1953, the agency's owners undertake "to ensure that Reuters shall not pass into the hands of any interest group or faction, that its integrity, independence and freedom from bias shall be fully preserved, and that no effort shall be spared to expand, develop and adapt the business of Reuters. . . ." During the years since 1941, the trustees had not been called on to take action to ensure that the agreement was respected, but the controversy surrounding the share flotation brought them into the limelight. One trustee, Lord Matthews, had been among the most active proponents of the share float. He took pride in having chivied Reuters into going public, as he said to a shareholders' meeting of the newspaper publishers, Fleet Holdings, of which he was chairman.

The suggestion that the trustees might turn out to be a toothless body aroused their chairman, Angus McLachlan, to issue an indignant statement in November 1983. "It has been inferred that since we were all in the first place nominated by newspaper companies that [sic] we shall rubberstamp anything that is formally proposed by the Board," he wrote in a press release issued by Reuters. "On the contrary, on becoming Trustees, we, all of us, accepted an obligation to conserve the objects of the Trust. . . . When any scheme is presented to us we shall seek independent legal advice as to whether that scheme is one with which we, as Trustees, should concur."

The scheme that emerged from Reuters in 1984 was one with which the trustees could hardly not agree. By creating a "Founders' Share" with overriding voting rights to ensure that the trust agreement was respected, it met the objections of those who had feared that the board might wave that document aside as an outdated legal formality that could be undone by agreement among the shareholders. At the same time, the number of trustees was expanded by the addition of the former British ambassador to Washington, John Freeman, now chairman of a London television company; Lord McGregor, the former chairman of the latest British Royal Commission on the Press; and, in a departure from the British–Australian–New Zealand tradition of the trust, Kingman Brewster, former president of Yale and U.S. ambassador in London.

News-Agency/ Government Relations . . . .

There is one group of subscribers from which the agencies are particularly eager to remain autonomous: governments. To a large extent, they have succeeded. Independence from official control is important both because of the strong tradition among members of the press that news organizations should be free from external influence, and because political independence is necessary if the agencies are to sell their services widely. But news agencies cannot simply ignore governments; their relationship with officialdom, both at home and abroad, is a multifaceted one that affects both the collection and sale of news. Governments subscribe to agency services, set the political environment in which agencies work, determine constraints (or the lack thereof) on agency reporting, and are of course a major source of information. They also set international communications rates through their control of national telecommunications authorities, thus affecting the costs to the agencies of both reporting and distribution of news.

For their part, news agencies from their earliest days have been a significant source of information to governments, often delivering information ahead of official services. In the Franco-Prussian War of 1870, for example, the French government's own information arrangements proved so unsatisfactory that it signed a supplementary contract for war news with Havas. In 1914, a Havas journalist reported the assassination of Archduke Franz Ferdinand to the French president. During the Spanish Civil War, the rebel headquarters learned of the bombing of Guernica through Reuters. In World War II, the British Ministry of Information picked up news of the Nazi advance in 1940 from UP. AP twice got into hot water with the allied authorities by issuing news of the D-day landings in France and the German surrender before the official release time. The British chief censor described the first incident as "the worst shock of my life." [3] At the end of the fighting in Asia in 1945, the AP's Stanley Swinton recalled going to see Ho Chi Minh. "There, in Ho's outer office, was a telegrapher dutifully copying the AP Asian report so Ho would know what was going on," Swinton remembered. Five years later,

UP provided the U.S. government with its first news of the North Korean attack on the South.

Improved communications in the 1950s and 1960s made the agencies even more competitive with official news services, particularly since their dispatches did not have to go through decoding or bureaucratic filtering. A 1963 study of U.S. government use of agency news reported that in fast-breaking situations agency stories were often received four to five hours ahead of State Department cables and, in some cases, a full twenty-four hours earlier. Defense Department officials questioned during this period said they often got their first news of events from agency teleprinters, while a member of the Senate Foreign Affairs Committee commented: "The tickers are used steadily; this is the first source of information—many hours before we read it in the press."

Diplomats interviewed for this book acknowledged the news agencies as one of their most important sources of information. In developing nations, the international services are sometimes the prime source of news for foreign ministries. In Communist countries, news from the Western services is circulated in restricted bulletins to top officials.[4] A study of news media and international negotiations in the 1970s revealed that, at one European foreign ministry, agency reports were torn off the printers and distributed internally every fifteen minutes. A foreign ministry official in an important European nation described how he waited by the agency printer until five minutes before the start of a briefing he was to give his prime minister on a developing crisis; he then rushed over to the prime minister's office with his arms full of agency paper. "Literally all we had on [the crisis] was from the agencies," he recalled.[5]

Despite their importance as immediate news sources, the agencies are regarded by most diplomats as having their limitations. "The agencies have a role initially," U.S. State Department spokesman John Trattner noted in 1980. "The way a story is cast, the first three paragraphs might make an initial impression on a policy-maker that would stay with him throughout what he later receives from embassies. But, generally, policy-makers in this government wait for what embassies report and what the intelligence community reports, and for analysis."

A detailed view of the role played by the wire services in keeping the White House informed was given by President Lyndon Johnson's press secretary, George Reedy, who—after cautioning that the character of the White House changes with each occupant—observed:

From my experience, the wire services were invaluable to the White House because they were usually ahead of the standard diplomatic channels both in terms of initial news breaks and subsequent flow of information. This puzzled me at first but a few simple enquiries brought the obvious answer. The only people authorized to provide information through the standard channels were invariably too busy handling the situation which gave rise to the need for information to compose messages about it. Furthermore, government channels are usually subject to exhaustive editing, which takes time.

The wire services, on the other hand, were not subject to such inhibitions. Their people on the scene were present only to gather information and to report it. . . . They did not exercise the scrupulous care which characterized diplomatic communications, but errors were surprisingly few. Of course, in the long run, the diplomatic communication would be more thorough as it could tap sources unavailable to the journalists.

Obviously, the wire services were insufficient for all Presidential purposes. But their speed was a definite factor in securing more time to prepare a Presidential response. I had four tickers in my office— AP, UPI, Reuters, and Agence France-Presse—and the President had three because he could not read French.[6]

While they have always supplied their services for internal government use, the agencies have taken differing attitudes toward selling news for reuse by official information services. After World War II, the AP and UP refused to supply news to the Voice of America because they did not want to become involved with their government's service, but Reuters had no compunction about doing so. Similarly, the AP declined to sell its service to the Spanish news agency, Efe, because it enjoyed a monopoly on news distribution in Franco's Spain. But the AP's initial decision to refuse to supply government-run news organizations was in jeopardy as soon as the agency expanded internationally; for many countries, there was simply no other buyer. Well before boycotting Efe, the AP was ready to sign contracts with TASS, which operated on the principle that information must serve the interests of the Soviet state, and with the Stefani agency of Fascist Italy. After 1945, there was no alternative to dealing with state agencies throughout Eastern Europe. If no contract existed, the radio transmissions used by the major services at that time made pirating simple and limitation of the service to paying subscribers impossible.

More recently, the Big Four have found it difficult to refrain from selling their services exclusively to official agencies in many developing nations, either because those nations' media are too poor to subscribe on their own or because their national agencies have legal monopolies over the reception of foreign news. Outside Latin America, where direct subscriptions are the rule, the AP, UPI, and Reuters had direct contracts with the press and broadcasting in 36 nonaligned countries and dealt with official agencies in 68, according to a count made in the mid-1970s by Edward Pinch of the U.S. State Department. Reuters, with its wide implantation in Africa and the Arab world, had direct contracts with the press and broadcasting in only 17 nonaligned nations and agreements with government-controlled bodies in 44—27 of these were in Africa and 10 in Arab states. The control this provides governments over what actually reaches the public is a matter that will be addressed later, in an examination of the agencies' role in the developing nations. What is relevant here is the way in which subscriptions from state bodies dominate the agencies' revenue sources in certain areas of the world.

Despite this, there is little evidence of widespread government attempts to use financial pressure to win favorable reporting. There have, however, been isolated instances of such pressures: for example, of governments' refusing to pay for agency services after expelling correspondents. In one case, an African government threatened to cancel its subscription to one of the Big Four if the agency did not send a correspondent to cover the country. The agency, which had suffered harassment there, refused; the subscription was maintained.

This is not to say that governments do not try to influence the coverage of their countries by the agencies. To the contrary, many use whatever means they consider suitable to try to stop bad news from being sent abroad and to promote the flow of "positive" reporting. But the methods used are more apt to consist of harassment and selective favors than financial blackmail.[7]

In one case, however, financial considerations prompted Reuters to accept an arrangement under which it ceded most of its Middle Eastern operations to an organization it knew to be funded by the British government. In 1954, when Reuters was earning £11,000 a year in the Middle East, the Arab News Agency (ANA) offered £28,500 a year for the exclusive right to distribute a Reuters-originated news file to the Arab world. ANA also offered Reuters one-third of any new revenues it collected in this manner, and undertook to buy the agency's assets in Egypt. For the financially pressed Reuters of the 1950s, the proposed seven-year agreement was most attractive. The British head of ANA was believed to have good relations with nationalist-minded Arab leaders. Reuters' reporting would remain independent. "The objection to the contract," general manager Christopher Chancellor told his board, "is the fact that the Arab News Agency is known to be subsidised by the British government."

This objection did not overly worry the board, and the contract was duly signed. As the years went by, ANA, which was renamed Regional News Service (RNS), not only distributed Reuters' news in the Middle East but became an essential pillar for the agency's reporting there. With the two organizations regarded virtually as one, Reuters and RNS renewed and expanded their agreement as the British-government-backed service drew up plans to extend its activities to Latin America. Although Reuters' executives subsequently expressed distaste for the link, they kept it going for business reasons, and not from any desire to serve British interests. Whatever its motives, however, Reuters had effectively abdicated its role as an independent supplier of information by handing over distribution of its news to an organization it knew to be financed by the British government. Whereas in the Soviet Union Reuters had no choice but to sell its service to TASS, in the Middle East it did have a choice, and it forsook independence for a subscription that netted £55,000 in 1968. In that year, the agency decided that it could do better by selling its services directly in the Arab world, and broke the agreement with RNS. At last Reuters was prosperous enough to be able to act for itself.[8]

Eight years after Reuters ended the RNS agreement, the London agency became the target of allegations that it had been used by another government in a different way. Leaks from U.S. congressional committee testimony by the director of the CIA, William Colby, hinted that a number of Reuters correspondents had worked for the agency. It looked as if the CIA had considered Reuters fair game because it was non-American, thus falling outside the CIA's pledges not to suborn the staffs of U.S. news enterprises.

No concrete evidence in support of the allegations was produced, but that did not stop the charges from resurfacing periodically in the following years. In 1981, a BBC television investigation of intelligence services reported that both Reuters and the CIA had been deeply embarrassed by the 1976 report, but no mention was made of the fact that it had been Reuters itself that first reported the Colby allegations, leading the CIA to deny them. In the same BBC program, former CIA officer Frank Snepp spoke of "the general assumption of my colleagues that a Reuters journalist is more likely than not to be tied in with British intelligence in some way." Snepp produced no evidence, but the allegation was one that, by its very nature, was impossible to disprove.[9]

It is quite possible that a number of correspondents working for Reuters or other major agencies have worked for intelligence services. Some have certainly been approached; one correspondent in East Africa, for example, recalls being asked by a U.S. embassy official after a tennis match if he would fancy working for another agency on the side. The fact that the news services have not actually discovered intelligence operatives in their ranks proves nothing, but it is remarkable that, despite the recurrent allegations, no evidence of infiltration of the major agencies by intelligence bodies has been produced.

The most notable exception to the general rule of government noninvolvement in agency affairs comes from France. The amount Reuters received from RNS was minuscule compared with the sums AFP gets annually from the French government. Unlike the terms of the Reuters–RNS agreement, no French state body exercises direct control over the AFP news flow. However, the facts that 60 percent or more of the agency's revenue comes from the government's information budget and that government-appointed directors have a blocking minority on the AFP board obviously expose the French agency to official pressures which the other three services escape.

Direct state interference in AFP is apparently rare, and, when it is exercised, it is directed much more toward the domestic French service than toward the agency's international operations. It is clear, however, that AFP feels sensitive about its special position vis-à-vis the state and the responsibilities this can entail. According to journalists at the agency, not all judgments made on AFP's stories are simple news decisions; in some cases, AFP's position as the national agency is also considered. Such sensitivity is maintained at AFP by occasional telephone calls from ministries or the Elysée Palace, and by reports of politicians' keeping blacklists of AFP journalists who have written stories they do not like. In the resulting editorial climate, the French agency tends to be more aware than the other three major services of the susceptibilities of whatever government is in power in its home country, and to shifts in political power. When the weekly newspaper *Le Canard Enchaîné* published a series of unflattering allegations against President Valéry Giscard d'Estaing in 1979 and 1980, AFP was slow to pick them up, but in 1982 it immediately covered stories by *Le Canard* reporting dubious electoral financing by a leader of the French opposition. The different reactions may have been partly a result of a sharper editorial performance the second time around, but the fact that the government had changed hands between the two stories is also likely to have had an effect. Embarrassing a client who pays more than half your revenue is never good business.

Government pressure on AFP has been most obvious in recent years at the very top of the agency, as demonstrated by events surrounding the appointment of the chairman/chief executive. Only a year after AFP received new statutes guaranteeing its independence, General de Gaulle established the Fifth French Republic. His first prime minister, Michel Debré, believed that AFP should play the role of a national institution in helping to rally the public behind the administration's policy in Algeria—and that AFP's boss, Jean Marin, was not the best man for this job. But the agency's board resisted Debré's attempt to change its chairman, and Marin was reelected. For the next fifteen years, Marin ruled the agency unchallenged, but by 1975 he had fallen into official disfavor. Some of AFP's domestic reporting had come to be regarded by the authorities as too left wing, and staff problems were mounting within the agency. The young politicians and civil servants around the newly elected President Giscard d'Estaing felt it was time to bring AFP under tighter control.

Six weeks before the board was to meet to elect a chairman for a new three-year term, the founder of AFP in its present form was told he would not have government support. Although the directors from the press vowed to support Marin, the government could block his reelection through the three government-appointed directors and two board members from the state broadcasting services. In the face of such opposition, Marin stepped down. The government picked its favored candidate, the French ambassador to Brussels, Pierre Hunt, who traveled to Paris, spoke to a few people who knew about AFP—and refused the job. Ultimately, Jean Marin's longtime deputy, Claude Roussel, was elected chairman and chief executive. It appeared that the agency and the press had once more beaten off the government.

But the new chairman's position was soon undermined by the government's use of its financial lever. Budget discussions between the agency and state officials became increasingly difficult as the government attempted to widen its involvement beyond strictly financial matters. President Giscard watched AFP in a way that neither of his predecessors at the Elysée Palace had done. Under de Gaulle or Georges Pompidou, according to one top-level AFP executive, government intervention was rare, while under Giscard the government intervened not for high policy but for immediate political reasons. Flash points included a story about alleged voting frauds involving French embassies and the publication of what the presidency considered to be overlong statements by Polisario rebels fighting Morocco in the Sahara. A high-ranking presidential aide suggested that the government might simply cut off its payments if AFP remained a source of annoyance. In the 1978 budget discussions, a Finance Ministry official even commented on the scale of AFP's coverage of the world soccer cup.

Thus it was no surprise when the government made it clear it did not want Roussel to serve a second term. The *doyen* of the AFP board, Hubert Beuve-Méry, founder of *Le Monde,* resigned in protest. A minister closely involved in monitoring AFP was reported to have approached a group of the agency's journalists standing in the courtyard of the presidential palace, mentioned Roussel's name, and twisted his hands together as if wringing a chicken's neck.

To replace Roussel, the board elected the head of the French regional press federation, Roger Bouzinac, who was acceptable to everyone involved. But seventeen months later he resigned, prompting fresh discussion at the presidential level about an acceptable replacement. The entirely logical choice was a former civil servant, Henri Pigeat, who had joined AFP as Roussel's deputy in 1976 after working in the Information Ministry and a government information department. "The Elysée will now have no more need to worry about what will be distributed across the world on the agency wires," wrote the spokesman on information matters for the opposition Socialist party, Georges Fillioud. "Freedom is encircled." Less than two years later, the Socialists were in office and Fillioud was minister of communications. In 1982, Pigeat was reelected for a second term with the unanimous backing of the state board members. His managerial performance and his plans to strengthen the agency outweighed any political reservations about his past allegiances. To that extent, the Mitterrand administration showed itself to be more open-minded than its predecessors, but there was little doubt that the chairmanship of AFP was still a political, as well as a professional, job.

AFP's ability to be acceptable to both conservative and left-wing regimes in France is in keeping with the national role that the agency sees for itself, and that is also seen by many French politicians and observers within the media. While he was chairman of the agency,

Roger Bouzinac expressed his satisfaction that "AFP journalists posted abroad have become true ambassadors of French thought." The manager of *Le Monde*, after criticizing the agency's evolution, expressed the hope that AFP would meet the requirements of foreign newspapers interested in receiving "the voice of France." Although in no way comparable with the state news agencies of Eastern Europe or authoritarian governments on other continents, AFP is undoubtedly part of the framework of the French state. The independence it enjoys is granted by the government, rather than being a basic factor in its existence. As a result, the agency is more aware of its national character than the other major services, but still retains a high degree of functional independence from its major client.

Such independence is essential for all four major agencies, not simply as a matter of operating philosophy but also to ensure their acceptability to as wide an audience as possible. Being tied to a government politically would compromise the global appeal that is a fundamental attribute of each of the major services. As will be seen, potential challenges from a number of alternate news sources have failed to develop precisely because those alternatives are vehicles for the propagation of official news. At the same time, the major agencies are well aware that, in order to function, they have to deal with governments. In many parts of the world, official approval is needed for them to run reporting offices, and officials decide on agency subscriptions. Simply ignoring government is not possible. Agency executives tend to take a subtler view of the world than extreme proponents of an American-model press, for whom what is good in Arkansas is automatically the best thing for Africa, but independence in reporting and editing remains a cardinal principle—albeit one that the exigencies of agency operations often make it more difficult to achieve for the Big Four than for their more comfortably endowed and less-exposed clients.

Secondhand News

The financial restrictions under which the four major news agencies operate are not immediately apparent from their files. Their wide-ranging datelines and varied subjects suggest organizations that can cover any event they consider newsworthy almost anywhere in the world. Critics have taken it as an article of faith that the agencies could do more and better if only they wanted to, and the agencies have found it difficult to dissent from this larger-than-life picture of themselves.

The impression of omnipresence is fostered by the particular approach to reporting that has been adopted by all four agencies. In order to obtain wide coverage with only limited means, they have evolved a reportorial style that ensures the maximum volume of news but also entails decided drawbacks, particularly in originality and depth. Their style, generally acceptable to subscribers, has become accepted as the prevailing model for reporting immediate events in much of the non-Communist world. But many subscribers—and the general public—are unaware of the extent of the limitations that affect the shape and content of the news services they depend on for much of their news of the world.

Small Staffs, Big Countries ....

Like most foreign correspondents, agency reporters are attached to capital cities, since it is there that the politicians and decision makers who most concern them congregate. Agencies report matters of visible power, and visible power is concentrated in capitals. Such cities are also where the greatest amount and extent of significant information is immediately available, and where outward communications work best. The result is a lopsided view of the world in which the lives of the nonpowerful are rarely glimpsed and in which the provinces are covered at secondhand—when they are covered at all. As Wes Gallagher, president of the Associated Press, said with reference to his own country in the mid-1970s: "The Washington politicians' view of what is going on in the United States has been substituted for what is actually happening in the country. The two are not always the same." If that was so in the United States, where the AP has hundreds of reporters spread across the country, it is even more the case in all the nations in which each agency has only one staff correspondent.

Periodically, the Big Four decide to do something about the neglected hinterlands outside capital cities. Reporters are urged to go on trips to the provinces—provided, of course, that money is available and (even more importantly) that nothing newsworthy is likely to happen in the capital. It may be a sound idea to dispatch a member of an agency's two-person Madrid bureau to investigate the situation in the Basque country, but when a sudden political crisis erupts in the capital, interviews with the inhabitants of Bilbao can be strikingly irrelevant to the basic job of maintaining a competitive hourly flow of the most significant news from Spain. Nobody is more lonely than the solo agency correspondent caught in the middle of a feature-gathering trip in the back country as the tanks roll into position around the presidential palace in his base capital.

This is not to say that agency coverage is entirely restricted to news from capital cities. Wire-service correspondents file stories originating from all over the countries they cover, relying on leads from newspapers or broadcasting stations. Part-time local "stringers" provide material from their areas to be written up by staff correspondents who inject the background and explanatory material necessary for international intelligibility. All this can be done most effectively in capital cities. For a one- or two-person bureau, operational efficiency is much more important than detailed knowledge of the country.

Even if they were able to spend the time needed to gain such knowledge (and their employers were able to pay the costs involved), agency correspondents would be able to make little use of intimate familiarity with locally significant matters such as agricultural conditions in the Nile delta or the state of the Scottish shipbuilding industry. In-depth stories, analyses, and feature material have their place in international news files, but they are far from being the agencies' raison d'être. What makes the greatest impact on subscribers and dominates the agencies' editorial activities is immediate coverage of significant events in terms that can be grasped straightaway by readers, listeners, and viewers—regardless of their prior knowledge of the subject involved. Agencies do not have time to deal in depth with any but the biggest events. Speed and simplicity are paramount; originality of thought and depth of analysis rank much lower on their scale of values, not because such qualities are disdained or distrusted in themselves, but because they conflict with three more highly valued elements in agency operations. First, the agencies try, day by day, to put out as many stories as possible in a limited period of time; there is neither time nor space for detailed explanation and interpretation. Second, they seek to appeal to as many subscribers as possible, and this goal can better be achieved by conventional, middle-of-the-road coverage than by new reportorial approaches. Finally, the agencies depend on their correspondents' producing more copy each day than would be possible if each story involved original thought and presentation.

Stereotypes and Simplifications . . . .

The resulting product is easy to caricature or deride. There is no doubt that the stereotypes pervading agency copy can mislead. Ideally, each news event should be seen as unique and reported as such, for generalizations serve only to distort. But in practical terms, individual editorial treatment of news stories is simply not possible. If the international news agencies had unlimited funds, staff, and transmission time, they could perhaps be more profound, although it is questionable whether their news would then be used more widely by subscribers who already feel they get too many words. And even if resources were unlimited, the agencies would find it hard to avoid generalizations and stereotypes in relaying unexpected events in unfamiliar parts of the world, for subscribers in a hundred or more countries, using a limited number of words—all the while maintaining clarity and accuracy.

Because they must attract the attention of their audience, the agencies like to begin each story with a sentence that makes clear why the report is worth reading. Because they know that many subscribers will pare stories down to their first few paragraphs—or even to the first sentence—the agencies try to tell as much of the story as possible in the opening lines. As long as they are competing for attention and serve subscribers whose foreign news space is limited, agency copy is inevitably going to be studded with formulas and stereotypes from the first sentence on.

173

In the process, each event easily becomes a "turning point," each detachment of soldiers a "crack unit," and each decision "critical." Agencies not only practice the journalism of exception on a worldwide scale, they also often feel a need to underscore the exceptional nature of the events they report, as if afraid that subscribers might otherwise miss the point. Agency folklore has it that, when Chinese troops fought their way through the United Nations lines in the Korean War, one of the American agencies began its story: "The vanguard of half a billion Chinese today broke through. . . ."

The agencies periodically attempt to purge their files of clichés and knee-jerk writing. In 1958, the AP carried out a campaign to improve writing quality, and proclaimed when it ended, "AP men ARE thinking when they sit down to write"—raising the disconcerting question of what had been going on previously. In 1964, the AP ran its file through a computer, which selected 371 expressions to be avoided, including "riot-torn," "limped into port," "marched to the polls," and "eyeball to eyeball." Two decades later, such expressions were still turning up in the agencies' files with what can be described only as inexorable regularity.

Whatever the disadvantages in terms of repetitiveness, the use of clichés and easily assimilated generalizations has obvious advantages for organizations trying to impose a single editorial approach on vast numbers of disparate events. "Without standardization," journalist Walter Lippmann once noted, "without stereotypes, without routine judgments, without a fairly ruthless disregard of subtlety, the editor would soon die of excitement." To which one might add that ordinary readers, listeners, or viewers would simply give up in a welter of uncoordinated words about unfamiliar subjects.

The other side of the coin is the distortion that may result from simplification. The lack of understanding evident in much of the coverage from Iran before the fall of the shah has been cited as a prime example of how stereotyped reporting masks reality. Clichéd descriptions of Cold War vintage have largely disappeared in coverage of major power politics, but the agencies have great difficulty in dealing with the job of reporting the developing world in terms immediately comprehensible to subscribers all around the globe. The resulting simplifications and stereotypes have been attributed, by advocates of a new world information order, to an attempt by the agencies to cater to the prejudices of the rich nations. But the problem goes deeper than that. A reader in Mexico may be just as much in need of familiar, easily understood phraseology in a report about

Zimbabwe or Bangladesh as a reader in Amsterdam. The agencies are continuously seeking to present news in a form that will attract people who are both ignorant of the subject involved and not necessarily very interested in becoming better informed. Individual agency correspondents may be acutely aware of the complexities of events they report, but translating such awareness into stories running to a few hundred words is often an impossible task if the reader's interest is to be attracted and retained—particularly given the pressure of a constant need for speed.

When correspondents manage to convey a real understanding of the complexities of a situation, their stories are at the mercy of editors who may not appreciate the value of a background paragraph or a carefully worded—but to them verbose—formulation selected by the correspondent in an effort to convey the flavor of an event or to hint at factors bubbling below the surface. Subtleties evident to a correspondent on the spot may appear as unnecessary wordage to a harassed deskman whose main concern is to clear a mounting backlog of stories in New York, London, or Paris.

To correspondents, desk cutting and rewriting can sometimes appear to be ends in themselves, giving rise to sour jokes about copy editors' needing to justify their existence by messing around with perfectly good copy. All correspondents think their stories are worth running as written. The constant need for desk editors to fit quarts of copy into pint-sized pots, to discard and cut amid the flood of material coming in from all over the world, is not apparent to reporters wrapped up in their stories thousands of miles away. Some have an instinctive idea of what each story is worth, but many file far more than subscribers could ever want, reinforcing the desk editor's conviction that each item should be looked at with an eye to improving its presentation. At the AP, there is a story of an ace rewrite man who finished a late shift one night by recasting a report to be issued the next day. On resuming work in the morning, he picked up the copy as if it had just landed in New York, and did a complete rewrite of his own rewrite. The tale is not regarded as apocryphal.

Without editing desks, agencies could not function. Because of the restricted amount of money that can be spent on editing, each desk provides services for a wide variety of regions and clients. The amount of detailed attention that can be paid to any particular country, or group of countries, is strictly limited, and the spread of simplification is thus increased. A story going to the subscriber with the most knowledgeable readers also goes to the client with the most ignorant audience. The file issued by an editing desk is not designed simply for the lowest common denominator among an agency's recipients, but it has to be acceptable to that lowest common denominator if the agency is to do its job properly.

The agencies take very little for granted when it comes to prior knowledge among the audience their clients serve. Life begins anew with the morning and afternoon news cycles; readers are assumed to have forgotten everything except the most important events of the previous days. Encapsulated background references are inserted again and again into running copy. Virtually identical sentences explaining how a crisis developed, or what is at stake in a negotiation, crop up repeatedly with only slight differences in wording. An agency file is thus accessible and understandable to almost everyone and—if read properly—is generally honest about its own limitations. The trouble is that not everyone notices what sources have provided what information.

The Sources of News. . . . .

The agencies are committed to accuracy, but firsthand, verifiable information is often unattainable. Even without the financial restrictions under which they operate, the agencies would not be able to be present everywhere that newsworthy events occur. Given their limited resources, they are able to witness relatively little of what they report, except for programmed events. Even then, a full-time presence may be unacceptably costly in time—no one- or two-person agency bureau, for example, could afford to have a staffer sitting permanently through parliamentary sessions.

The result is that most international agency news is secondhand. The agencies often reconcile this handicap with their commitment to accuracy by quoting their sources of information, but they do not always do this. For an agency bureau that picks up a report of a newsworthy speech in a parliament from the national news service or the press, to quote the source would appear naive. But when direct knowledge of an event is unattainable, or when the facts are in doubt, sourcing enables the agencies to breach the gap between their thin representation and the wide scope of coverage they offer.

While the agencies do not claim to collect all their news by using their own resources, what they do try to do is pass on information from others who are in a position to know the facts. Rather than taking direct responsibility for the information in a story, they assert that some person or organization reported those facts. An agency does not say that an aircraft has crashed, killing a hundred people; instead, it reports that an airport spokesman has announced such information. In one of the biggest agency scoops of 1984, Reuters carried a report of Soviet leader Yuri Andropov's death seven minutes ahead of AFP and nearly half an hour ahead of the U.S. agencies. The story came from Brussels, not Moscow. The source was the French foreign minister. The order in which the story's opening sentence was put together was significant: "French Foreign Minister Claude Cheysson told a meeting here today that the Soviet leader Yuri Andropov had died." Reuters was reporting not that Andropov had died, but that Cheysson had said that Andropov had died. Naturally, Reuters had reason to believe that Cheysson was likely to have reliable information. But, if the French minister had turned out to be mistaken, Reuters could have run a follow-up story saying Andropov was still alive, despite an earlier statement from Cheysson that he was dead. Accurate attribution to sources of information is not only honest, it is also wonderful protection against being held responsible for originating false news.

While attributions are vital to the agencies, both practically and philosophically, their impact on the general public is probably minor. It is the plane crash that remains in people's minds, not he fact that it was reported by an airport spokesman. This tendency is reinforced by the common practice of naming the source at the very end of the opening sentence, or by dropping it down into the body of the story. When the source itself requires some explanation, it is simpler to use expressions such as "was reported to have . . . ," and to reveal only later the fact that the report came from a guerrilla leader who went over to the government two weeks earlier after falling out with his comrades. In other instances, a simple formulation may cover the whole chain along which a story has passed. The statement "First reports were that the plane crashed into an electricity pylon" may indeed be accurate, but if elaborated might read, "A farmer who had been plowing his fields half a mile from the crash site staggered into the local police station an hour later and managed to blurt out, before collapsing from shock, that the aircraft had hit an electricity pylon."

Reuters reported both the agreement to end the Algerian war and Britain's entry into the European Economic Community on the basis of hand signals made by informants inside the negotiating areas to correspondents waiting outside. Explaining such sourcing would be difficult indeed. A multitude of artful arrangements are hidden behind such innocuous phrases as "reliable sources reported" or "according to informed sources here today."

Sourcing is an essential element in the agencies' quest for neutrality. By placing the responsibility for statements of fact on others, agencies can avoid involving themselves in controversy. They report partisan opinions, but are careful not to be caught putting forward any of their own. At one point in their history, they were so pathological about the need for external attribution that anonymous "observers" were conjured up to be tacked on to perfectly straightforward statements of fact. Self-confidence grew somewhat in the 1960s and 1970s, but the nature of agency reporting is unchanged; the abhorrence of anything that could enmesh an agency in controversy is as strong as ever. Neutrality and objectivity are the watchwords, and sourcing is the primary means by which organizations with limited resources can attempt the job of covering an unlimited range of events with a minimum of exposure.

Agency correspondents learn to be discriminating about which sources they can trust and which they should treat with caution. There are few sharper journalistic dilemmas than that of the agency reporter who receives a sensational news item from a source that cannot immediately be verified. The inner conflict between the competitive urge to file and the desire to check out the story is a classic source of ulcers, or at least of a search for wording cautious enough to enable the story to be issued.

National Agencies, National Problems . . . .

The major agencies depend heavily on national news organizations[1]— particularly state-run agencies—for their information, and in many cases in which such sources are used they either cannot check the information or do not think it worth spending the time doing so. Although an agency may include the appropriate reference to the origin of the information in a story, the fact that it is issued under the credit line of Reuters, the AP, United Press International, or Agence France-Presse gives it added authority. What is not made clear to either the subscriber or the reader is that the agency is often simply passing on information from others without having done anything more than packaging it in a form acceptable to a world audience.

The secondhand nature of agency news is particularly characteristic of reporting from Communist countries and nations in which the national news agency enjoys a virtual monopoly over domestic coverage. In the Soviet Union, for example, there is generally no way of knowing what is going on unless TASS or the official media report it. In China, agency correspondents in Peking can be completely ignorant of momentous events occurring 100 or 1000 miles away. Where the state does not control information in such a rigorous manner, the sheer size of the territory that agencies try to cover often means that they have to rely on others to keep them informed. How can a two-person bureau in Delhi hope to keep track of what is happening in the whole of India, except by depending on the Indian media? Even if he or she reads every word in the local press and on the national agency's wire, how can a lone correspondent in Lagos do more than scratch the surface of what is going on in Nigeria?

This makes the major agencies keen supporters of the development of strong national news services, particularly in the Third World. The more news that such national organizations are able to provide, the easier the task of the Big Four in reporting their countries. Ideally, the major agencies would like national services to adopt an impartial, factual, nonpolitical approach to reporting. In practice, they accept that this is unlikely to be the case all the time. But any news service is better than none at all.

When the agencies undertake original reporting, they sometimes find themselves in trouble if what they write is unpalatable to governments. Such problems occur rarely in the developed world, but are an ever-present factor in agency operations both in the Communist nations and in parts of the developing world. Official harassment takes many forms, from refusal to transmit photographs of communal violence to the threat of beheading (in one extreme case). Between 1965 and 1973, to take the French agency as an example, ten AFP correspondents were jailed or assaulted overseas. In 1980 alone, the AFP correspondent in Bolivia was arrested and expelled for having talked to opposition leaders, the Reuters correspondent in the Central African Republic was arrested for having written a story that displeased the authorities, agency reporters were refused entry into Nigeria, Reuters' chief correspondent in Lebanon was wounded by a gunman, and UPI's bureau chief and two AFP reporters in Moscow were arrested and had their cameras confiscated for covering an attempted one-man demonstration in Red Square. In 1979, a Reuters reporter covering the trial of former premier Ali Bhutto in Pakistan wrote that correspondents were "tailed by Special Branch police . . . and several . . . were cited for alleged contempt of court in private petitions that quoted from their outgoing telex despatches.'' In Iran in 1980, Reuters' office was closed down and correspondents were warned that they risked execution for having reported the location of a military headquarters in the fighting with Iraq. The story had emerged as a result of an officially sponsored trip to the war zone. Five days later, the closure order was canceled without explanation. In May 1985, Iran expelled the Reuters correspondent in Teheran for "false and biased reporting,'' leaving AFP as the only major agency with a staff reporter in the country.

A foreign correspondent who falls afoul of the local authorities may be expelled. A journalist who works for a newspaper or broadcasting station in an authoritarian country and who oversteps the officially approved line is in danger of losing his job, going to jail, or otherwise suffering a worse fate than being bundled onto the first outgoing plane. The London-based International Press Institute reported at the end of 1984 "a continuing increase in the number of journalists expelled, jailed or murdered.'' The Institute's country-by-country report for the year said conditions had worsened in 43 countries and improved in 10. Just before the report was published, an AP correspondent in India, Brahma Chellaney, faced prosecution in the Punjab for having quoted unnamed police and military sources as saying that the number of dead in a battle between the Indian army and Sikh extremists was as high as 1200, double the total announced by the government. In March 1985, the AP bureau chief in Beirut, Terry Anderson, was kidnapped in what a telephone caller said was part of a campaign to rid Moslem areas of Lebanon of "foreign spies.'' After two television newsmen were killed by Israeli tank fire in March 1985, an Israeli army statement simply warned that "if journalists enter territory in which armed terrorists are located, they take on themselves the risk of getting hurt.'' Such cases make it clear why news agencies place little faith in the idea of special cards requesting protection for their correspondents under the auspices of an international body like UNESCO. It is difficult to imagine that Anderson's abductors would have paid much attention to a piece of pasteboard stamped with UNESCO's emblem. And, since a fair proportion of the harassment agencies suffer comes from governments, is it reasonable to expect protection from international organizations which pay attention to such governments as part of their membership?

Harassment and expulsions present the agencies with a particularly knotty problem. If a newspaper correspondent is expelled from a country because of a story, his paper knows it will still get coverage from the agencies, but if an agency is closed down, it has nothing to fall back on. While clients may appreciate the story that provoked the closure, they may be less keen on the ensuing lack of news from the country concerned—particularly if it is one that interests them and if the expelled agency was their only foreign news source. There is, as a result, a tendency among agencies to try to maintain their presence as long as possible. The point at which this is impossible is sometimes reached—some agencies, for instance, refused to staff Ethiopia for periods in the mid-1970s because continual uncertainty about their correspondents' safety made anything other than relaying official communiqués virtually impossible. [2] But if the agencies were to give up transmitting news from countries with reporting restrictions, they would cease to cover much of the world. Summing up its experience in the late 1970s, UPI concluded that correspondents encountered obstacles in gathering news wherever they worked. "It can be said that, as a generalization, Africa is the most difficult continent for international news services to cover today," UPI added. "A few countries, such as Kenya, are permissive, but all require a visa which often takes weeks or months to arrange. Some countries refuse most requests; others simply ignore all cables and letters on the subject." Even when a visa was obtained, there was almost universal censorship. If a correspondent's copy did not meet official approval, the correspondent might be detained, expelled, or simply admonished. "Restrictions in Eastern Europe, the Middle East, Latin America and Asia run the gamut from general or selective refusal of visas in most of the Communist countries of Asia to surveillance or even harassment in some Eastern European countries," UPI reported. "Outside of the U.S. and Canada, Latin America and Western Europe probably are the easiest areas in which a foreign correspondent can work. Even in Latin America, there have been recent examples of kidnapping or detention without charges or warning."

The combined effects of limited resources, dependence on secondhand news, and official constraints on reporting substantially restrict the ability of the four major services to operate as truly worldwide collectors and suppliers of news. In many countries, they cannot do the job they would like to do because of their dependence on officially controlled sources of information; in others, their restricted budgets mean they must rely on part-time local correspondents who can often do no more than relay government-approved stories. Even in states where they are free to report as they wish, the pressures of their continuous deadlines and inadequate staffing limit the amount of independent reporting correspondents can do.

By attempting to cover so much ground, the major agencies have deprived themselves of much of the freedom of action they would have enjoyed had they been more selective. By catering to so many subscribers of different cultures and interests, they have limited their editorial choices to the standardized format that will be most acceptable to the largest number of recipients. In each case, the result has been a flow of world news conditioned by the limitations of the resources made available by the recipients. It has been one of the triumphs of the major agencies that these limitations have been disguised for so long. But their success has created expectations that the agencies cannot meet, and fostered deep misunderstandings that obstruct the improvement of the flow of independent news around the world.

Under Fire

The international news agencies attracted little attention for more than a century. Their activities went largely unobserved; their services were taken for granted by most recipients, and the autonomy and style of their news files remained unquestioned. While individual shortcomings were occasionally noted, the overall character of the major services and the effects of their commercial approach to distributing the news internationally were not considered matters of concern. History and their worldwide scope had turned the Big Four into institutions that seemed to be above politics or controversy.

The 1970s changed all that. From the beginning of the decade, criticism of the agencies evolved along four main lines.[1] From an economic point of view, the Big Four are now seen as exercising a monopoly based on their assumed financial strength and their commercial approach to news. Moreover, they are accused of perpetrating a predominantly negative picture of the Third World—one dominated by coups, crises, and disasters. Third, the services they distribute to developing nations are viewed as constituting a one-way flow of information that floods poor nations with inappropriate news formulated according to precepts irrelevant or even destructive to their development. Finally, the agencies are accused of reflecting the viewpoints of their home countries from behind a smokescreen of highly touted impartiality. Such activity, UNESCO's director-general has alleged, "borders on cultural aggression," and runs counter to the nonaligned movement's desire to build a new economic order in the world.

By the early 1980s, the agencies found themselves at the center of a debate carried on primarily in political rather than journalistic terms, with their contributions toward the development of national news agencies in the Third World rarely acknowledged. Their motivation in providing such help was not simply altruistic; as has been noted, the major agencies have a strong interest in the development of viable national news sources that can provide them with the basic material for their reports. But no matter what the level of their self-interest or the revenues they may have drawn from providing advice and assistance, the scale of their aid to developing countries has undoubtedly played a significant if unrecognized role in helping to develop Third World media. Agence France-Presse, for example, was instrumental in developing national news agencies in Francophone Africa. United Press International was involved in the Persian Gulf area, and the Associated Press in Nigeria. Reuters staff took part in seventy-two assistance projects and training schemes in forty-five developing countries over a twenty-five-year period. In 1982, the London-based agency established a "Reuters Foundation" to award one-year university fellowships to Third World journalists under a £1 million plan designed, in Reuters' words, "to help narrow the gap between industrialized and developing countries in the use of information technology, and to provide opportunities for academic research to promising journalists."

The lack of recognition paid to such assistance from the Big Four went hand in hand with the general absence of Third World media professionals from the debate about world information. This was not entirely the fault of those pressing for a new world information order. Enthusiasts for the Western-model media were guilty of bombast and oversimplification, which alienated at least some journalists from the developing nations. Slogans about freedom of the press, while valid in themselves, spilled over all too easily into breast-beating and pat solutions to complex problems. Such attitudes left the major agencies uneasy. It was noticeable, for example, how senior representatives of most of the Big Four shied away from the more sweeping resolutions advanced by self-styled "representatives of the independent press" at a meeting held in the autumn of 1983 in Talloires, France, to draw up a response to the new world information drive.[2]

Ideological rhetoric has masked many of the problems facing the major agencies and has undoubtedly affected the flow of world news. Most of this rhetoric has come from proponents of a new information order, and a sizable amount of it has flowed through the documents and research of UNESCO, an organization in which the concerns of governments are of paramount importance. This ensures that questions concerning news and information will be viewed through an unsuitably political prism. The resulting criticisms of the agencies are based largely on misapprehensions, assertions of doubtful factual value, or—most frequently—fundamental differences between the philosophical approaches of the agencies and their critics, as discussed in chapter 1.

Nevertheless, a basic question (although rarely addressed as such) has been raised: will news services based on the concept of delivering a single account of newsworthy events to commercial subscribers all over the world continue to enjoy general acceptability in the increasingly diverse conditions of the 1980s, or are alternatives emerging that could replace the Big Four? In considering this question, we must first examine the most widely heard criticisms of the major agencies in light of the way in which we have seen the agencies develop as well as the way they currently operate.

Development News . . . .

For proponents of a new world information order, news should be used for distinct national and political purposes. It must be both responsible and responsive to national aims as articulated by a country's leaders, so that it can be employed to aid development and foster progress.

This view of news as a tool is wholly unacceptable to the major agencies as far as their own reporting and editing are concerned. While denying that they are hostile toward the Third World, they can hardly preach the virtues of news as a development tool without abandoning the neutrality they consider so important. An agency may devote resources to covering a development program, but it approaches the story in the same way as any other piece of reporting. Coverage of a dam project in Africa is measured according to its potential interest to subscribers, just as the construction of a new airport in Belgium would be.

The concept of "development news" that emerged in the Third World during the 1960s and 1970s is thus philosophically foreign to the major agencies. They devote relatively little news space to such coverage. Part of the reason is purely practical; it is not possible for the Big Four to orient their coverage specifically toward development projects or to monitor, even in a general way, the progress being made by poor countries. Both the desire and the means to do this are absent and are likely to remain so. As our analysis of their history and present positions has made clear, the agencies exist to supply news of interest to as many subscribers as possible, not to support development—however laudable it may be.

The resulting philosophical rift between the agencies and proponents of development news is deepened by the commercial forces affecting the major services. The agencies do not carry as much development news as their critics would like, but even the restricted amount they do issue is too much for many of their markets. While the agencies enjoy a great deal of autonomy in their news judgments, it is clear that they are obliged to bear in mind broad market requirements, and the experience of the past two decades has been that news from the developing world is not widely used outside its immediate region. This is a reflection of the importance of two factors influencing news judgments: geographical proximity and national connections. The effects of both on news distributed in the developed world has frequently been noted as a matter for concern in recent years, but they apply equally to the emerging nations. It is questionable, for instance, whether the Asian media have a significant interest in Africa, or vice versa. In a sample of fifteen Asian newspapers in 1977, news from Africa accounted for only 7 percent of the stories from the Third World, and reports from Latin America only 4 percent.[3] Such statistics can be qualified by invoking the responsibility of the agencies— if they had sent more news from Africa and Latin America to Asia, the percentages might have been higher—but the fact remains that development news, like all news, is most likely to be of strong interest when it occurs close to home.

Neither can the major agencies become worldwide channels for news regarded as positive by the leaders of developing nations without undermining the market-serving function that is the basis of their international operations. If there emerged an identifiable group of subscribers who wanted a service that concentrated on news of development—and was ready to pay for it—the agencies would no doubt respond. Reuters at one point ran a special service of news from the developing countries for the World Bank.[4] But there has as yet been no sustained demand from the market in the Third World to match the recurrent political demands of the past decade.

Such demands ignore the realities of the agencies' financial positions and resources. The assumption is that the major services report the developing nations in a patchy fashion because, as Western organizations, they are uninterested in doing better. In fact, as has been stressed, the agencies' resources for international general-news coverage are already fully stretched in both finances and staffing, not to mention the practical difficulties of reporting from considerable numbers of developing countries. Certain African nations that have criticized the major agencies for their lack of local coverage have at the same time refused to admit reporters from at least some of the Big Four.[5] Even when there are no restrictions on entry, agency correspondents often find it hard to gather information in developing nations. This may be because of difficult physical access to news, poor communications, or the absence of a strong domestic information system, rather than overt official hindrance. Whatever the reasons, the major agencies do not provide a rounded, detailed picture of most of the nations of the world, simply because they are not able to do so. With the exception of the highly profitable Reuters, no substantial expansion of the resources at their disposal is likely. All that can be hoped for, therefore, is a qualitative improvement in their Third World coverage.

Such a conclusion is not going to satisfy the body of critics who accuse the big agencies of swamping poor nations with news from the industrialized world that is either irrelevant to their needs or a manifestation of information imperialism. "We receive hardly any regional news from the Western news agencies—that is, news about our neighbors, with whom we have close cultural, historical, and economic affinities," a chairman of the pool of nonaligned news agencies, D. R. Mankekar of India, wrote in 1979. "The news we receive from the rest of the world is a one-way imbalanced flow of news, overloaded with news about America and Western Europe. Research has established that 75 percent of the news received on the international wires originates from the West, of which 63 percent is from America." Such remarks reflect the firmly established view that the four major agencies are conduits through which Western news and Western values flood into the developing nations.[6]

There is undoubtedly an imbalance in statistical terms between the overall amount of news carried from the West and the quantity originating from the developing countries, if only because the agencies' clients tend to be more interested in Western Europe and North America than in Africa or Latin America. But the image conjured up by Mankekar, and by UNESCO's International Commission for the Study of Communication Problems, is an exaggerated one.[7] Nine different studies of international agency services to the Third World, considered together, show that the West as a whole provided 44 percent of copy; the figure for North America in this total was 23 percent.[8] The charge that the agencies do not circulate news of neighboring countries to the developing nations is not borne out by studies of the Big Four. The high proportion of regional content in agency services to Latin America was noted in chapter 5. Reuters has always tried to keep the African content of its services to that continent at 50 percent or more, and while it has not been uniformly successful, neither has it always fallen short. A study of agency services in Asia by the Hong Kong Chinese University showed that about half of all stories were concerned with news from the developing nations; of these, 58 percent originated in Asia outside the Middle East.[9] There *are* agency services that contain only a modicum of regional news; the AP and UPI, for instance, send relatively little African news to Africa because their clients there are so few in number that it has not been economically feasible to provide them with substantial area coverage. On the other hand, Reuters and AFP, with their much larger numbers of African subscribers, have made a point of providing all the local coverage they can manage for Africa.

It is generally true that reports from the developing nations occupy only a limited place in agency services distributed in the industrialized world. There is, as a result, an imbalance between the amount of news from the West that goes to Africa and the amount of African news that goes to North America or Western Europe. This imbalance is perhaps not as great as critics of the agencies imagine—one striking U.S. study done in 1979 showed that, contrary to the reigning orthodoxy, 60 percent of foreign stories carried by the AP on its regional U.S. circuits were from underdeveloped countries.[10] This figure needs to be qualified by the fact that it referred only to foreign stories, and so took no account of news from the United States—which figures so prominently in international services. But it is yet another indication that the flow of news is not a one-way street, however much the combination of power and regional concerns gives North America, Western Europe, and (to a lesser extent) Japan the lion's share in statistical studies of the origins of agency copy.

The attention the agencies pay to the developing world in their services to the industrialized nations is, like everything else they do, a function of subscriber requirements, as judged by correspondents and editors, and there is no indication that this judgment is mistaken. Indeed, interviews with agency writers and executives show that the agencies are aware that they are providing more than the Western media want from the developing countries. Each agency has stories of lining up series after series of reports on particular aspects of Third World development, only to find that they are little used in the developed countries.

Too often, the agencies are judged on the basis of news choices

made by their subscribers. For instance, in 1975 Reuters was casti-
gated as an alleged example of the way agencies ignore significant
Third World events in order to run trivia from the West. The events
in question were a meeting of nonaligned nations in Peru and the
escapades of the wife of the Canadian prime minister. Reuters carried
voluminous coverage from Lima and only brief reports on Margaret
Trudeau, but newspapers in the West ignored the first story and played
up the second. Reuters was blamed. In 1980, to cite another example,
a Latin American critic of the existing news system, Fernando Reyes
Matta, drew attention to the lack of coverage in Latin America of
statements made to the United Nations about "mercantilism and profit-
seeking which is currently invading the pharmaceutical industry."
Reyes Matta, director of the Division of Communications Study at
the Latin American Institute of Transnational Studies, noted that only
Mexican newspapers printed the story, and even they treated it as
being of negligible importance. "The media considered the information lacking in newsworthiness, preferring an exhibition of the
[photographs of] Caroline Kennedy to the health of millions of human
beings subject to the consequences of the commercialization of med-
icine," he added in a paper submitted to UNESCO.[11] This, he concluded, was a result of the way in which "the news agencies and the
newspapers validate the persistence of the traditional information
structure in the Latin American press." But—as was evident from
Reyes Matta's paper—both AFP and the AP had carried the story to
Latin America. His evaluation of "the agencies" was based not on
what they had issued but on what their subscribers had done with the
copy. The amount of material the agencies carry from the developing
countries may indeed be limited, but it is wrong to judge them on
the basis of the even more restricted amount of Third World news
that actually gets into the press and onto the airwaves.

The Power of Politics . . . .

Agency reports from the developing and developed areas of the
globe have one thing in common: they are dominated by political
reports that focus on the wielders of power, wherever they may be.
The importance of political news in agency services as a whole was
demonstrated in chapter 5 with statistics showing that international
and domestic politics took up 45 percent of the contents of services
studied between 1974 and 1980. A detailed study for this book re-

vealed that 69 percent of the coverage of Latin America in five agency services concerned politics; from Africa, the figure was 33 percent. Other recent studies of agency services tell the same story.

The emphasis on reporting what national leaders do and say is at least as great in the developing world as in the industrialized countries. In part, this is a product of the national information systems through which the agencies get much of their news. When such systems are dominated by the state, the government tends to get maximum play, and it is often difficult to learn what opposition politicians are saying. Relaying stories of presidential speeches, official statements, conferences, ministerial visits, and national ceremonies constitutes the staple fare of agency reporting from the Third World. These are the events that are easiest to cover and that involve the least risk in politically sensitive countries. In most cases, such stories are simple reports of what was said and done, presented without comment. Nobody reports in a flatter, more factual style than a local agency stringer in an authoritarian country.

The fact that these stories often pass through London, Paris, or New York on their way from one part of the developing world to another—or even from one part of a region to another—is seen by critics as sinister, opening up coverage to distortion introduced in Western capitals.[12] What is ignored is the fact that most Third World coverage is relayed from agency headquarters as received. The two U.S. agencies' Latin American operations, for example, direct as much copy as possible through computerized systems from reporting offices to clients without editing it on the way. Reuters' African service, which has been edited in Nairobi since 1983, transmits as many African items as it can without desk intervention. The reason is partly economic: redirecting copy is cheaper and quicker than altering it. But the practice also stems from the fact that much agency staff coverage of the developing world is so straightforward in presentation and content that it needs no attention from editing desks. Communications routes do not alter editorial content, whether they run through London or New York or go straight from Nairobi to Lagos. What matters is the availability of information and the way it is reported from its origin.

Also ignored by critics is the fact that agency news rarely reaches the media of the developing countries directly. In most of the Third World, the major agencies sell their services to national agencies that edit, translate, and distribute news as they wish. In some countries, the national agency has a legal monopoly over the reception of foreign news. This is most common in Communist nations, but also applies to parts of Africa and elsewhere; a scheme to channel all incoming news through the national agency was put forward in Malaysia in 1983. The image of the big agencies indoctrinating the people of the developing nations with a barrage of unsuitable news is a seductive one for proponents of a new world information order, but it is palpably false. The agencies do indeed determine most of what the national news agencies in poor nations receive, but what happens to the news after that is beyond their control. National agencies can cut copy, rewrite it, or ignore it completely. They can replace the neutral terms used by the major agencies with descriptions that suit their own political outlook, substituting "terrorist" or "freedom fighter" for the agencies' "guerrilla" according to their viewpoint. As a study of agency copy carried out by the North Carolina School of Journalism noted: "Very little Western wire copy contains the kind of ideological labeling that people found so offensive in the 1960s. By far the greatest part of such labeling is added at the national news agency level."[13]

Since many national agencies in the poorer countries are under more or less direct official control, the governments that complain about the approach to the Third World taken by the major services often have the power to ensure that unsuitable or destructive copy does not get through to their people. Doing this means exercising censorship, and even authoritarian governments that censor the news closely are loath to admit it openly. But it is a demonstrable fact of the relationship between the major agencies and the Third World that the final decision on what reaches the public often lies with national news organizations subject to official influence.

Bad News . . . .

Despite the ability of governments to control the news, and despite the agencies' emphasis on official political reporting, the assertion that the Big Four portray Third World nations unflatteringly—both to one another and to the developed world—has gained wide currency in recent years, becoming a cardinal element in criticism of the major news services. It is therefore an assertion that should be fully examined. The agencies are alleged to report the developing nations "in the most unfavorable light, stressing crises, strikes, street demonstrations, putsches, etc., or even holding them up to ridicule," in the words of Mustapha Masmoudi, president of the Coordinating

Council for Information of the nonaligned countries, in a document submitted to UNESCO in 1978. As summarized by D. R. Mankekar of the nonaligned news pool a year later:

> What is given [from the Third World] is mostly "destructive" news such as military coups, ethnic strife, terrorist acts and national calamities.
>
> The Western news agencies project a distorted image abroad of developing countries. With an unempathetic approach, they concentrate on failures and deficiencies, poverty and squalor, while ignoring achievements in the field of developmental progress—the kind of news which affluent TV listeners [sic] and newspaper readers find entertaining but the developing countries characterize as an unbalanced picture often amounting to "invasion of cultural privacy."[14]

The journalism of exception practiced by the major agencies prompts them to report the one train that crashes and not the thousands that arrive safely. Stories of misfortune stand out as isolated events, to be absorbed quickly by the agencies and their clients before they move on. The agencies report what happened, but not—in most cases—why it happened; their files are filled with news of immediate events, not of the processes underlying those events. When a river overflows its banks and floods thousands of farms, the agencies do not explore in any depth why the disaster occurred, both because they do not have the time to find out and because they doubt their subscribers would use a lengthy explanation. Theirs is essentially an instant business. Even if it were less so, there is no guarantee that their reporting would be any less "unempathetic." Depth does not always mean approval.

Given the undoubted penchant of many of their clients for news of violence, unrest, crime, and disaster, what is striking about agency files as a whole is that they do not contain higher proportions of items about catastrophe or adversity. Our analysis of five services issued by Reuters, the AP, and UPI to Western Europe, Africa, and the Middle East showed that stories involving violence, unrest, accidents, crime, and disaster accounted for 17 percent of these files. At UPI an internal study of its service to Latin America found that 27 percent of the file consisted of such items. The review of the four major agencies by the University of North Carolina included somewhat lower figures in services to Latin America. The study of Asian services by the Hong Kong Chinese University put at 16 percent the average amount of news of war, crime, accidents, and disasters from the

Third World distributed by the major agencies, while English academics Oliver Boyd-Barrett and Michael Palmer reported in the mid-1970s that "sensational" news, including conflicts, crime, and catastrophes, made up 20 percent of the AP service to Africa and 24 percent of the Reuters file to South Africa.

On the basis of such studies, it appears that as much "bad news" originates in Western Europe and North America as in the rest of the world. The survey of five services carried out for this book, for instance, revealed an almost exactly equal flow of negative news from the rich and the poor nations. But such an equation may be misleading, since the agencies run more coverage overall of Western Europe and North America than they do of each region of the Third World. They can thus be expected to run, in absolute terms, more bad news from the West than from the Third World. In our study the political and international violence category accounted for 16 percent of coverage of developing nations compared with just under 6 percent of items from North America and Western Europe. In the category of natural disasters, Africa had a near monopoly, although such reports made up only a very small proportion of the file from the Third World in general.

Neither of these findings should come as a surprise. The high proportion of natural-disaster reports under African datelines occurs because catastrophes such as famines strike more frequently there than in the developed countries. It is deplorable that these events occur, but it is not the agencies' job to sweep them under the rug simply because they happen in countries that believe such reporting harms their image in the rest of the world. As for the category of violent events and political turmoil, it is undeniable that internal politics in parts of the developing world are conducted in a more turbulent manner than in the industrialized countries. If the agencies report numerous coups in Latin America and Africa, this is because these are regions in which coups frequently take place. The localized wars and guerrilla conflicts of recent years have occurred in the developing nations, not in Western Europe. To take the agencies to task for covering them is like criticizing the Big Four for having given the United States a bad name by reporting the assassinations of the Kennedys and Martin Luther King, Jr.

The origin of a large proportion of agency coverage of national and international violence in the developing world is, therefore, only to be expected. Whether it is logical to categorize such reporting automatically as bad news is questionable. To do so—and then to attack the agencies for carrying too much news in this category—is to condemn them for having paid too much attention to liberation struggles in which violence was used against colonialism. The overthrow of Idi Amin was achieved by a military invasion of Uganda, undoubtedly an entry in the "bad news" column. By the same token, street demonstrations against dictators or strikes for higher pay by Third World workers are presumably "bad news," and the agencies are disseminating an unsympathetic picture of the developing world by reporting them, however much they may be glorified by later regimes.

On the other hand, much news that is not generally labeled "bad," since it deals with official pronouncements on international relations, politics, or economic affairs, could reasonably be regarded as having a decidedly unattractive character. An announcement of a breakdown in international negotiations to boost aid, the fall of a government, or a rise in the rate of inflation might well prompt fewer cheers than the violent overthrow of a vicious dictator. Even within other apparently straightforward "bad news" categories, there are nuances undreamed of by those who seek to sift agency stories into categories of positive and negative reporting. The arrest of a murderer goes down as an entry in the negative column because it concerns crime; if he had remained at liberty, the "bad" statistics would have been smaller. Without news coverage of major floods or earthquakes, what would be the spur for individuals and institutions to organize relief? Without reports of the evil doings of repressive governments, how could international public opinion be mobilized to exert pressure for improvement? If the agencies should fail to report torture and repression in South American military regimes, they would no doubt be accused of kowtowing to dictators rather than commended for having taken a step in the direction of positive news.

While the incidence of violent international and internal political events is higher in coverage from the Third World, stories about crime and accidents are much more common from Western Europe and North America. In our 1980 study, such items accounted for 5.2 percent of the total file from the Third World, and 9.2 percent of North American–Western European coverage. Of crime stories, nineteen came from Asia, Latin America, and Africa; twenty-six from Western Europe; and thirty-two from North America. This may show that criminals in the industrialized world are more innovative or daring than their peers in the developing countries—or only that they are better reported. It certainly does not provide support for suggestions that lawbreaking plays a significant part in agency coverage of the Third World.

Among accident stories, forty-eight came from North America and fifteen from Western Europe, while the developing nations produced twenty-six. It is reasonable to assume that industrialized societies will, as a rule, suffer more accidents of a scale likely to command attention abroad than underdeveloped nations, and agency coverage reflects this. They certainly do not place undue emphasis on news of accidents in the Third World; Africa, for instance, provided only one accident story in fifteen daily files studied. Indeed, not only was the number of items on accidents from North America alone far higher than from the whole of the Third World, the average length of stories in this category from the United States was almost twice that of similar reports from Asia, Africa, and Latin America, reflecting both the dimensions of the accidents involved and the greater availability of information about them.

Taking all the negative news categories together, the proportion of space they occupied in reports from the Third World in our study was considerably higher than the proportion in coverage of Western Europe and North America—23.1 percent compared with 15.2 percent. But an important qualification needs to be made to put this statistic into perspective. The priority accorded by the agencies to news of an international political character ensures that, within the "bad news" category, certain types of stories encountered more frequently in the Third World than in industrialized countries will be given extensive space. This is not a matter of strikes, demonstrations, natural disasters, poverty, or squalor; it is not even a matter of coups, terrorism, or ethnic strife, or of other, less significant events. Some "negative" items in coverage from the Third World are there because their international implications and connections are of great interest to the worldwide news audience. In the 1980 period studied for this book, reports of fighting in Afghanistan and of an Israeli raid on Palestinian positions in Lebanon were among the major stories reported by the agencies. The treatment they received was equivalent to that accorded important events in other news categories, and they naturally earned more coverage than the run of crime and accident stories from Western Europe and North America.

A strong case can be made for regarding stories such as those about Afghanistan and Lebanon as constituting a special category in which events cannot legitimately be tied down to their geographical origins. Neither of the two stories in question was about the Third World, although the events prompting them occurred there. The view the general public takes of the developing countries is not much affected either by the situation in Afghanistan or by the Arab-Israeli conflict; it is because of the external interest involved that such stories are internationally newsworthy. Properly, they belong outside any strict geographical classification.

The allegations about unfavorable reporting from the Third World are likely to live on in criticism of both the news that the agencies report from the Third World and the services they distribute there. The agencies will continue to protest, releasing figures such as those contained in a recent AP board report to the effect that only 5.6 percent of that agency's international news concerned violence compared with 23.4 percent on economic matters, or Reuters' calculation that, in the second quarter of 1979, stories involving violence, disaster, and catastrophe from the Third World took up just 1 percent more news space than news of misfortune from the West. The "bad news" argument is too seductive not to be kept alive. To some extent, this is simply a measure of how difficult it is to resist blaming the messenger of bad tidings. It also reflects a confusion between events and the reporting process that informs the world about them but by no means creates them. The "bad news" approach also coincides neatly with the conspiracy theory of agency operations; a conspiracy can produce only unwanted results.

But perhaps the most important reason for the strength and longevity of the "bad news" thesis is that it diverts attention from more fundamental questions. For leaders to blame their countries' negative national image, international ignorance, or lack of influence on the news choices made by the agencies goes beyond merely seeking a scapegoat; shunting information problems into a ghetto of their own by identifying them as the product of pernicious foreign organizations also provides a convenient way of avoiding the deeper ideological and practical questions raised for societies, both individually and collectively, by the way they inform themselves. The "bad news" thesis itself, the wish to structure news by geographical origin and subject matter, and the assertion that journalism must be supervised combine to produce a dense smokescreen. Behind it, governments that permit no opposition can castigate the news agencies for monopolistic behavior, while at the same time the heads of their state-run national news agencies can put their names to reports advocating greater independence for the media and a freer flow of information.

All this could easily be dismissed as the normal coinage of politics.

While the agencies have become somewhat more aware of the need to report the developing world better in recent years, neither side in the argument takes much real notice of the other. The overall effect on agency files has been small. Proponents of an information order in which news will be responsive to national criteria take no account of the amount of space the agencies already give to government leaders and official information. Both sides could quite comfortably maintain a dialogue of the deaf so long as it does not affect their vital interests.

The victims are the media of the developing world. Those who espouse the Western-model approach to news risk finding themselves cast as renegades by their governments, as allies of the politically alien news style propagated internationally by the major agencies. Those who believe that there are alternative ways of reporting within the Third World—*without* falling under official control—are even more isolated.

One Style for Different Worlds? . . . .

Statistics such as those presented above, collected from counts of stories falling into subject or geographical categories, do not reveal the way in which agency reports from the developing world are formulated. For the most part, such stories are handled as straightforward reports of what happened. More rarely, they include descriptive and analytical material. In either case, stories are presented according to certain reportorial conventions, but this standardization does not mean they are any less accurate or fair.

Each agency has its own individuality, but there is a broad common style based on the shared editorial values noted earlier. Whether this style is as acceptable to the nonideological media in Africa, Asia, and Latin America as it is in Western Europe and North America— or whether there is a need for a different editorial approach that takes account of varying cultures, educational levels, and subjects of interest in different parts of the world—is an important question facing journalism in the 1980s. It is a question that goes deeper than the currently argued issues of the agencies' devoting enough space to one region or another, or running too many negative items from Africa or Asia, would suggest. Because of their shared working philosophy, the Big Four report the world's news in a basically uniform manner. Competition among them has led them to concentrate their attention on those areas of the world in which the chances for earning substantial revenues are greatest; without this concentration, they could not have survived in their present form. The heavy predominance of Western press and broadcasting organizations among their subscribers means that their reportorial style is always going to be the one that is the most satisfactory to the industrialized nations.

On top of that, the major agencies undoubtedly reflect values in their reporting and editing that are most common in the West. They often employ local reporters, but the coverage that a Brazilian or a Malaysian correspondent provides is presented in the standard agency style. This uniformity of coverage is one of the agencies' great strengths, for it enables them to be widely accepted, professionally if not always politically. And, as agency executives like to point out, even some of their most vociferous critics depend on their services for a fast and reliable account of world events, proving just how far their acceptability reaches.

This is a cause for disappointment to those who believe the developing world should have access to news reported according to different, but still nongovernmental, standards. The upshot is that agency files of the highest professional standards may not fully satisfy subscribers in the developing world. As an Indian editor, Nihal Singh, put it:

I think the four international news agencies on the whole do a commendable job. But one of the basic problems that arises as far as the Third World is concerned is that stories are naturally written with a primarily Western audience in mind. This is understandable since the agencies have to satisfy a majority of their subscribers. For the non-Western audience, this approach suffers from two kinds of constraints: the type of stories that are written and the overemphasis on Western news.

It is necessary to separate the two strains of criticism often made about the news agencies. One is the desire of many Third World leaders to see laudatory references about themselves and their countries and their aversion to critical references. The other is the more legitimate criticism that Third World countries live and struggle after their own fashion.

The strength of the major Western news agencies is the wide network of correspondents they have round the world and their standard of professionalism.

To be sure, the ethos of the parent country, if not a particular government's policy, does influence each of the agencies—another reason why so many Third World countries hanker after a non-Western orientated and controlled news agency.[15]

The editorial approach adopted by the Big Four is clearly not the only one that could be used in reporting the world. While it has proven widely acceptable, it could be complemented or superseded by other styles, other priorities, and other values. It is remarkable that, after more than a decade of debate and criticism, the major agencies remain so firmly the predominant suppliers of news to the world. Much of the reason for this lies in the wide acceptability of the services they issue, but it can also be attributed to alternatives that have emerged in recent years and that will be examined in the next two chapters.

CHAPTER 11

Alternatives

Alternatives to the major agencies can be divided into two broad categories: those that (like the Big Four) have distinct reporting and editing operations of their own, and those that act primarily as communications channels for national or regional services. The Western-based alternate services, the big Communist agencies, and two regional initiatives in Latin America and the Caribbean fall into the first group; the majority of recent efforts carried out by advocates of a new world information order are in the second. This chapter will examine those alternate services that, despite wide differences in character, follow the basic pattern of collecting and distributing news themselves. An examination of their recent history and present position clearly shows why no alternate agency, operating either on the Western model or along the state-controlled lines of the Soviet agency TASS, has emerged to challenge the Big Four.

Second-Tier European Agencies ....

Three agencies based in Western Europe—Deutsche Presse-Agentur of West Germany, Efe of Spain, and Agenzia Nazionale Stampa Associata of Italy—distribute international news on a substantial scale outside the continent.[1] Their operations often seem very similar to those of the Big Four, but each claims to offer something different from Reuters, Agence France-Presse, the Associated Press, and United Press International. Analysis of their files shows, however, that their reportorial approach is indeed akin to that of the major agencies. Differences occur mainly in the choice of material they offer and in their character as representatives of their home countries on the international scene.

West Germany's postwar economic revival might be expected to have produced a new and significant force on the international news-agency scene. As a stronger economic power than either Britain or

France, and with prosperous domestic media, West Germany today looks like a logical setting for one of the world's major news services. Indeed, as long ago as 1954, a director of Reuters discussed with his board the "strong nationalist element on the DPA board who were in favour of building up DPA as a world news agency." But thirty years later, the West German service has yet to reach full world-agency status.

DPA was begun in 1949 when the separate services operating since the end of the war in the British, French, and U.S. occupation zones were combined. It moved into what were expected to be temporary headquarters in the offices of the British-zone agency in Hamburg. "We decided not to go to Bonn, but to wait until German reunification and go straight to Berlin," the agency's editor in chief, Dr. Hans Benirschke, recalled. "We are still waiting."

A private company whose capital of 5 million marks ($2.2 million) is owned by 200 shareholders, DPA serves West German newspapers and broadcasting stations with both domestic and foreign news. From its earliest days, the agency had foreign correspondents of its own, but it has always viewed a link with one of the major English-language agencies as an essential part of its operations. "The West German media have always insisted on having their own international cover," according to Benirschke. "But we never had the ambition to do everything with a network of correspondents of our own, which would have been impossible. We always felt the need to be part of an international agency."

As a result, DPA received the Reuters service for two decades, an arrangement facilitated by Reuters' postwar decision not to develop its own distribution in Germany as the two U.S. agencies had. When a mixture of financial factors and Reuters' desire to establish an independent presence brought that arrangement to an end in 1971, UPI was busy closing down its local European services. A tie-up between DPA and UPI was the natural outcome; it was all the more attractive since the American agency could deliver both textual news and photographs.

In addition to maintaining close links with one of the major world agencies for general-news purposes, DPA has fifty-five staff correspondents abroad. With the help of part-time stringers, the agency receives coverage of its own from seventy-nine countries: the whole of Europe (except for Albania), eight countries in Africa, seventeen in Asia, the United States, Canada, Australia, and all of Latin America except for Guyana, Surinam, and French Guiana. In 1981 the cost of this news team came to 20 million marks ($9 million), 27 percent of the agency's annual budget of 75 million marks ($33 million).

The maintenance of a considerable foreign reporting network, and the production of a regular flow of news intended for the domestic German market (but also of interest to media elsewhere), soon pushed the fledgling DPA into international distribution. The agency instituted a German-language service for foreign subscribers in Scandinavia, Austria, Switzerland, Belgium, Luxembourg, and Holland in the 1950s. East European countries, eager for information about the Federal Republic, took the fuller domestic West German service. An English-language service for Africa and Asia followed. DPA then entered the crowded Latin-American market with its own Spanish-language file. In Cairo, the Egyptian Middle East News Agency (MENA) began to edit and translate DPA news, although transmission takes place from Hamburg. In 1985, DPA reported that it served 1500 subscribers, including 60 news agencies, in 85 countries. Agency executives said DPA's foreign services went to 186 direct recipients, 95 percent of them news agencies, newspapers, and broadcasting stations. Of the total, 76 were in Latin America, 59 in Europe, 28 in Africa, 20 in Asia, and 3 in Australia/New Zealand. In Latin America, most clients were newspapers and broadcasters served directly, but elsewhere, delivery was mainly to national news agencies, which frequently provided their own services in exchange.

Such exchanges between second-tier international agencies and a large number of national news services produce the illusion of a major world network operating alongside the Big Four. DPA has agreements with 60 foreign news agencies, ANSA with 53, and Efe with 22. But even though the number of words sent daily by national agencies to DPA, Efe, or ANSA is enormous, the use made of copy received under such arrangements is usually small because it is not dictated by consistent need. Thus, despite its geographical scope and diversity, this news in no way competes with the files of the Big Four. "We don't use their copy much," a senior Efe editor remarked of the national news services. "Very sporadically, in fact. They are often late. We use them only if something big happens in their country." On the opposite side of the coin, the second-tier international services are of somewhat greater value to the national agencies, since they offer occasional alternatives to the Big Four. Such diversity is welcomed, although again the actual use of copy is limited.

Efe executives today speak of belonging to the ranks of the top agencies, but the gulf between such services as Efe and the Big Four remains wide, even though the scale of coverage is sometimes similar. DPA's English-language service to Africa, for instance, not only covers major world events but also provides detailed target coverage for subscribers. The Spanish and West German agencies both run large amounts of material from Latin America in their services to the continent, and Efe is a major partner in a Central American agency. An ANSA editor claimed: "We have the same geographical network as the bigger agencies. We are even stronger in some places." Although they still depend on the Big Four for some of their world coverage, these agencies could theoretically develop into equal and fully independent sources of international news. But such a development is unlikely to occur for two related reasons: the essentially national nature of the second-tier agencies, whatever their foreign distribution, and the lack of demand for a Western-model addition to the ranks of the major international agencies.

The financial position of the general-news operations of the Big Four clearly shows that there is no great untapped market waiting for DPA, Efe, or ANSA. The scope of such agencies is bound to be limited by the saturation of the market as a whole, although they may find particular corners they can fill. In general, government backing is needed to make their foreign distribution possible, just as it is at AFP. Such backing enables the second-tier agencies to sell at low subscription rates without going broke. They cannot replace the Big Four, but a newspaper executive faced with the choice between taking, say, three big agencies or two big agencies plus a cheap second-tier service may well opt for the second alternative.

The government money that agencies in Western Europe receive is, to some extent, the result of a genuine commercial transaction. Ministries, official bodies, and embassies receive useful news services from them for which payment is only to be expected. What are not straight commercial matters are the sizes of the payments, the ways in which they are determined, and the coincidences between the decision that certain embassies need a national agency's service and the countries in which that agency wishes to expand its distribution.

In Italy, the Foreign Ministry decided in the early 1950s that, instead of forming its own information service for diplomatic missions abroad, it would be more efficient and economical to work through ANSA. A contract with the national agency, to supply a service of specially selected Italian news to embassies, followed. This gave ANSA the financial cushion for international expansion, and underwrote the cost of establishing communication links abroad.

203

In Spain, Efe has a contract with the state, under which the government pays an annual sum fixed after the agency has determined its costs. The agency is owned in equal parts by the state, by newspapers and private shareholders, and by the National Industry Institute, which is under ministerial control. "We don't want to be the agency of the government, but of the state," Efe's administrative manager Indalecio Diaz Sánchez has said.

DPA enjoys an arrangement under which the Bonn government pays for communications with developing nations from which the agency would be unable to recoup its investment via subscriptions. In 1981, 4.5 million marks ($2 million) were budgeted for this purpose. As a result, DPA has been able to offer services for a few hundred dollars a month to countries halfway across the world. "We had a choice between that and leaving out some areas," Benirschke commented. "As a private company we wouldn't supply areas such as Pakistan, Sri Lanka, Burma, and Central America." He noted that as part of the arrangement West German embassies in the countries concerned are able to get the DPA service by wire or satellite rather than in airmailed bulletins. "We try to coordinate government requests to get the service to certain embassies with contracts with the national agencies," Benirschke noted.

DPA, ANSA, Efe, and other national agencies with foreign distribution say they have something original to offer, particularly to those who identify agencies with their home countries. "We don't reflect the point of view of the big powers in this world," the head of DPA's Latin American service commented. "We have things, especially from Europe but also, for instance, from China, which other agencies don't have." Despite such claims, the developing world receives no more attention from DPA than it does from Reuters or AFP. On a typical day studied, the DPA English-language service for Asia and Africa contained 63 items running to 12,100 words. Of these, 36 stories, amounting to 7500 words, came from Western Europe. The Middle East provided 10 items, Central Asia 6, Eastern Europe 4, the Far East 3, Africa 2, and North and Latin America 1 each. As with the Big Four, politics dominated the DPA file, providing 36 items and 8375 words; 11 items were economic, while 6 concerned crime and violence.

However great the attraction of an ever-growing plurality of information sources might seem, the reality of the environment in which the agencies operate is such that there is little possibility for the growth of one of the second-tier international services into a major-league operation. There are limits to what state financing can buy, and limits as well to the funds governments are willing to supply. As Benirschke, with a budget half that of AFP and a fifth that of Reuters, recognized in 1981:

> The present size of DPA corresponds to our domestic base and the interests of our shareholders. We have no ambitions for further expansion. We have had our four foreign services for ten years and there won't be any expansion. I can't see the economic basis for expansion. I can't see any area of the world where there is enough revenue to support expansion.

Economic considerations do not weigh heavily on the biggest state-funded international agency, TASS of the Soviet Union.[2] TASS is sometimes classed with the Big Four, as, for instance, by UNESCO's 1980 Commission for the Study of Communications Problems. But the Soviet agency cannot be included in the same club for several reasons. Its position and development as a source of international news are ruled primarily by political factors. TASS is an integral part of the Soviet state system and proclaims the promotion of that system as one of its prime objectives. TASS reporting of the Soviet Union and the rest of the world is framed to advance Moscow's interests. The Big Four may fall short of impartiality on occasion; the partiality of TASS is evident in virtually every dispatch.

The distribution and, more important, the use of the Soviet agency's services is highly uneven. Most recipients are in the Communist world, or in states that align themselves with Moscow. Elsewhere, TASS is used primarily as a guide to official thinking, as the official mouthpiece of one of the superpowers, rather than as a twenty-four-hour-a-day news source.

In Kenya, elaborate installations undertaken by the Soviet agency for the country's postindependence news requirements were virtually ignored from the start in favor of Western-based services. In France, the newspaper *Le Monde* takes TASS merely to be able to get full texts of major Soviet statements, and staff at the Communist daily, *l'Humanité*, say they use the Soviet agency "for reference." TASS itself, on the other hand, regularly draws on the four Western agencies as a source of international information. Some of this material is issued in its general service within the Soviet Union; more is reproduced in two restricted services, "White TASS" and "Red TASS," issued to keep senior Soviet officials abreast of what is really going on in the world.

The Latin Experiment[3] . . . .

The arrival of DPA, Efe, and ANSA in Latin America during the 1960s and 1970s gave the continent the widest choice of news services of any area outside Western Europe. For the established commercial agencies, the newcomers posed the threat of decreased profits or increased losses. For recipients of printed or broadcast news, the heightened competition failed to bring about improved selection, since the new services (although they differed in volume and price) offered much the same basic diet. Only one agency, Inter Press Service, attempted to provide something different. (Its efforts will be examined later in this chapter.)

Latin America had always appeared—particularly to the U.S. agencies—to be a region in which the classic agency approach to news was eminently acceptable. The American services formed close links there with major clients, links that in some cases went beyond the simple delivery of news services. UPI, for instance, ran domestic agencies in Chile and Argentina; the latter, a loss-incurring operation, was closed down by President Juan Perón, to UPI's secret relief.

Although conventionally classed as part of the Third World, Latin America has a long press history, and publishers there are distinctly displeased at the region's being lumped together with emerging African nations in which the only newspaper may be a government-sponsored sheet. The importance of the region's press was recognized by the U.S. agencies when they began to distribute in Latin America after breaking Havas's cartel monopoly; the role of *La Prensa* in Buenos Aires in UP's international development, for instance, has already been noted. The agency's head in the 1940s, Hugh Baillie, noted that at that time the Argentine newspaper was still UP's largest single newspaper client, in terms of the money it paid and the service it received.

By contrast, the British and French agencies were weak in Latin America once the Havas monopoly under the cartel had ended. In the early 1950s, Reuters did not have a single staff reporter in the region; it decided to stop distributing there in the middle of that decade in the face of losses of £40,000 a year. There were occasional suggestions that the region's media might organize a news service of their own. The material received from the AP and UPI through their Latin American desks in New York was criticized by some outside observers as too conservative in its political tone and inattentive to social forces at work within the continent. The criticism was not voiced by the press owners who paid the subscriptions; most of them were conservatives who often played a prominent part in local politics. As a U.S. observer, Peter Barnes of the Lowell (Mass.) *Sun,* remarked in an examination of AP and UPI services to Latin America in 1964:

> There is no doubt that most of the publishers who provide the agencies with their Latin American revenues would be shocked and offended by a fairer treatment of the changing social forces at work in modern Latin America. . . . A UPI correspondent in Brazil, for example, wrote a story several months ago that was mildly critical of rightist Carlos Lacerda, Governor of Guanabara. This provoked *La Prensa* of Buenos Aires into protesting vigorously to UPI headquarters in New York, which relayed the protest to the correspondent with a "never again" advisement attached.

Similar reports of pressure from Latin American clients still surface sporadically, as do allegations that individual correspondents prefer to avoid trouble by ignoring controversial matters. It is clear that both the AP and UPI generally operate very much within the area of consensus set out by their clients in Latin America. Calls for the establishment of an alternate regional service reflected the Latin Americans' desire to cover the continent for themselves, rather than political discontent with the North American agencies by media owners.

This did not mean that journalists were always happy with what they received. As long ago as 1926, delegates at a Pan American journalists' congress called for the establishment of a regional agency, and in 1961 a conference organized by UNESCO in Santiago advocated the establishment of a cooperative Latin American agency. Nothing came of either of these appeals. But a meeting of the Inter American Press Association (IAPA) in Bogotá in 1969 led, albeit indirectly, to the establishment of the only continental agency owned by media operating on a commercial basis with an independent editorial structure and a supply of international news from one of the Big Four. At Bogotá, a number of Latin American publishers had bemoaned their dependence on the AP and UPI for regional as well as world coverage. Their complaints might have been dismissed as mere ritual if a top Reuters executive had not heard them and decided to take the publishers up on what they were saying.

The executive, Patrick Crosse, had impressive credentials, having established Reuters' reporting and distribution network in independent Africa in the 1960s. His presence at the IAPA meeting was the result of Reuters' decision in the late 1960s that it must reestablish itself in Latin America in order to be a truly worldwide service. The problem was the potential cost of getting back into the area—not to mention the unattractiveness of competing head-on with the entrenched American services.

Crosse found what looked like an ideal way to satisfy the Latin American publishers and solve Reuters' problems: the Latin American newspapers should set up their own agency with Reuters' help. The new agency would have its own correspondents throughout the region, an editing desk in Buenos Aires, and a world news report from Reuters. It could sell its regional report to Reuters for inclusion in the London agency's world files. To help the agency get started, Reuters would provide management and would help to drum up shareholders and subscribers. A group of major Latin American newspapers would take shares in the new venture, but none would be dominant, and the agency would be free from government or partisan influences. At last, Latin America would get a news service of its own. Its name, of course, would be Latin.

The new agency, founded in 1970, issued its first service in July 1971. At one time or another, its Latin American shareholders, or *socios,* consisted of *El Mercurio* and *La Tercera* of Chile; *Diaro Popular, O Estado, Jornal do Brasil,* and *O Globo* of Brazil; *Excelsior* of Mexico; *El Tiempo* of Colombia; *La Verdad* and *El Nacional* of Venezuela; *Excelsior* of Costa Rica; *El Comercial* of Ecuador; *Editora Siglo* of Bolivia; *El Comercio* of Peru; and another Peruvian newspaper, *Expreso,* whose share was taken over personally by its owner, Manuel Ulloa, when his newspaper was expropriated by the government. Reuters also took a share, which grew steadily from its original 8 percent.

The larger newspaper shareholders each paid $3500 a month for the Latin service; others were charged $1500. In either case, the figure was generally less than shareholders' subscriptions to the North American agencies. But despite the savings, and despite its character as a new organization for Latin America, the agency was not universally welcomed by potential subscribers; indeed, even the enthusiasm of some of the *socios* was in doubt. The head of *O Estado* in São Paulo refused to see senior Reuters managers when they toured South America to help launch Latin. "We were the poor at the gate," Crosse (who left the agency business soon after Latin started) recalled. "We were treated with contempt sometimes. We just couldn't get to see important people. We were rather like people flogging vacuum cleaners. We had to establish ourselves and put ourselves on the map.''

That could be done only by widening the range of the agency's editorial service. Latin had to deal with the hugely entrenched positions of the AP and UPI, the competition of AFP, Efe, and DPA, and resentment from some editors who saw the new agency as a service imposed on them by its owners, diverting money that might otherwise have been spent on developing their own operations. The lack of a photographic service was a big drawback. There was also, inevitably, the initial disbelief that such a cooperatively owned service could actually function—despite missionary work on its behalf by one of the leading Latin American publishers, Agustín Edwards of Chile's *El Mercurio*.

Overcoming such drawbacks, Latin's service expanded steadily in both the coverage it offered and the number of subscribers it signed up. By 1975, it had 130 clients. A study of copy used in six Latin American newspapers in 1972 and 1973 showed that Latin accounted for 31 percent of credited agency material. The file contained the usual agency weighting toward politics and economics; foreign relations took up 22.4 percent of Latin items in a 1973 survey, and economic items 19.3 percent. The agency's style and writing standards were praised, and it tried to develop interpretative and analytical coverage to go with the spot news provided by its own fifteen correspondents and the world network of Reuters.[4] But two problems were emerging that would prove the agency's undoing. One was a matter of politics and personalities. The other concerned money.

The newspaper bosses who had come together in 1970 at the urging of Edwards and Crosse were men of considerable substance in their own countries. Some were politicians. Manuel Ulloa had been finance minister in Peru and would later be prime minister. Agustín Edwards was deeply involved in Chile's turbulent politics. When Edwards was forced out of his influential national role by the victory of Salvador Allende, he also retreated from taking an active part in Latin, according to one close observer. Following the coup d'etat that overthrew Allende, Edwards returned to Chile, but he had become something of an embarrassment, a man caught up in allegations of backing from the CIA and the bringing to power of a bloody military dictatorship. In Peru, Ulloa's association with Latin made the agency suspect to the military rulers who supplanted him and his associates. It operated behind a Reuters front in Lima for some time, until a report of fighting between military units led to the closing of Reuters and the expulsion of the Reuters-Latin (or Latin-Reuters) correspondents.

Other shareholders operated on a less lofty political level. One employed a private security firm to investigate the backgrounds of the agency's journalists and handed in a report on their political activities as students. Government pressure was a recurrent problem; at least one correspondent was withdrawn after official protests about his coverage. Shortly afterward, Latin signed a transmission agreement with the government in question.

The majority of Latin shareholders favored the status quo, but political divisions—for a time—beset the agency's board. The conservatives thought Latin should confine itself to spot news and eliminate interpretation and analysis. The opposing view, for which Julio Scherer García of Mexico's *Excelsior* was the spokesman, was that Latin should go beyond the news diet offered by the AP and UPI to provide background, analysis, and features and to support politically progressive movements. For a while, Scherer's influence predominated. He became president of the agency in 1973, pushed for the development of costly new communications circuits in Central America, and got his candidate installed as editor of the agency over the opposition of other *socios* and of Reuters.

Soon, however, a more conservative approach took over. Scherer's editor left, and Scherer himself faced a growing opposition to his political stance within his cooperatively run newspaper. In 1976, he was ousted from *Excelsior*. Since he had been one of the few active journalists on the Latin board—a fact that had contributed to his strong influence—his departure left the agency in the politically conservative hands of newspaper owners and their representatives.

By then, politics was of little importance. The agency's financial position, which had been undermined early on by the departure of two *socios* and the failure to sign up significant new shareholders, had become precarious. In 1974, the *socios* met in Buenos Aires, where managers from Reuters told them that Latin's accumulated losses amounted to $1 million. The agency's overdraft facility had been exhausted; it was involved in expensive communications arrangements, and was having trouble persuading some subscribers to pay their bills. Reuters was meeting many of its debts. Something needed to be done.

The possibility of raising subscription rates was mentioned hesitantly by the Latin management—and quickly dropped in the face of immediate hostile reaction. Latin was past its high point; while costs would inevitably rise, the initial surge of sales of the news service had subsided. The broadcast market offered a fleeting hope, and Latin launched a rip-and-read service for radio, but strong competition in this area from U.S. and European agencies meant that rates had to be set unprofitably low—down to $200 a month. One growth area did exist: special-traffic transmissions of copy for clients. However, because of Latin's limited communications facilities, this service entailed leaving the teleprinters of all subscribers but one on a given circuit silent while copy was moved for a single recipient.

In 1976, Latin recorded a net loss of just over $100,000 on gross revenues of almost $2 million, and it was predicted that the deficit would jump considerably in 1977. Somewhat more than half the agency's 1976 revenue came from a contract with the Venezuelan government, under the terms of which Latin supplied its service and a ministerial bulletin to embassies around the world. Latin's management believed that the Venezuelans might underwrite the agency for five years. The board discussed whether or not to accept fresh official backing in the form of government shareholders.

Nothing came of such schemes. Latin's losses mounted. The emergence of subregional news networks in Latin America, enjoying financial assistance from governments, further increased competition and diminished the agency's ability to maneuver commercially. There was growing competition on the special-traffic transmission front as well. Latin's owners would not pay its bills, so its managers at Reuters picked up ever-increasing tabs. Only a few *socios* remained actively interested in the agency. By November 1977, earlier hopes for widespread commitment of the Latin American media had evaporated, and Reuters announced that the "boards of Reuters and Latin have agreed to integrate the general news reporting and distributing operations of the two agencies in Latin America."

Despite the careful wording of the announcement, the decision amounted to an operational takeover of Latin by Reuters, with the manager of Reuters in Buenos Aires now the dominant figure. The announcement specified that "ownership of Latin will continue to be shared between Reuters and the 15 existing Latin American shareholders. Reuters will increase its shareholding but the majority of the stock will continue to be held by the Latin American shareholders." This majority was barely more than 50 percent. Most of the Latin American founders had effectively abdicated. Absorption by Reuters was only a matter of time. In May 1981, Reuters announced that "Reuters and Latin, its associate agency in South America, will merge fully on July 1. All company activities in Latin America will be carried out in the future in Reuters' name, although the regional Spanish-language news service will continue to use the Latin-Reuters tag.''

The word "tag" seemed more than a little inconsequential given the original hopes for and potential of Latin. An initiative that could have offered a real alternative to the existing news services had died because of divisions and a growing lack of commitment among its owners, the strength of the competition, and financial problems from which there was no exit. "We were getting into something we didn't fully understand," Patrick Crosse reflected afterward. The Latin experiment showed that, in the end, information is expendable, for private media as well as for governments. Building a regional agency to meet Latin American needs was simply too much trouble for the press, which could continue to exist quite happily with the U.S. news services. Commercially, Latin had quickly run into the familiar problems of inadequate revenues and steadily rising costs. Keeping the agency alive required a degree of selflessness that proved to be beyond the Latin American media. The lesson is obvious: calling for alternatives to the Big Four is one thing; paying for them is quite another.

Success in the Caribbean[5] . . . .

At about the time Latin was being formed, pressure was also building for the establishment of a regional news agency in the Caribbean. The initial impetus came when Caribbean heads of government urged the regional media to consider forming such a service in 1967. Nothing happened, partly because many of the newspapers and broadcasting stations in the area were unhappy with the idea of acting under government pressure. But the same officials returned to the subject four years later, raising the possibility of proceeding with their idea on an interstate level as part of a general movement toward integration within the Caribbean. Predictably, the regional media responded that they would have nothing to do with any government-run news service; they would prefer to continue using their existing news sources. These consisted of their own reporters in the region and Reuters' Caribbean service, which was edited in Barbados and which contained a certain amount of regional coverage (20 percent, according to one study) as well as international news.

The deadlock was broken by UNESCO. A project set up by the international organization to improve communications in the Caribbean won the confidence of both governments and media. The result was the formation of the Caribbean News Agency (CANA), which—despite considerable difficulties—has probably proven to be the most successful regional news agency launched in the developing world, and one that has shown UNESCO playing a valuable practical role in contrast to the usual picture of the organization simply as a forum for politically motivated rhetoric.

Founded in 1976, CANA grew out of Reuters' Caribbean service. Reuters was not motivated by philanthropy. It had been eager to close down its loss-incurring operation in the area, and CANA took over both the infrastructure and staff. The new agency's general manager had previously worked with Reuters both in the Caribbean and in London. CANA depended on Reuters for its world news—a dependence that remains great, although the agency has broadened its sources to include the news pool of nonaligned countries and Cuba's Prensa Latina. The editorial philosophy adopted by CANA could have come straight out of any Western agency: "CANA is only concerned with the reporting of fully substantiated, well-sourced or eye-witnessed facts, as well as attributable conclusions or comments, always endeavoring to balance the latter whenever they contain a controversial element." [6]

The need for CANA to remain independent of its owners and subscribers was particularly acute because of the wide variety of approaches to news that exists within the Caribbean. The agency's sixteen shareholders in the Caribbean media varied all the way from ardent advocates of commercial media independence to newspapers and radios owned by governments that believe information should be used to serve narrowly defined national ends. The agency's success in avoiding major ideological problems is a tribute both to its own standards and to the restraint of its subscribers.

From its inception the agency suffered editorially from uneven coverage, particularly of the smaller countries in the area. In some cases, it appears that correspondents held back on controversial stories—an inevitable problem in a region with some countries in which information is often seen in very direct and personal terms. The agency's regional file contained much in the way of immediate news items and political news but was short on features, in-depth stories, and analysis. Despite such difficulties, however, CANA grew steadily in scope and professionalism. When the agency had become firmly established, Reuters withdrew its correspondent from Barbados and entered into an agreement under which CANA provided the London-based agency with Caribbean coverage. By 1978, the proportion of Caribbean news in the CANA service had risen to around 40 percent, and the agency had virtually saturated the Caribbean market, prompting an investigation into the prospects for entering new areas such as economic-news services.

There is no doubt that CANA has been helped along by a number of factors—the history of bids for cooperation among Caribbean nations, the strength of the independent media in the region, its relationship with Reuters, and the limited geographical area involved. CANA was also helped by a $1 million grant between 1982 and 1985 from the West German government through UNESCO. Singly or together, these are factors that do not universally apply in other areas of the developing world. But CANA has shown so far that it is possible to establish a locally based news agency that seeks to meet specific regional needs while retaining a sizable degree of independence from both its owners and government.

Inter Press Service:
A New Approach?[7] . . . .

Latin grew out of predominantly capitalist and conservative media in association with one of the Big Four, while CANA built on an existing Reuters operation and continued to depend on the London agency for its world news. A third service that set out to meet developing world needs, Inter Press Service (IPS), was established in complete independence from the major agencies to carry out a specific political mission. The nature of this mission has changed drastically during the two decades that IPS has been in existence, but it remains the leading example of a nonstate news agency operating on the basis of a news ideology that its owners and journalists believe is appropriate for the developing world.

IPS, with headquarters in Rome, was established in 1964 by the Italian and West German Christian Democratic parties to act as a link between Western Europe and Latin America. At the time, hopes that Christian Democracy would provide an alternative both to Western-style capitalism and to Communism were high. The backers of IPS wanted to provide a means of reporting from the Christian Democratic viewpoint, and of enabling Latin American governments—notably that of Eduardo Frei in Chile—to make their achievements widely known. For the Frei administration, IPS arranged to distribute a daily news bulletin to Chilean embassies around the world. It also concluded an agreement with the Italian government to transmit news about Italy to Latin America. Communications agreements with other South American governments followed, and IPS was reported to have received financing from the European Economic Community and West German development funds.

But the eclipse of the Christian Democrats in Latin America in the later 1960s deprived IPS of its raison d'être. The agency, which had few media clients for its news service, lost some of its communications contracts, including a particularly lucrative one with Argentina. Under Salvador Allende, Chile began to use the Cuban agency Prensa Latina as well as IPS for its international transmissions. Reuters, with its new computerized message-switching system, became an aggressive competitor in the special-traffic business.

Under these changed circumstances, IPS found a new role. It was reorganized as a journalists' cooperative, and declared its aim to be "the diffusion of the economic, social, and cultural processes of the developing countries and their organizations." It would also "facilitate bilateral or multilateral information exchange among those same nations, acting as a channel for multiple communication and information services."[8]

Today IPS stresses the need for "horizontal" communication between developing nations interacting as equals, rather than "vertical" communication in which a news supplier imposes its services on others. "With a view to contributing towards a *real* process of communication IPS has directed its energies towards the horizontal linkage of Third World countries in the field of information," according to the chief of the agency's Office of Research and Information, Phil Harris.

> The aim of IPS is to escape the traditional vertical processes of communication. . . . While IPS does not deny its manifestly political orientation, the agency's view is that, since this orientation is the product of journalistic interaction, it escapes the problem of traditional vertical structures in which one power or authority invests the news organisation with a particular orientation.

To rectify the deficiencies of coverage of the developing world by the major agencies and other organizations involved in "vertical structures," IPS, according to Harris, has "adopted a style of journalism which focuses directly on the processes of development. This alternative style is an attempt to provide systematic and processual

Table 8	Origins of IPS News Files in Two Languages During Six- and Four-Day Study Periods, 1980	
	Spanish Language: Six Days (Rounded to Nearest %)	English Language: Four Days (Rounded to Nearest %)
Origin		
Latin America	54[a]	29[a]
Europe	27	29
International organizations	16	33
Asia	1	3
Africa	0	3
North America	1	1
Middle East	1	3

[a]The Dutch study of IPS found that 45 percent of the items over a four-day period came from Latin America.

coverage of the successes and problems of development in the various Third World countries.''

IPS listed thirty ''major customers'' in eighteen countries at the start of the 1980s. In addition, it exchanged news with eighteen national agencies. Its strength, as far as use of its own copy is concerned, remained very much in Latin America and among international organizations; three of its ''major customers'' in Western Europe said they used none, or hardly any, of its copy. Dutch researchers who studied IPS in 1977 found that the six biggest users of its copy were all in Latin America. Mexican subscribers accounted for 31.4 percent of all IPS credited copy, Peru 18.7 percent, and Colombia 11.8 percent. In Europe, Portugal took 7.1, Britain 2.4 percent, and Italy 1.7 percent.[9]

IPS provided fewer and longer reports than the traditional services—around twenty a day in its English-language service and twice that number in Spanish. For an agency that proclaims a Third World orientation, its geographical scope was remarkably limited and quite as distorted, in its own way, as that of any of the Big Four. An examination carried out for this book in 1980, in which six days of the IPS Spanish file to Latin America and four days of the English service sent to Africa, Asia, and Europe were monitored, showed that the great majority of reports came from Latin America, Europe, or international organizations. (See table 8.)

While politics and economics are as prominent in IPS news files as they are in files of the Big Four, IPS pays much more attention to social issues, which constituted, in the 1980 study period, 29 percent of the Spanish file and 21 percent of the English service. It is clear, therefore, that the agency is breaking away from traditional coverage patterns in some ways. In others, however, it remains a prisoner of protocol news, programmed events, and statements by national elites. The 1980 study showed that about half the stories issued concerned leaders of one kind or another (the 1977 Dutch analysis found that "political elite news" far outweighed "nonelite news"). A large proportion of the agency's English file was taken up with reports of UN sessions and other international meetings—reports consisting mainly of textual excerpts from speeches and procedural details. The subjects covered, and the space allotted to them, were different from those of the Big Four, but the style in which they were reported generally did little to illuminate the development process on the ground or to explain what was happening outside the confines of international meetings or UN projects.

In addition to its reporting, IPS has developed a substantial business in transmitting copy for national news agencies and UN bodies, and a smaller business covering UN conferences and projects in return for a fee or payment of editorial costs. Earnings from the United Nations and its agencies shot up from $3300 in 1977 to $75,232 in 1978 and $415,782 in 1979, and played a major part in keeping the agency in business as it swung between a loss of $98,802 in 1977, a profit of $134,951 in 1978, and another loss of $140,343 in 1979. Total revenue jumped from $724,034 in 1977 to $1,635,151 in 1979.[10]

The UN material carried by IPS mainly concerns meetings and projects. The copy carried for national news agencies is equally aimed at getting a message across on behalf of Third World governments. Domestic and international political events from a few countries dominate. In our 1980 study of the IPS Spanish file for Latin America, 100 of the 203 stories from national agencies came from Yugoslavia's Tanjug or Libya's JANA agency. Thirteen of the national services using IPS facilities sent only one story during the whole six-day period studied, and thirteen others put out fewer than six items each.

The editorial approach adopted by these national agencies was, for the most part, about as far removed from an alternate style of reporting as could be imagined. Deadpan relaying of official statements, proceedings of conferences, and stories tracking the movements of ministers made up the bulk of copy from agencies that pay to use IPS transmissions. This material may be moving horizontally between national agencies hooked into the IPS network, but it is cast in the communiqué style of reporting. Its predictability and superficiality exceed anything the Big Four offer, illustrating once again the error of confusing communications links with the information that moves through them.

IPS sees itself as a cog in a new world news system. It has won friends in the developing nations and international organizations as a communications vehicle whose reporting is generally sympathetic. The cooperative's journalists are genuinely eager to evolve new ways of reporting the developing countries to one another; the problem is that the service's outlets for its own news are highly restricted. It has not found the necessary pool of newspapers and broadcasters eager to replace the Big Four with a service using the IPS approach, so it has been forced to depend on its special-transmission business for national agencies and the United Nations for much of its revenue, and this has not been sufficient to enable it to develop a full and independent alternative to the Big Four even within the developing nations.

Restrictions of one kind or other are a staple of the news agencies' world. They hamper the alternatives to the Big Four just as much as they affect Reuters, the AP, UPI, and AFP. Money is the biggest single limiting force in almost all cases. But the potential alternative services also suffer from other restrictions, whether in the form of political direction, lack of commitment from owners, or the simple (and sensible) recognition that the appetite of the world's media for foreign news is limited. The CANA experience shows what can be done on a regional basis, given the right combination of circumstances. But to expect any alternative to the Big Four to emerge on a worldwide basis is an illusion that can be sustained only by the belief that change must always upset the status quo. As it is, the Big Four have quite enough problems maintaining the operations they have built up since World War II. As if in recognition of the huge difficulty of establishing an international agency operating on different lines for a predominantly different audience, recent initiatives in Africa, Asia, and Latin America have taken the form of news-exchange agreements, which differ fundamentally from the classic news agency pattern. It is now time to look at these initiatives and how they meet the need, often expressed by Third World countries, for a new world information order to promote development and international understanding.

CHAPTER 12 ....

News Exchanges

Exchanging information on a noncommercial basis is an easier process than producing news and trying to sell it. Geographical proximity, shared interests, and the growth of regional economic and political organizations have encouraged national agencies to swap their news for information from similar agencies in adjoining countries for many years. Implementation of the concept on a multilateral basis dates back to just before World War II, when agencies in six smaller European countries formed an exchange association known (after the foundation year) as "the group of '39." In the postwar period, this group expanded to take in other national agencies from Eastern and Western Europe. Members meet regularly to exchange technical information and to cooperate on sports news and photographs, but their association has had little impact on their individual relationships with the Big Four.

In Scandinavia, the four Nordic agencies have gone much further in exchanging news and in appointing joint correspondents abroad.[1] They share an international communications circuit to carry news services into and around Scandinavia, set up in cooperation with Reuters in 1960 and known as Scanplex. Their joint foreign coverage began in 1962 when a Danish journalist went to Brussels to cover the Common Market for the four Scandinavian agencies. Later, a Swede was posted to Moscow, a Norwegian to the United States, and—in the mid-1970s—a Finn to Peking. The four Scandinavian agencies also send correspondents abroad on short-term assignments fifteen or twenty times a year, sharing the cost. There are, of course, linguistic problems; "after all, we have to translate copy written in Norwegian just as much as English material from Reuters," a Swedish agency editor noted. But the system between the Nordic four has been a success and would be expanded were it not for financial considerations.

The managing directors and foreign editors of the Nordic agencies meet regularly to coordinate their dealings with the major world agencies and to keep one another informed of changes in subscription rates. In 1985, they planned to upgrade their communications links by switching from the 25-year-old Scanplex system to a new circuit developed by Reuters, Nornet. Given the desire of each agency to retain its independence of action, the Nordic effort is a rare example of how far cooperation can go. But it has not produced any upsurge in coverage of Scandinavia, let alone an increase in shared regional consciousness.

Most recent associations of news agencies have occurred in the developing nations, where political influences have played varying roles, sometimes spurring cooperation, sometimes provoking disruption. Collaborative projects, offering the prospect of building up the flow of news of specific regional interest at minimal cost, generally take the form of news pools to which participants contribute selected items from their domestic files.[2] Editorial decisions lie with the originators; there is little or no feedback from recipients. Thus a country's agency determines what news from its country will go to other members of the pool. When the contributing agency is under government influence, the report fed into the pool reflects the officially approved picture of the country. Even when a country's contributing agency is politically independent, the pool's material is restricted to items selected by that agency. There is no plurality in reporting. Such services increase the volume of information available to recipients, but pool systems give contributing agencies a monopoly power not enjoyed by competitive news sources.

Africa . . . .

Despite this advantage to governments and others interested in propagating controlled news reports, the establishment of news pools can be a lengthy and tortuous affair, as the history of the attempt to found a cooperative news system for black Africa demonstrates. The idea of a Pan African News Agency (PANA) dates back to the independence period of the late 1950s and early 1960s.[3] The Ghana News Agency (GNA), set up in 1957 with advice from Reuters, was seen as a possible foundation-stone for a wider organization. GNA's declared objective was "to serve as a means of minimizing . . . Ghana's dependence on the foreign news media for information and thus [to] be able to serve fully the needs of Ghana, unfettered by foreign interests or influences.'' Encouraged by the Pan Africanism of Ghana's first president, Kwame Nkrumah, and the idea of forming an African news agency, GNA established offices in 1961 in Lagos, Abidjan, Cairo, London, New York, Dar es Salaam, and Ouagadougou. At the same time, a Ghanaian took over as head of the agency from the previous British general manager, who had come from Reuters.

The idea of an African news agency moved ahead in the mid-1960s when the Organization of African Unity (OAU) adopted statutes for the projected service and called together experts to examine the technical and financial problems involved. Both kinds of problems proved formidable. The Union of African News Agencies insisted on the importance of ''liberating Africa, which was still in the hands of the foreign news agencies,'' but such declarations did nothing to resolve practical matters. Politicians expressed the desire to break the power of the Big Four, although Reuters was among the sources that had provided an early blueprint for a Pan African agency with an independent, highly trained staff and guaranteed income. Like other schemes of the time, this proposal got nowhere.

Progress was, in any case, gravely hampered by the absence of a continental telecommunications system. Colonial routings dominated African communications. A message sent by cable from Togo to neighboring Ghana had to go through Dakar, Paris, and London before reaching Accra; telegraph communications from Kinshasa to Brazzaville, across the Congo River, went through Belgium and France.

Finances were another problem. It was estimated in the late 1960s that a Pan African agency could be set up for £10 million, but no such funds could be found. The African agencies, numbering about twenty by the mid-1960s, needed all the money they could get to develop on a national level; they had nothing to spare for the still-nebulous continental project. Governments also proved unforthcoming, as political differences intruded on the Pan African ideal. Deliberations by experts convened by the OAU ended in 1965 with a classic nonresult: the establishment of a subcommittee for continuing study.

The choice of headquarters for the projected PANA symbolized the differences between the potential partners. Anglophones and Francophones argued for East and West Africa respectively. Ethiopia pressed its claims for Addis Ababa, where the OAU headquarters were located, while Idi Amin of Uganda announced that Kampala would be the best site for the new agency's base. Eventually, Dakar was selected because of its communications links and Senegal's political status.

Since central direction by an independent editorial management was unacceptable to the governments involved, a contributory pool system was the only way PANA could operate. Although politically expedient, this format raised fresh practical problems. As one news executive closely involved in developing national agencies in Africa observed at the end of the 1970s:

> There are around forty African nations with agencies or news services. If each ran 10,000 words a day, this would produce 400,000 words of input. Cut it by a factor of ten and you still get 40,000 words a day. Nobody can deal with that much copy. But if you have selection somewhere, that imposes difficult decisions on local journalists on political grounds. God help the editor who makes a head of state ask: why the hell am I paying for this agency?

By the late 1970s, there had been some advances in telecommunications, but a huge technical gap still existed. The Pan African project was refined into a series of regional pools all around the continent. Each would provide an exchange of news within its region. All would be linked to a central headquarters that would act as a coordinator and a channel for the exchange of relevant items between the different regions. Meeting in Addis Ababa, African information ministers decided on an initial budget of £850,000. Member agencies were to subscribe according to population and their "ability to pay," with UNESCO contributing £250,000.

The chairman of the information ministers' conference, Major Girman Yilma of Ethiopia, kept the ideological flame alive. He told the Addis Ababa meeting that the all-African agency "must be an organization that exposes imperialist and colonialist conspiracies in Africa and should be an organization that draws Africans into the struggle against imperialism and colonialism." Other delegates were more down-to-earth, pointing to the difficulties caused by ideological and national divergences between participant states. The agency, they said, risked becoming a clearinghouse for propaganda; what kind of impartiality, for instance, could have been expected in coverage by either Ethiopia or Somalia of fighting between the two nations? The only safeguard against this possibility would be the creation of an independent journalistic group to report and edit the news in an impartial manner. But this was not at all what the proponents of PANA had in mind; nor, it appears, was it a goal that UNESCO felt any inclination to support. Thus, as planning for PANA went forward, each member agency was left to produce its own report of its national affairs. State sovereignty reigned supreme, reducing news exchange to a mechanistic, one-way process without much regard for the recipients.

In June 1980, PANA's Inter-Governmental Council announced that the planned launching of the agency at an OAU summit the following month had been postponed in order to build a more solid technical foundation. Too much haste would compromise the agency's future; further studies were needed to develop telecommunications between the different regional pools. A year later, a launch date was finally set: PANA was to start operations in late 1982, issuing 25,000 words a day each in English, French, and Arabic. Member states would contribute 20,000 words. The rest would come from inter-African and international bodies engaged in development activities.

The Conference of African Ministers of Information was confirmed as the agency's governing body; it would meet every two years to set general policy, programs, and budgets. An Inter-Governmental Council, made up of fourteen elected members plus representatives of the OAU and of the host countries of PANA's headquarters and regional offices, would act as the agency's guiding body between ministerial meetings.

PANA's initial annual budget was put at $2.5 million, with another $939,525 needed for capital investments in Senegal and the five regional centers in Lagos, Lusaka, Kinshasa, Khartoum, and Tripoli. The money was to come from contributions from member states and from outside bodies. The new agency submitted a request for $1.5 million to UNESCO's International Programme for the Development of Communication (IPDC) but received only $100,000 at IPDC's first project support session in January 1982, followed by a pledge for an additional $125,000 at the end of 1982. In May 1983, UNESCO reported that it had contributed $910,000 to PANA during the previous six months to buy equipment. As well as helping the news-exchange system, UNESCO drew up programs to help national news agencies in seven West and Central African countries. UNESCO's efforts were boosted by grants of $2.5 million and $2 million from, respectively, the West German government and Arab Gulf countries. The new agency's annual communications bill was put at $500,000 in 1984, not including staff costs or other associated expenses. The regional poll centers filed material into Dakar by telex. The outgoing PANA service was sent from Senegal by radio. The inward and outward communications costs each amounted to about $180,000 a year. A report by the director of the London-based International Press Telecommunications Council, Oliver Robinson, in June 1984, underlined the need to reduce the telex costs. Robinson also noted that the radio transmission charge made by the Senegal telecommunications authority, Telesenegal, seemed "somewhat excessive" compared to fees in some other poll countries such as Zambia and Nigeria.

PANA is based on the principle that news should be used for definite ends. The new agency says it exists "to promote the aims and objectives of the OAU for the consolidation of the independence, unity and solidarity of Africa." It is to "assist the liberation struggles of African peoples against colonialism, imperialism, apartheid, racism, Zionism and all other forms of exploitation and oppression," and to work for the integration of African countries and the correction of "the distorted picture of Africa and . . . its countries and peoples resulting from partial and negative information published by foreign press agencies." [4]

The Far East . . . .

Japan proposed the establishment of a Far Eastern news agency as long ago as 1960, at a meeting arranged by UNESCO in Bangkok. The regional reaction, confirmed at a second meeting a year later, was that it was too soon to envisage an enterprise that risked duplicating the efforts of the major world agencies. In the mid-1960s, however, the idea of forming a news organization to link developing nations in Asia began to gain proponents. The head of the United News of India agency, Kudlip Nayar, complained to a meeting of the Press Institute of India in 1964 that

> what the news agencies generally pick up and disseminate in Asia and elsewhere is a story of some riot or of hungry and famished Asians. These are correct stories. But there are so many other things happening. . . . Seldom do Western news agencies report the progress we have made toward development. . . .

Progress toward establishing a system of news exchange in the Far East and Central Asia was almost certainly slowed down by the attention the major agencies paid to regional interests, which made the need for an alternative less pressing. There was also a dichotomy, affecting both requirements and outlook, between the majority of Far Eastern national agencies and the Japanese media. As a result, Japan was not the motivating force that its wealth and experience might otherwise have made it. There had long been speculation that Japan's Kyodo agency might develop into the main news distributor for the Far East; by 1980 its budget had reached $110 million, more than that of either Agence France-Presse or United Press International.

With forty-four correspondents in thirty countries outside Japan, Kyodo had the potential nucleus of coverage for an international service. But its impact remained limited. It distributed a worldwide service in English for three hours a day and a fuller, sixteen-hour-a-day service to Asia. The number of recipients remained small, however, and most media subscribers were national news agencies, often as part of reciprocal arrangements to exchange services. In 1983, Kyodo began to insert a daily average of sixty primarily economic stories into the Dow Jones retrieval service in North America. Kyodo termed this its "full-fledged entry into the field of new transmission overseas." It remained a modest entry for the main agency of such a major economic power as Japan, but there was no indication that Kyodo's world role would grow significantly in the near future.

In the early 1970s, a group of journalists set out to establish an Asian news service in order to report the continent from an Asian viewpoint. But the effort was short-lived; financial problems and a lack of subscribers brought the venture to an end after eighteen months. Further developments in Asia took place within the context of exchanges between national agencies, first bilateral and then paralleling the wider political links of the Association of South East Asian Nations (ASEAN).

In 1979, the national agencies of Indonesia, Malaysia, the Philippines, and Thailand agreed to establish a system of news-agency links. In the same year, delegates at a meeting organized by UNESCO in Kuala Lumpur decided that setting up news exchanges within the Asian region was a priority project. There followed a meeting in New Delhi, attended by representatives of all agencies in the Asia-Pacific region (including the Soviet Union), at which Asian agencies were urged to increase their ties, either by using existing communications lines or by establishing redistribution centers from which copy received from Asian agencies could be disseminated. It was suggested that the Organization of Asian News Agencies (OANA), a body representing agencies from non-Communist Asian nations, should act as coordinator and, as such, should widen its membership to include all agencies in the region, including Australia and New Zealand. As in Africa, the essential precondition to such an exchange agreement was that there should be no supranational supervision or control. Once again, the sovereignty of nations and their news agencies was reinforced as the price of agreement.

Latin America[5] . . . .

In Latin America, with Latin fading as a regional force, the role of governments in regional news exchanges was acknowledged in an arrangement established by a dozen countries, including some in the Caribbean, in 1979. The avowed aims of the National Information Systems Network—ASIN, after its Spanish acronym—were to enable members to exchange information, to help toward the decolonization of news, and to dispel distortions detected in coverage from the major news agencies. The new agency enjoyed the backing of a West German grant-making body, the Friedrich Ebert Foundation, which planned to finance a German-language edition of the ASIN service for distribution in Europe.

ASIN strongly reflects both the recent call for the creation of new "transmitters" to augment and replace the existing Western-dominated information system and the central role that developing countries accord their governments in achieving a new world information order. Speaking to UNESCO's General Conference in 1980, ASIN President Luis Javier Solana reaffirmed his organization's belief in "the right of governments to inform and be informed directly, and to be more deeply integrated though information . . . The so-called 'mass communication' has been nothing more than a one-way street, especially in the international sphere," he charged, adding, "One cannot speak of communication nor of freedom of information while there is only one transmitter and millions of passive, inert receivers."

The close relationship between ASIN and its members' governments was clearly demonstrated during the election of officers at the organization's 1981 conference in Mexico City. Javier Solana, who was chosen to head the organization, was general secretary of social communication for the Mexican president. The two vice-presidents were the director general of planning for the Venezuelan Information Ministry and the minister of information of Guyana, a country that had been particularly active in bringing the media under official influence to ensure that they worked toward official goals. As a product of the drive for a new information order, and strongly influenced by some of that movement's most convinced ideologues, ASIN is clearly an organization that believes in governmental direction of news. It might be argued that this ideology is a realistic one, since in many developing countries there is no alternative to official financing and direction. "Better to have government involvement than nothing at all," as one UNESCO official working to promote the development of Third World media put it. But experience shows that governments are generally reluctant to relinquish control over the media once they have achieved it. On a more philosophical note, one might wonder how the rights of governments to inform and be informed, as championed by Javier Solana, can be reconciled with the liberation of "millions of passive, inert receivers." The "one transmitter" denounced by the proponents of a new world information order occurs, overwhelmingly, in the shape of governments, not of commercially based media.

Like the Inter Press Service, which acts as its "operating secretariat" and sells ASIN communications facilities, the Latin American/Caribbean system represents an attempt to provide an alternative to the major news services. It aims not only to fill a technical news-exchange gap, but also to supply a flow of information different from that of the traditional news agencies. A study by ASIN of topics covered in 1981 shows economic and political subjects in the majority, reversing the order of predominance of news topics noted earlier for the major world agencies. It also reveals a huge gap between economic-political items and stories on subjects such as culture, science, and education, although not as great a gap as that seen in the files of the major agencies (see table 9).[6]

The Oil-Producing Countries and the Middle East . . . .

The Asian pool and ASIN were joined in the summer of 1979 by a service representing the oil-producing countries, which had decided it was time to spread their view of themselves to the rest of the world. Meeting in Vienna, the Organization of Petroleum Exporting Countries (OPEC) declared:

The Conference, conscious of the efforts undertaken individually and collectively by the Member Countries in cooperating with other developing countries, and of the need to inform other countries of the

Table 9	Types of Stories Appearing in ASIN Service in 1981

	Percentage of ASIN Files
News Category	
National economy	28
International economy	19
International policy	19
National policy	15
Culture and communications	7
Education	6
Science and technology	4
Other	2
Total	100

world of the true scope and magnitude of such efforts, as well as of other news of general interest regarding the Organization and the Member Countries and in order to counteract the manipulation of information by some of OPEC's detractors, has given general support to the idea of establishing an international news agency—OPEC News.

The agency was to voice OPEC's point of view on all problems relating to oil, the world economy, and the Third World. OPEC's public relations director, Hamid Zaheri, forecast that it could become "the first major independent news agency designed to serve the developing countries." Asked by a Reuter correspondent at OPEC's Vienna headquarters to comment on regional news agencies and the news pool of the nonaligned nations, Zaheri responded:

There have been several lonely attempts to do something in this regard. But when have you ever seen a news pool correspondent here? It's time we put our efforts together to build one strong, efficient news agency on a noncommercial basis.

So far, however, the OPEC initiative has shown no sign of growing into anything more than a channel for news put out by a special-interest group to a limited number of recipients.

Many of OPEC's members were also involved in the bumpy history of regional agency cooperation among Arab states. Politics were never far below the surface. In February 1979, delegates at a meeting of the Union of Arab News Agencies called for a balanced and objective flow of news that presented the facts about Arab nations without distortion. At the same meeting, the Middle East News Agency of Egypt and the SUNA agency of Sudan, which was considered close to Egypt, were suspended. The official reason for the move against MENA was a failure to pay subscriptions, but a more realistic reason for the isolation of the Egyptian agency lay in Arab ostracism of Egypt following the Camp David agreement with Israel.

MENA has long been the leading Arab agency, involved in training and cooperative agreements with a large number of other regional services, supplying its own news file, and translating the Arabic services of AFP and Deutsche Presse Agentur. The repercussions of Camp David were thus significant and not confined to the Arab world. Attempts to foster links between Arab and European news agencies, begun at meetings in 1976 and 1977, were disrupted. MENA's presence at a subsequent conference in Vienna, attended by twenty-four European agencies, produced a boycott by the sixteen other Arab services. The meeting lasted fifteen minutes.

The Middle East was, naturally, on the agenda at a conference of Islamic mass media organizations held in Djakarta in September 1980. Opening the meeting, President Suharto of Indonesia set the tone for the subsequent discussions by complaining about a flood of news and world opinion "tinted by the interests of the advanced countries." The secretary-general of the Islamic Conference, Habib Chatti, followed with the statement that "only" 30 percent of world news emanated from Moslem countries. "Apart from this highly reduced information, in terms of quantity, produced by the giant foreign agencies, one must also insist on the partisan if not hostile and wholly mendacious character of information involving the Islamic world," he told the meeting. The source of the problem, Chatti concluded, lay in "the large bias of a world press mostly controlled by Zionist lobbies, whether in the United States or elsewhere." [7] The conference expressed its support for a new order in world information but—like the majority of meetings on the subject—left the means for achieving this vague.

The Nonaligned News Pool[8] . . . .

For many of the developing nations, the most promising step toward a new system of exchanging world news appeared to be the establishment of a news pool embracing the national agencies of all of the nonaligned countries. As a result of a series of governmental meetings and of initiatives taken by the Yugoslav agency, Tanjug, such a pool came into existence in the mid-1970s. After nearly a decade of operations, however, its role remains limited, particularly in view of the hopes it once aroused.

Tanjug had been convinced for some time that the nonaligned movement needed its own news organization to help bind it together and to enable its members to exchange information independently of either Western or Eastern news channels. According to Tanjug's director at the time, Pero Ivacic, the agency was getting requests regularly in the early 1970s from the Yugoslav media for Third World news—requests that it was unable to satisfy using its existing sources (mainly the Western-based agencies). "There was a lack of information from countries which were in the process of development and were nonaligned," Ivacic recalled. "In particular, there was no flow of information among the nonaligned nations. We depended entirely on multinationals based in a few developed countries."

Nonaligned leaders meeting in Algiers in 1973 approved a resolution calling for an exchange of information about their achievements, a move that, as Ivacic later said, "gave us something on which to base our initiative." Consultations followed among the heads of national agencies in a dozen nonaligned nations: Yugoslavia, Algeria, Tunisia, Iraq, Egypt, Sri Lanka, Indonesia, Cuba, Mexico, Ghana, Zambia, and Mali. By 1974, the way was clear for a preparatory pool arrangement to begin operation. Instead of inviting the participation of the nonaligned movement as a whole, Tanjug and the other agencies involved decided to proceed on their own. "Eleven of us came to the conclusion that we should not hold a conference of all the nonaligned countries, as some people had proposed, because we knew it was very difficult to come to a concrete conclusion at a conference," Ivacic recalled. "Instead, [we] decided to begin to exchange information among ourselves."

A limit of 500 words per agency per day was set, with each participating agency sending what it considered its most important news items to Tanjug in English, French, or Spanish. The Yugoslav agency translated this material into the other two languages and transmitted it internationally, using its own communications and crediting such items to the pool. In all, pool material accounted for about two hours a day of Tanjug's seven-hour English-language service.

With this arrangement in operation, the eleven partners invited news agencies in other nonaligned nations to join them. Nonaligned foreign ministers, meeting in Lima in 1975, noted the launching of the pool with satisfaction, and a conference of information ministers was arranged for New Delhi the following year to draw up formal statutes for the new organization.

The news pool that emerged full-blown from the Delhi meeting is highly decentralized. As described by a former chairman of its co-ordinating committee, D. R. Mankekar, it "has no central head-quarters or general manager or board of directors, or even a financial budget and staff." The Coordination Committee, whose chairman is replaced every three years, provides what top-level management structure there is. This lack of central authority has two important implications. On the one hand, as viewed by those involved in the arrangement, it respects the separate identity of each participant by avoiding the imposition of "vertical" authority. At the same time, the looseness of the arrangement means that no national agency, information ministry, or government need surrender any of its sovereignty.

Governmental considerations pervade the news-distribution system evolved by Tanjug and its partners. The pool owes its formal creation in 1976 to a meeting not of news-agency heads but of information ministers, whose decisions in Delhi were ratified later that year at a nonaligned summit in Colombo, Sri Lanka. Many of the pool's members are directly influenced by their governments. The organization's statutes require that members select the items they transmit "on the basis of mutual respect and common interests." This edict can be taken as a warning against issuing propaganda aimed at other pool participants, but it also represents a call for discretion tantamount to self-censorship. Since the pool's philosophy decries supranationalism and sees news in essentially national terms, the whole arrangement has been subject to political influences arising from the relations among states and having little or nothing to do with news.

The Camp David agreements were a case in point. Shortly after the conclusion of these accords, Syria and the Federation of Arab News Agencies spearheaded an attempt to expel the Egyptian agency MENA from the pool, just as it had been suspended from the Union of Arab News Agencies. This proved impossible, since Egypt remained a member of the nonaligned movement, and the news agencies of all member states were eligible to participate in the pool. But delegates to a pool conference in Belgrade, Yugoslavia, in November 1979 still managed to penalize the Egyptian agency. As one of the most highly developed national agencies in the Third World, with its own foreign distribution to other Arab countries, MENA had been an automatic member of the pool's Coordination Committee. At the

Belgrade meeting, representatives of most Arab states insisted that MENA be dropped from the committee. In addition to its role at Camp David, MENA had taken part in discussions aimed at the establishment of a new form of agency for the Third World. At issue was a proposal by a former UPI editor in chief, Roger Tatarian, now a journalism professor, for a new agency to be set up to cover the developing world with Western help. Merely to have participated in a meeting at which the Tatarian proposal was considered was viewed by the more militant members of the pool to be tantamount to selling out to the West. MENA, referred to in official conference records simply as "Egypt," was duly thrown off the Coordination Committee. "It was politics that counted, not professional questions," MENA's chairman, Mohamed Gawad, commented. The pool was confirmed as an instrument of states, an organization in which the interests of government would always predominate.

The financial arrangements according to which the transmitters of information in the nonaligned news pool pay the bills reinforce this characteristic. In the commercial system, the readiness of recipients to pay for news is a guide, however imperfect, to whether they really want what they are getting. In the pool, there is no such element of choice. Recipients get what suppliers decide to send them.

"We are not competitive with the big systems, but they are not competitive with us either," Ivacic, who became chairman of the Coordination Committee in 1979, commented. Even "if they improve the quality and quantity of their information from the nonaligned world, they will still not be capable of understanding all the processes as national sources can." This is an idea put forward repeatedly by advocates of a new world information order: that Indians can best report on India for the rest of the world, Africans on Africa, and so on. It is no doubt true that nationals of a country will know more about that country than foreigners arriving as correspondents for one of the Big Four. But it does not necessarily follow that nationals are therefore better interpreters of national events for the rest of the world. Apart from the question of whether a citizen can be objective about national events about which he or she may have strong personal feelings, the influence of governments on Third World coverage ensures that the picture of a nation disseminated abroad through the nonaligned pool is the official one. To take an extreme example, should the world have depended on officially controlled reporting of Uganda by Ugandans during the Idi Amin regime, or did coverage by the Big Four, incomplete as it was, give a more accurate picture of what was happening? Is the best reporting of the Soviet Union necessarily that of TASS, or the best coverage of the United States that of the AP and UPI?

The pool fosters "the idea of giving . . . national sources [a chance] to be present in other countries, not only to fulfill the right to be informed, but also to use the right to send information about yourself to others," Ivacic comments. "You have to give an equal right to everybody to send information about themselves to the rest of the world. This is the difference between the pool and the big agencies." Mankekar adds:

> We are concerned with regional news, news of socio-economic progress, of cultures, economic, agricultural and industrial development; news about social change and about measures taken and successes achieved, or not achieved, by our countries in their efforts to improve the quality of life of the common people, and the abolition of illiteracy, poverty and unemployment; and of developing countries' continuing struggle against colonialism, neocolonialism, racism and economic exploitation. This is the kind of news the Western news agencies we subscribe for do not care to supply us.[9]

These lofty aims need to be assessed in the light of the material the nonaligned news pool issues. An examination of pool contents by Edward Pinch of the U.S. State Department in 1977 revealed that 47 percent of pool items concerned Third World development, while another 17 percent reported on the Middle East, 6 percent on the nonaligned movement, and 5 percent on Southern Africa. A study carried out for the present book on pool material transmitted in Spanish, French, and English in 1980 and 1981 showed that stories on politics and economics were predominant, as they are in other agency services. The two surveys also yielded data on the number of contributors to pool files. A six-day sample of the pool's Spanish service to Latin America in 1980 included stories from twenty-four contributors, while in a three-day sample of the English, French, and Spanish services, taken in 1981, thirty different national agencies were represented. Most contributed only one or two items in each sample, as can be seen from table 10.

A survey of pool material distributed in English, French, and Spanish by Tanjug, during three days in June 1981, confirmed the predominance of political and economic news and of stories from Latin America, Africa, and the Middle East, the great majority of them

Table 10	Results of Two Surveys of Nonaligned News Pool Material, 1980 and 1981	
	Number of Items Contributed	
	1980 (Six Days; Spanish Only)	1981 (Three Days; English, French, and Spanish)
Agencies Contributing		
1 item	12	11
2 items	5	7
3–5 items	5	11
6–10 items	1	0
10+ items	1	1
Regional Sources		
African agencies	7	10
Latin American agencies	4	7
Middle East agencies	3	5
Central Asian agencies	6	4
Far Eastern agencies	1	1
European agencies	2	1
United Nations	1	2

reporting government statements or the activities of ministers and officials (see table 11).[10]

It often happens that one major event accounts for a relatively large proportion of items in the pool service at any given time. For the period reflected in table 11, reactions to Israel's raid on an Iraqi nuclear power plant contributed to the high percentage figures for international relations and stories from the Middle East. Had this particular event not occurred, it is probable that some other single international event would have been a major source of copy. An examination of the pool service distributed in Latin America in May 1980, at the time of President Tito's funeral, revealed a similar predominance of politics and economics, and again there was a marked inclination toward the elite of the nonaligned world. A remarkable 70 percent of pool stories sent to Latin America, for instance, dealt with rulers, officials, governments, and others in authority.

Opinions on the nonaligned news service from participants generally stress the pool's function as a counterbalance to the Big Four. "We believe that this experiment is an effective formula for making

Table 11	Type and Origin of Stories Appearing in Nonaligned News Pool Files During Three Days in 1981	Percentage of Pool Files
Classification		
International relations		59
Economics		15
Domestic politics		11
International violence		6
Social		4
Miscellaneous		4
Art/Culture		1
Total		100
Origin of Stories		
Middle East		21
Latin America		19
Africa		18
Eastern Europe		14
Central Asia		11
International organizations		6
Western Europe		5
Far East		5
North America		1
Total		100

the developing nations aware of the realities existing in each country," an executive of NOTIMEX of Mexico commented. "It is at the same time a means of catalyzing information which has been manipulated and put out after the stamp and style of the big information systems." The amount of use actually made of pool material, however, remains highly uncertain. Under the financial system adopted by the pool, the supplier pays the bills; there are no subscriptions and no attempts to raise revenue. Pool information is not treated as a marketable commodity; if it were, it is doubtful it could command much of a price. The governments and news executives who set up the pool want to move away from the marketplace philosophy of the Big Four. Their aim is a different one: to give voices to those nations they believe are excluded from the world news system. The emphasis is on providing a channel through which members can send messages free of outside influence. The physical existence of the channel is the paramount concern; what is sent through it is of less importance, as is shown by the gulf that exists between the actual content of the pool service and some of the claims made for it by its chairmen.

Pool participants were reticent about expressing their opinions when approached for this book. Among the few agencies that did express a view, the Tanzanian news agency judged the pool service "at an infant stage, but vital to bringing a new international information order." The Associated Press of Pakistan found it "fairly satisfactory." The Petra agency in Jordan hoped the pool would become "more specific, more organized." Mohamed Gawad, still smarting over the treatment of MENA, said: "If we want it to be a news agency, let us work at that. But getting records of events twenty-four hours behind the news—history, rather than news—is something . . . we don't need." In 1977 (in the early days of the pool), a survey of media editors in Sri Lanka and Bangladesh revealed widespread distrust of the arrangement because so much pool material originated from government sources.

A particularly interesting view of the service was provided in 1978 in an "impact report" prepared by the pool's India desk in New Delhi. Much of the news provided by pool contributors, according to this report, was of a local political nature, and much was outdated by the time it was received, although stories reflecting the nonaligned countries' activities at the United Nations were timely and useful. It was in the area of economic news that the Indian press made the best use of pool material, since economic news was "generally ignored by foreign wire services, [which] mainly concentrate on political developments," the report said.

Outside the nonaligned countries, the Kyodo agency of Japan received the pool's service, but, according to the director of the Japanese agency's international department in 1981, did not actually use it because of poor reception or the slow nature of the service. The Swedish agency, Tete, formerly subscribed to the pool on a trial basis; its managing director, Sven Gerentz, recalled, "We simply did not find it good enough, but we are willing to try again." A spokesman for the Polish agency, PAP, commented: "We use it on a very limited scale because it pays too much attention to propaganda."

Both the strengths and weaknesses of the nonaligned news pool are products of its character as a loose grouping of national agencies. Participation is uneven. A small number of partners dominate in terms of the amount of material they supply, the communications facilities they contribute, and the training services they perform. Executives

236

of such agencies recognize the need for improvement, but progress in any area other than the technical sphere is limited by the tenets under which the pool was established.

Although any other form of news cooperative would have been unworkable, the result of the existing arrangement has been to restrict the pool to a diet of official and often largely protocol news that has little bearing on the aim of fostering international understanding. Despite the thousands of words transmitted daily and the many high-flown declarations of intent, the pool's contribution to the goal of establishing fresh news channels that adequately report the developing world and inform its peoples in ways different from the major services is questionable. The nonaligned news pool does not offer an alternative that is tailored to specific Third World requirements. Indeed, the pool's character and content, like those of most other alternate services, serve only to perpetuate the need for the Big Four.

CHAPTER **13** ....

Present and Future

The raison d'être for the international news agencies is simple: to collect and distribute news of interest to as many subscribers as possible, in the form most digestible to the greatest number of recipients willing to pay the cost. A news agency is a service organization; it has no reason to exist except for its users. Its general-news role is a wholesale one, and the yardstick of its success or failure should be the use made of its news by recipients, quantified by the sums they are willing to pay for subscriptions. This simple view of news agencies was perceived clearly by the founders of the main European services. No doubt it was also evident to the commercially acute newspaper bosses in New York who founded the Associated Press, even if the equation was expressed in terms of members sharing costs rather than clients paying subscriptions. At United Press, E. W. Scripps was never a man to overlook the importance of commercial profit.

In the present century, however, the basic rationale for the agencies has become obscured by a patina of other roles and responsibilities. At the same time, the major services have allowed the international costs of their operations and their revenues from the media to get out of balance. In short, the Big Four have ceased to be straightforward commercial organizations. Between the two world wars, they developed aspirations that went beyond simply supplying news. Reuters prided itself on the intimate link Sir Roderick Jones envisioned between its activities and Britain's world role, and the AP's belated entry into foreign news distribution was expressed in terms of a crusade. More recently, Agence France-Presse hears itself being described as the voice of France by the politicians who ensure its survival as a world agency.

The size and international nature of the major services, and their claim to provide news files that rise above partisan divisions, have led to their being regarded as something akin to informational nursemaids, responsible for the well-being of mankind in general and its least-favored peoples in particular. Since information is a politically charged subject, the agencies are automatically cast as participants in the political and economic relationships between rich and poor nations. They are assumed to have responsibilities that not only are far beyond their basic function but are incompatible with their fragile commercial position as well.

To a degree, the agencies have accepted these assumptions as forming the context within which discussions of their activities should be conducted. As a result, there has developed an image of the Big Four that bears little relation to the realities of their existence and operations. The agencies' lack of resources, their operational restraints, their vulnerability to harassment and pressure, and their lack of direct access to the public are ignored by those who see them as giant enterprises doing less than they could or should for the developing nations. And the agencies themselves have been unwilling to face the impossibility of producing, from a newsworthy event, a single report acceptable both to those who accept and to those who reject the commercial press model. When their services are found unacceptable, the agencies tend to blame arbitrary political factors. "What we have to offer is so much better than anything else available," AP president Keith Fuller declared in 1981.[1] This may be true, particularly when the situation is assessed through American eyes. But it does not mean that the major agencies' way of reporting the world is the only possible one.

The confidence of the Big Four in the correctness of their editorial approach and the absence of true alternatives have fostered the by-now familiar image of monopolists exercising a stranglehold on the circulation of world news. Because they have been so successful at providing a prolific and dependable flow of news with limited funds and staff, the major agencies have made the need for other services much less pressing. At the same time, most of the news arrangements that have evolved in the developing world have failed as satisfactory alternatives to Reuters, the AP, UPI, and AFP. In the absence of such alternatives, the Big Four have been left, de facto, in a monopoly position, and are likely to remain there. When the Pan African News Agency (PANA) hits its stride, for example, Reuters and AFP will still be indispensable sources of world news for the African continent. Normally, a service organization depends on its ability to attract clients. In the case of Reuters and AFP in Africa, or the U.S. agencies in Latin America, the dependence is the other way around: the agencies could continue to function without any subscribers at all in, say, East Africa, but the national media of Kenya, Tanzania, or Zambia would be severely handicapped without the agencies.

Criticism of the Big Four for concentrating too intently on the industrialized world, in both reporting and distribution, suggests ignorance or willful misconception on the part of the accusers. What is surprising, in view of the financial conditions under which the agencies operate, is that the bias toward the developed world has not been even greater, and that the agencies continue to produce services for areas that offer little or no prospect of substantial revenue. If the agencies were to follow strict commercial logic and cease to pursue unprofitable international operations, they would be spared a lot of trouble, since they would close down the services that are currently attracting criticism.

The Big Four have refrained from taking this step because they believe they have a role as providers of information to the whole world and, as such, should make their services available everywhere. Reuters felt obliged to go back to Latin America in the 1970s, and to stay there after Latin failed, despite an extremely unpromising competitive situation. AFP felt called upon to break into East Africa at the same time, although Reuters dominated the market. Despite its lack of progress over the years, the AP is still trying to establish itself in black Africa. Since the agencies' primary source of both news and clients is the developed world, it is inevitable that they devote most of their resources to reporting those areas and to producing services for them. At the same time, however, they are trying to provide subscribers everywhere in the world with a full service of international news. Playing a world role not only opens up the agencies to accusations of monopoly, it can also fly in the face of commercial logic and commit them to serving areas whose needs can be met only imperfectly.

Each client, of course, sees the service it receives in isolation. It is not concerned with how the agencies apportion their editorial budgets, or whether international services for the media are underwritten by domestic members, business services, private owners, or the state. A subscriber in a poor nation, paying a minimum fee, expects the service it gets to meet its requirements, just as a client in West Germany or Japan, paying a higher rate, does.

Given their restricted resources, the agencies manage to go a considerable way toward satisfying everybody, but there is no doubt that, on the whole, their services meet the needs of the media in the industrialized world more fully than they do those of newspapers and broadcasters in the developing countries. This is the result of many factors mentioned in previous chapters: finances, the editorial approach taken by the agencies, the environment in which they operate, problems of access and communications, and the absence of any clearly defined alternate news requirement from the media. The outcome is a mutually unsatisfactory situation. The agencies are committed to a job for which they have inadequate resources, and subscribers in the poorer nations must depend on services that, while preferable to any existing alternatives, do not entirely answer their specific needs.

The wave of criticism of the world's information system that crested in the 1970s came at an awkward moment for the Big Four, since financial pressures were pushing them toward retrenchment. After shrugging off the initial attacks, their general reaction was to stress the help they had given to national agencies in developing countries in the form of editorial training and technical advice. This had been appreciable in some cases, but the response fell on deaf ears—or worse, was seen as proof that the Western-based services had sought to insinuate their editorial philosophies into the Third World. The major agencies expressed their willingness to give whatever further professional help they could, but it was clear that the practical extent of this offer would be limited. When an agency manager said his organization could help to train two or three Third World journalists, the offer was hardly likely to offset the wide-ranging accusations of monopoly and manipulation that reverberated throughout conferences on international communications.

The agencies felt, quite genuinely, that they were doing all they could for the Third World. Indeed, in occasional moments of exasperation they complained that they were doing too much, and that their efforts were being unfairly and ungratefully pilloried. "Nobody could give a damn about [a report of] a new hospital opening in Lusaka," a top UPI executive observed in 1980. "We subsidize those countries in any case because we don't take any money out of them." At the same time, UPI's foreign editor reflected gloomily on the editorial interests of his major group of clients. Taking the U.S. embassy siege in Teheran as an example, he asked:

If Americans had not been involved, how much would the American media have cared? Experience suggests the answer is, not very much. Readers are captive to editors' perceptions of the world and these

perceptions seem too often bound up in mostly outdated stereotypes—
Englishmen wear bowler hats and speak la-di-da; Mexicans wear som-
breros and snooze under cactus bushes. . . . If no Americans are concerned, who cares what happens to these people?

With many editors in the United States subscribing to this view,
it is easy to understand why the American agencies tended to believe
they were already doing as much as they could in reporting the
developing nations. And Reuters and AFP, with their larger staffs in
the Third World, felt the same way. They were certainly under no
pressure from subscribers in their main markets to increase coverage
of Africa, Asia, or Latin America, except when events in one of
those regions directly concerned the industrialized world. The AP
and UPI, for instance, stepped up their reporting of Southern Africa
in the mid-1970s not because they had suddenly decided the area was
of interest per se but because the U.S. administration had become
involved in the diplomacy of the region and Cuban troops were
fighting in Angola. The main motive for Reuters' setting up a two-
person reporting bureau on the Ivory Coast in 1979–80 was that its
profit-making economic services needed more commodity news from
the area.

The financial situation in which the Big Four found themselves in
the mid- to late-1970s precluded augmenting their reporting of the
developing world for the developing world. Even in the more lucrative
markets, the overall pattern was one of careful cost control. Reuters,
with its booming profits from business services, began to open a
string of new bureaus in the early 1980s, mainly with the needs of
its rich clients in mind. On the other hand, UPI closed down its
European-language services, and the AP got out of independent distribution in Italy as manning international reporting offices became
increasingly expensive. The AP and UPI both cut their editorial staffs
in Europe. Estimating that its Prague office would cost £40,000 a
year, Reuters decided to shut its doors there in 1980. In the preceding
decade, the agency had thought it worth spending the necessary money
to keep a constant watch on Czechoslovakia, with its dissidents,
hooligans who harassed correspondents at official bidding, and civil
servants who claimed foreign agencies would do best to rely on the
state-controlled service for their news. As praiseworthy as this might
have seemed to those who believe the agencies have a responsibility
to monitor the world, nobody was going to back such high esteem
with cash. As an editor for Reuters put it, "There is not £40,000

worth of news in Czechoslovakia.'' That being the case, how much could there be in most of the African countries?

The areas in which the agencies could look forward to increasing revenues were not only outside the developing world; they were outside the international general-news field altogether, most notably with Reuters' business retrieval services. The AP and UPI pressed ahead with distribution by satellite in the United States and the development of new computerized services for the domestic press. AFP took another look at the possibility of going into electronic business services.

The reality of the 1980s is therefore likely to be—at best—a standstill in international agency reporting and distribution for the media. Indeed, if Reuters does not maintain its high business-service profits, if the French government reduces its payment to AFP, or if the AP decides to eliminate some marginal foreign activities that matter little to its members, the result could well be a drop in the volume or quality of their world services. UPI's international presence depends on its ability to avoid financial collapse through restructuring in its domestic market. For all four agencies, news and commerce will continue to go hand in hand internationally. The poor nations, by definition, are not of great commercial potential.

Naturally, this situation is unacceptable to those nations. For at least some of them, the fact that the only news style available (apart from government-run services) is one formulated according to Western standards is equally unacceptable. On the other hand, the extent to which Third World media reject the editorial approach adopted by the major agencies should not be overestimated; some newspaper editors in Asia, for instance, object to the division between Western and non-Western standards, saying that what is really at issue is the difference between a free and a controlled press and that they prefer the free model, wherever it may originate. But it also remains true that not all the world wants to have its reporting couched in concepts designed primarily for the media of the North Atlantic area, however neutral and objective these try to be.

For reasons that have been made plain in this book, it is probably illusory to expect major news agencies to change in any substantial way. They are wedded to a one-track approach to reporting the world. They cannot accept editorial diversity within their services, no matter how many subjects they cover or media markets they serve. By their nature, they must see news in objective terms—as an end in itself; they cannot work for external political or developmental purposes.

If there exists a circle of dependence in the world in which the majority of poor nations is subjugated to the industrialized minority, it is not the job of the major agencies to rectify this situation but only to report it, covering bad news as well as events and statements of a more positive nature. They should not discriminate in the news they report from different areas; nor, according to an examination of their files, do they do so. In their news services, as in their operations as a whole, the agencies reflect the world as they find it, portraying it in terms acceptable to their subscribers. Far from attempting to make the globe a better place, they do not even aspire to change it.

Having cultivated for so long the image of themselves as truly worldwide organizations, the major agencies are experiencing some difficulty in adapting to the more modest role their situation prescribes. In discussions at UNESCO and elsewhere, they do not spell out the limited resources at their disposal, nor do they ordinarily draw attention to the restrictions that have resulted from their primarily wholesale role vis-à-vis the world media. They often appear unwilling to admit their limitations. Defending their coverage of Africa in 1979, American agency executives produced figures for the number of staff correspondents in the region to rebut allegations that they had no interest there, but ignored the fact that more than half the total were posted to South Africa and Rhodesia (Zimbabwe). It was only at the start of the 1980s that Reuters' editor in chief made the admission his predecessors could never bring themselves to acknowledge: that the agency had never really been able to provide a fully comprehensive service of world news for the whole world.

The call for alternatives to fill the information gaps left by the Big Four are both timely and healthy. They should relieve the major agencies of responsibilities they cannot fulfill. However, as has been seen, the various formats in which the alternatives to the Western-model news system have emerged in recent years have represented, at best, only partial answers to the question of how developing nations can be better informed about the world and one another. This is not surprising, given the origins of these alternatives. Political perceptions usually produce politically motivated solutions, and the several contexts within which alternatives to the major agencies have emerged in the 1970s and early 1980s have been formed by ideology and the practical concerns of the rulers of nations. For politicians, news is too important to be left to journalists; it must be subsumed within a wider political framework, as an objective. Thus, most systems that have emerged in recent years deal in news only in the most mechanistic sense; at heart they are systems by which sovereign powers exchange messages. The sender is the prime element; the recipient has little or no influence.

It was not until late 1981 that the suggestion was put forward at a UNESCO meeting that participants in the nonaligned news pool and similar regional arrangements should assess the use being made of the information they exchanged.[2] For most of the national agency managers, ministers of information, and international civil servants involved in promoting the recent exchange arrangements, the question of use had been secondary; transmission was assumed to be sufficient. The existence of an exchange justified its purpose. As had been noted, there are strong underlying reasons for this approach, reasons having little or nothing to do with news or information. It leaves each participant with the last word and avoids the inconveniences of choice and selection inherent in true news operations.

News organizations alleged to be lacking in sympathy and understanding are thus replaced by systems that admit no qualification or questioning of the information produced by national news sources. Such arrangements are agencies in the true sense of the word. Acting as passive agents between originator and recipient, they do not combine the roles of originator and supplier as the major agencies do. Their role is technical: a communications function between national news organizations subject, in the majority of cases, to governmental or national pressures of varying degrees of forcefulness. As such, they may be regarded as useful by the leadership in countries in which the mere act of transmitting certain items of information is valuable in itself. All the evidence suggests that the recipients of material communicated through arrangements of this kind print or broadcast little of it on its merits as news, although use may be increased by the political environment within which the recipient operates, by official directives, or by the belief that information originating from Third World national agencies should be given privileged treatment as a matter of principle. What is evident is the operational and conceptual gulf between the exchange agreements developed in recent years and the international news services.

The cornerstone of the services produced by the Big Four is the control exercised by an independent editorial process. The essence of the nonaligned news pool and regional exchange arrangements in Africa, Asia, and Latin America is the absence of any such control.

245

The two systems are not in competition with each other. To the contrary, they fill radically different roles dictated by different sources of revenue and support.

For those countries politically aligned with one side or the other in the information debate, there is no problem; the nonaligned news pool is no more likely to be seen as a model for news organizations in the United States than the AP or UPI are likely to be adopted as shining examples for media development in Iraq or Tanzania. But for many developing countries, monolithic state direction is not preordained, nor is the notion of the media as a more or less independent force entirely lost. Then, too, substantial segments of the press and broadcasting in industrialized nations could benefit from coverage of the Third World offering greater quality, if not necessarily increased quantity. But neither the major international agencies nor the exchange arrangements of recent years offer any real prospect of progress on this score.

What is needed is a new agency, free of the financial constraints that tie the Big Four to the industrialized world yet independent of government influence in the countries where it reports and distributes. Such an organization would have to be able to square the circle between editorial freedom and financial dependence. The editorial side of the equation is resolvable on the professional level, given a clear understanding of what such an organization would be mandated to do. Its role as a reporter and analyst of the developing world would have to be realistically unambitious. It would have to be aware of the limitations on the events it could actually cover and of the complaints even such restricted reporting would inevitably arouse. Its very existence would connote a certain political choice, stemming from several beliefs: that the developing world would otherwise suffer from a shortage of news reported and edited with its media in mind, that such a shortage would be unfortunate, and that the best remedy lies in the development of an independent news flow free of the influence of governments and national news agencies.

The basic obstacle to even preliminary discussion of a development along these lines has been the conviction that governments would refuse to contribute the financing necessary to supplement the subscriptions of Third World media without demanding in return the means of influencing news put out by such an organization. The history of government-financed news organizations has all too often borne out such fears, although the success of the Caribbean News Agency shows that tight official control is not inevitable.

There has, however, been little sign of any concerted desire in the developing world to establish such an agency. National control has been the preeminent concern. Among the developing countries there has been no indication of a consensus, beyond the broadest of principles, that could enable an effective international, or even regional, agency to be established with both editorial and operational independence from its owners. UNESCO's International Programme for the Development of Communication (IPDC), launched in 1981 to boost media development in the poor nations, demonstrated all too clearly the dual problems facing the creation of a new and independent agency for the developing world. Funds pledged to IPDC in its first six months totaled a little over $2 million; by contrast, requests for assistance amounted to a staggering $51 million. By 1983, the IPDC budget still stood at only $1.9 million.

Despite having initiated the IPDC idea during Jimmy Carter's presidency, the United States, under the Reagan administration, increasingly favors direct, bilateral aid rather than putting money into a pool from which it might go to purposes that conflict with American free press ideas. The desire of at least some Western governments to have a say over how their money is being used is, naturally, denounced by those who consider that rich countries have a basic duty to underwrite the development of the media in poor nations as a matter of principle. This cuts little ice with an American administration that had grown thoroughly frustrated at its inability to influence UNESCO in sensitive policy areas and decided to withdraw from the organization. Without the prospect of major financing from the United States, IPDC's future looks bleak. At the end of 1983, the IPDC chairman, Gunnar Garbo of Norway, warned not only that funds were out of all proportion to the needs of developing countries, but that the shortfall was such that there was no assurance of completing projects that had already been launched.[3] IPDC's financial problems did not explode the notion that international benefactors would be willing to sink substantial funds into multilateral schemes to help the media of the poor countries. In 1984, information ministers of nonaligned nations called on UNESCO and other international bodies to study the establishment of a new fund to compensate telecommunications authorities in developing countries for offering facilities to the media on a cost basis. But funds remain small. For 1986–87, UNESCO plans to fund IPDC with $676,300 from its regular program and, at a meeting in Paris in March 1985, UNESCO member states pledged another FFr 10 million ($800,000) in voluntary help. France was the biggest contributor, followed by Japan, India, and the Soviet Union. France said its assistance would go toward helping African projects, including PANA.

Even if IPDC were miraculously to receive much larger funds, it would still suffer from an inherent flaw that its original American sponsors appear to have overlooked. The bulk of projects submitted for IPDC help are state-backed.[4] The major news-agency request for assistance came from the Pan African news exchange scheme. By its nature, UNESCO and its offshoots such as IPDC deal predominantly with state organizations. The men and women who decide on aid grants either are direct government appointees or owe their positions to negotiations between governments. An international governmental organization like UNESCO is unlikely to see the promotion of private, commercial media as part of its mission, particularly if such news-papers or broadcasting stations might challenge state information monopolies. The initiatives taken by IPDC, however limited finan-cially, can be welcomed if they really increase the flow of information, but the nature of the program ensures that government concerns will remain dominant. In most of the developing world, news will continue to flow through officially supervised channels, and will be conditioned by the interests of the supplier rather than the recipient.

This means that the four major agencies will continue to exercise their de facto monopoly, dominating the reporting and distribution of instant information for the media in both poor and rich nations. They will defend their independence and continue to compete without too much regard for commercial logic. Nor will their limitations disappear, although it is to be hoped that rather more realism will surround future discussion of their roles and activities. In the absence of viable alternatives, the four major agencies simply turn out to be the best practical means of ensuring that the world receives a rea-sonable flow of information about itself.

Notes

Chapter 1: News of the World

As is the case with the whole of this book, much of the material in this chapter is based on interviews and conversations and on the reading of books mentioned in the Bibliography, in particular UNESCO works and documents charting the development of the nonaligned approach to news.

1. Denis MacQuail, *Analysis of Newspaper Content*, Research Series 4 (London: Royal Commission on the Press, 1977), pp. 245 et seq.

2. *Many Voices, One World: Report by the International Commission for the Study of Communication Problems* (Paris: UNESCO, 1980), pp. 58–62.

3. Frank Barton, *The Press of Africa* (London, 1979), pp. 11–12.

4. See, for example, speech by D. R. Mankekar, former chairman of the nonaligned agencies' pool, to conference in Athens, Ohio, in July 1979, which said:

A major objection to the pattern of news services proffered by the Western transnational news agencies is that between them, they hold a monopoly of international news and the developing countries are abjectly dependent on them (whose news policies are identical because they are on the same side of the ideological fence) to know what is going on in the world, and that the four news agencies are, between them, in a position to decide what the developing countries should (or should not) read, and in what shape and from what angle, about events and developments in the world.

To which the then managing director of Reuters, Gerald Long, responded that Mankekar "used a phrase which struck me and I'd like to transpose it a little and tell you that cows hold a monopoly on the production of milk and that babies are abjectly dependent on them."

5. *North-South: A Programme for Survival* (London, 1980), p. 30.

6. *Thinking Ahead: UNESCO and the Challenges of Today and Tomorrow* (Paris: UNESCO, 1977), p. 19.

7. When an American reporter, Paul Chutkow, organized a meeting with UNESCO delegates from the Third World on the information issue and reported their views in the Paris-based *International Herald Tribune*, he aroused criticism from developing countries, which, apparently, disliked the fact that they were not a monolithic bloc. Some reacted to Chutkow's article by saying that this proved the need to regulate the press.

8. M'Bow to International Commission for the Study of Communication Problems, 1977, quoted in a speech by Frederico Mayor to the International Press Institute General Assembly, Athens, June 1979. This speech by the UNESCO deputy director-general was largely instrumental in rousing the then Reuters managing director, Gerald Long, to a sustained attack on UNESCO. Long's copy of Mayor's speech carried the annotation "Power and Lies" opposite the quoted passage from M'Bow. In a statement to the IPI meeting the following day, Long said that the "manipulation" statement was "nonsense" and went on:

I would be very interested to see some support given by UNESCO to the very wide-ranging and high-sounding affirmations that are made and for which no example whatsoever is adduced. I would like the Director General to tell us how the manipulation is brought about, how it works, to give us some examples of it. I know of none.

I know many examples where governments have attempted to manipulate the world and world events through the use, or rather the abuse, of information. That is something that happens all the time. There are outstanding examples of it that I will not quote here, but not by the media themselves.

Furthermore, as far as I am concerned, and I can speak only for my own organisation, the mechanism by which one would direct or manipulate is totally absent. I can manipulate nothing. And I take good care that neither can anyone else in my organisation. I think in that I act in common with my colleagues in the other few similar organisations. This idea of direction, of manipulation of information, by the major international news organisations, is created by UNESCO for UNESCO's own purposes, purposes which appear to me extremely suspect.

Let me say immediately what I think those purposes are. If you wish power to be organised, power to be transmitted, power to be handed over, that power must exist. It therefore has to be suggested that this power exists in the world in order that it may be regulated and directed, one has to suppose by UNESCO.

9. From my own experience, Reuters had difficulties of an acute nature at least twice because of the speed with which agency copy returns to the country of origin. In Ethiopia, in the mid-1970s, after the overthrow of Haile Selassie, Reuters was regularly in trouble with the authorities. American newspaper correspondents, who wrote equally critical copy, came in for less criticism. An information ministry official explained why: "We see your copy on the printer the same day. American newspaper reports take weeks to filter back."

In Nigeria, the Reuters correspondent was expelled in a particularly unpleasant way after a failed coup attempt against the military government. (He and his wife and children were held in detention for several days and then driven in separate military vehicles to the Niger River, put into a dugout canoe, and cast off. Arriving on the other side of the river in Niger, they were put in prison again as suspect arrivals and held for a week before being released to fly back to London.) A Nigerian information ministry official later told me that Reuters' real fault had been "to be too quick with the news. You knew about the coup before we did. So, of course, we thought you must be part of a British-inspired plot against us. And so you had to suffer.'' The official added that, if the correspondent in question was sacked and Reuters announced the fact, ''a normal relationship'' could be resumed.

Chapter 2: Origins

1. Each of the major agencies has its own historian, though their books were all written some years ago. On the history of Havas/Agence France-Presse, see Pierre Frédérix, *Un Siècle de Chasse aux Nouvelles de l'Agence France-Press,* (Paris, 1959); on the Associated Press, see Oliver Gramling, *AP: The Story of News* (New York, 1940); on United Press, see Joe Alex Morris, *Deadline Every Minute: The Story of the United Press* (New York, 1957); on Reuters, see Graham Storey, *Reuters' Century* (London, 1951). Other books relevant to the early period of agency history are Henry Collins, *From Pigeon Post to Wireless* (London, 1912); Gerd Kulle et al., *Paul Julius v. Reuter* (Kassel, 1978); Michael Palmer, ''De l'Information Étrangère dans la Presse Quotidienne Française: Les Agences de Presse et le Journalisme Anglo-Saxon 1878–85,'' *Revue d'Histoire Moderne et Contemporaine* 22 (April–June 1976), on late-nineteenth-century agencies and the French press; Richard Schwarzlose's investigations of the origins and predecessors of the AP, ''Harbor News Association: The Formal Origins of the AP,'' *Journalism Quarterly* (Summer 1968), and ''The Nation's First Wire Service,'' *Journalism Quarterly* (Winter 1980); George Scott's account of the formation of the domestic Press Association agency in Britain, *Reporter Anonymous* (London, 1968); the memoirs of AP general manager Melville Stone, *Fifty Years a Journalist* (Garden City, N.Y., 1921); and *History of ''The Times,''* vol. 2 (London, 1939). Sir Denis Wright's book on Persia throws light on Reuters' activities outside the news business (*The English Amongst the Persians* [London, 1977]). Andrew Wynter's pen portrait of Paul Julius Reuter gives a vivid picture of Reuter in his early days in London (*Our Social Bees* [London: Robert Hardwicke, 1861]). Fritz Stern's superb book on Bismarck and Bleichroder contains the best account in English of how Wolff's agency was taken under the state's wing and of the prevailing press context in Germany (*Gold and Iron* [London, 1977]). Useful material on the background to Wolff is contained in Robert Keyserlingh, *Media Manipulation: The Press and Bismarck in Imperial Germany* (Montreal, 1977). The major collection of French documents is in the Havas archive in Paris; see Isabelle Brot, *Les Archives de l'Agence Havas* (Paris, 1969), for catalog.

2. See Schwarzlose, ''Harbor News Association: The Formal Origins of the AP,'' and ''The Nation's First Wire Service.''

3. See Wright, *The English Amongst the Persians,* pp. 102–6, 136; Storey, *Reuters' Century,* chap. 6.

4. For a more detailed study of Havas's early years, including its position vis-à-vis the state, see Oliver Boyd-Barrett and Michael Palmer, *Le Trafic*

des Nouvelles (Paris, 1981), pp. 104 et seq. This book, as could be expected from Palmer's unrivaled knowledge of French news agencies, is a major source for detailed material on Havas and Agence France-Presse.

5. Quoted in Storey, *Reuters' Century,* p. 2.

6. *History of "The Times"* records that it was Reuters' financial service that first attracted the newspaper's manager Mowbray Morris:

> The expense of the daily American cable incurred in the summer of 1858, however, induced Morris to reconsider Reuter. The daily American cable was primarily a City [of London] requirement. As the collection of Stock prices was merely a matter of routine, and as the figures could easily be checked, reliance on Reuter in commercial matters was felt to be justified. When, therefore, Reuter offered The Times an American money-market service, Morris was at last interested. The charge on cables from the paper's own correspondent was two sovereigns for each word—to Morris a most extravagant tariff. The use of Reuter for a limited purpose was an unexceptionable economy, and when the first American cable failed Morris gave Reuter his first month's general trial as a European agency—in October, 1858.

The function of the agency was to supplement the paper's own service. If Reuter could quote Stock prices and summarize foreign newspapers he could shoulder the burden of transmitting all news "known to persons of average information." In what was to become a *Times* tradition, Mowbray Morris rated news agencies as very much as inferior beings beside the newspaper's own correspondents. In a letter to Reuter in 1861, he wrote: "I have had frequent occasion to remonstrate with you against the flimsy, stale and even ridiculous character of some of the intelligence which you send to the *Times.* I call this stuff 'intelligence' by a great stretch of courtesy." (*History of the Times,* vol. 2, pp. 272–73).

7. For 1859 pact, see Frédérix, *Un Siècle de Chasse aux Nouvelles de l'Agence France-Presse,* p. 102 et seq.; Havas, *Archives* 5-AR 411 (Paris: Archives Nationales).

8. The rivalry and agreements among the three agencies are covered in Storey, *Reuters' Century,* chap. 4; and Stern, *Gold and Iron,* pp. 263–64, 267–70. Havas, *Archives* 5-AR 411, contains texts.

9. Stern, *Gold and Iron,* p. 268. For similar later evidence, see Storey, *Reuters' Century*, pp. 145–46.

10. To Reuters shareholders' meeting, 1870.

11. Kent Cooper, *Barriers Down* (New York, 1942), p. 7.

12. The map appears to have been lost or destroyed, but former directors of Reuters recall having seen it before World War II.

13. Havas, *Archives* 5-AR 411, contains texts. Fragmentary documentation has survived in the Reuters archives at the agency's head office in London.

14. For cable development, see J. L. Kieve, *Electric Telegraph: A Social and Economic History* (Newton Abbot, England, 1973), particularly chap. 5.

15. Reuters shareholders' meeting, May 27, 1908.

16. Paul Julius Reuter, appropriately, chose as the motto for his coat of arms "Per Mare et Terram." See Storey, *Reuters' Century*, p. 61, for details.

17. Scott contains a full account of the establishment of the PA-Reuter arrangement. Also see Storey, *Reuters' Century*, pp. 47–48.

18. This paragraph is based mainly on Kruglak, *The Two Faces of TASS*, pp. 13–15, which contain interesting material from a TASS account of 1955, *Osnovii Informatzii v Gazetta*.

19. See Gramling, *AP: The Story of News*, pp. 100 et seq.; Stone, *Fifty Years a Journalist*, pp. 212 et seq.

20. See Reuters contract books for 1893 in Reuters archives in London; Stone, *Fifty Years a Journalist*, pp. 216 et seq.; Storey, *Reuters' Century*, pp. 115–17.

21. Stone, *Fifty Years a Journalist*, p. 216.

22. Ibid., pp. 235 et seq.

23. Morris, *Deadline Every Minute*, p. 21.

24. Ibid., p. 20.

25. Ibid., p. 36.

Chapter 3: From Cartel to Competition

The agency histories mentioned at the start of the notes to the previous chapter are also invaluable sources of material for the years covered in this chapter. Lees-Milne and Adam Smith give insights on the way Reuters was run. The Havas archives in Paris are particularly useful for the interwar period. The memoirs of Baillie, Cooper, and Jones give their stories of events at United Press, the Associated Press, and Reuters, and of the break-down of the cartel. I am indebted to Reuters for giving me access to relevant board minutes. John Lawrenson and Lionel Barber, *The Price of Truth* (Edinburgh, 1985), contains a definitive account of Reuters' links with the British government in 1938–41.

1. See Reuters' share offer document of April 20, 1912, p. 3, for high hopes resting on the banking business. Graham Storey, *Reuters' Century* (London, 1951), pp. 87 et seq., deals in detail with Reuters under its second baron.

2. Jones note to Reuters board, July 1934. Despite such gaps in Reuters' network, Jones proclaimed the agency to be on "the throne of international ascendancy" (speech to annual general meeting, July 5, 1937).

3. Kent Cooper, *Barriers Down* (New York, 1942), p. 35.

4. The story of Japanese news agencies up to 1945, with particular reference to The Associated Press–Reuters battle, is admirably covered in S. Iwanaga, *Story of Japanese News Agencies* (Tokyo, 1980).

5. See Havas, *Archives* (letters from Señor Armato of Fabra (June 22, 1933; September 17, 1934), and letter from Rengo agency, August 29, 1934, on dumping.

6. Roderick Jones's attitude is evident from a reading of his memoirs (*A*

Life in Reuters [London, 1951]). James Lees-Milne, *Another Self* (New York, 1970), pp. 122–31, gives a close-up picture of Jones that is unflattering to say the least. Reuters board minutes for the period just before World War II and after the outbreak of fighting show Jones expressing no concern about the growing links with the government. The novelist John Buchan had been appointed deputy chairman of Reuters by Jones in 1923 and continued his work at the agency after becoming a member of Parliament, another indication of how little Jones saw wrong in linking news and politics. Buchan evidently took a relaxed view of his obligations at Reuters. During the parliamentary recess, he would come to London from his country home on only one day a week for business at the agency. Janet Adam Smith, *John Buchan* (London, 1965), pp. 229, 312.

7. A "heads of agreement" document was drafted on December 5, 1940, setting out these ideas. While negotiating with the government, Jones had told his board that the underlying idea was that "Reuters should have the British Government behind them without being in any disabilities of a semi-official agency" (minutes of board meeting of September 12, 1939).

8. See Storey, *Reuters' Century*, pp. 213–14. My account of the events at Reuters in 1939–41 is based mainly on the papers of the late Lord Buckton, who became chairman of Reuters after Jones's resignation, having previously served as a director. I am greatly indebted to his son, Sir Richard Storey, for placing these papers at my disposal. They give a full account of the board's growing unhappiness with Jones, the way in which it finally steeled itself for action, and then the immediate disagreements over what form Reuters' future ownership should take, between those who wished to retain PA control and those who wanted to broaden ownership to include the national press. I also interviewed surviving participants of the fight to get Jones to go and to reform Reuters. They did not wish to be named, but I am no less grateful to them.

9. Pierre-Marie Dioudonnat, *L'Argent Nazi à la Conquête de la Presse Française, 1940–44* (Paris, 1981), pp. 89, 91.

Chapter 4: Uniformity and Diversity: 1960–80

1. See Mustapha Masmoudi, *The New World Information Order* (Paris: UNESCO, 1980), particularly p. 4, for agencies.

2. *APME Red Book* (New York: Associated Press, 1978), p. 10.

3. *APME Red Book* (New York: Associated Press, 1976), pp. 17–18.

4. Reuters marked the 125th anniversary of its founder's arrival in London by erecting a statue of him opposite his original office in London. Soon afterward, busts of the first baron were sent to major offices around the world to be put on display.

5. Reuters World Service (RWS), as the general news division was now called, was designated within the company as a "cost centre," which, financially, was simply required to remain within an agreed annual budget approved by the board. Other parts of Reuters, including North America,

which bore editorial costs of its own, were designated "profit centres," which were meant to make money. RWS costs were not directly related to the money earned from the media. This gave RWS freedom to operate and expand, within its agreed budget, which remained static in real terms, increasing only in line with inflation. On the other hand, it cut RWS off from its market and made it less pressing, in practice if not in theory, to adapt services to changing customer needs.

6. One *Los Angeles Times–Washington Post* senior executive told me in 1981 that Agence France-Presse copy did not represent more than 1 percent of material run on the service.

Chapter 5: Operations

Most material in this chapter came from interviews and observation of agency operations, together with elements from the author's own experience. For reasons explained in the text, there is a lack of precision about some agency statistics, notably the total number of recipients of agency news. Each agency periodically changes the structure of its services, so there may be variations since this chapter's description of services, but the general picture remains the same.

1. Figures for agency clients refer to textual news. Reuters' current move into photo services has somewhat expanded its media base.

2. See UNESCO, Report by the International Commission for the Study of Communication Problems, working paper 11.

3. Studies are by University of North Carolina, Chapel Hill, of the Associated Press, United Press International, Agence France-Press, Reuter/ Latin services in Latin America over five days in 1979; idem, study of Reuters to Middle East and AFP to Africa over five days in 1979; Boyd-Barrett and Palmer of Reuters to South Europe and South Africa, AP to Europe and Africa, AFP and UPI to Europe 1974 (three days); Fenby study of Reuter services to Africa and North Europe, AP to Europe, Africa/Middle East, UPI to Europe three days in 1980.

4. Studies quoted are contained in Wilbur Schramm, *Mass Media and National Development* (Paris: UNESCO, 1964); Gehen Rachty, *Foreign News in Nine Arab Countries* (Medford, Mass.: Tufts University, 1978); Edward Pinch, *A Brief Study on News Patterns in Sixteen Third World Countries* (Medford, Mass., 1978); Denis MacQuail, *Analysis of Newspaper Content,* Research Series 4 (London: Royal Commission on the Press, 1977); respectively.

5. North Carolina study.

Chapter 6: Business News, Photographs, and Television

Again, most of the information in this chapter came from interviews and observation. Reuters' share flotation prospectus contains valuable material on business news.

1. I had a vivid experience of this when working for Reuters in Paris in

the early 1970s. The state broadcasting network was trying to save money on editorial costs. As well as Agence France-Presse, it took Reuters and the two American agencies. It had decided to drop one of the American services, but had to make further cuts. If it retained Reuters, it would still be obliged to take an American agency to get still photographs for use on the television service. It was, therefore, logically forced to drop Reuters, whatever its opinion of the merits of the service, in favor of an American agency that gave it both words and pictures.

2. Reuters' internal company magazine, *Reuters World,* reported the manager in charge of the photograph project as saying in June 1983 that "setting up a news photo service could be a major step in expanding Reuters' position in world media markets." Photographs, he noted, "can now be handled by a method similar to textual video editing. They can be retrieved on computer screens, altered and transmitted to appropriate centres at the touch of a button." The internal announcement of the United Press International deal at Reuters contained the statement: "We shall continue the plans already announced for investment in advanced picture transmission technology."

3. See Reuters' share prospectus in *Financial Times* (London), May 16, 1984.

4. When Reuters offered its executives a special share scheme in November 1983, ahead of the stock market flotation, options were offered to 124 staff. Of these, only 16 were from editorial, compared with 34 from general management, 28 from sales and marketing, 22 from technical management, and 24 from other sectors of the company.

Chapter 7: Finances
As noted in the text, some financial data can be found in Reuters' annual reports and Associated Press board reports. The Information Commission reports to the French National Assembly have only the barest of information about Agence France-Presse, but more can be obtained from the commission's working papers and internal AFP documents. United Press International remains highly secretive about its finances. My requests for information before the ownership change in 1982 were met with the statement that UPI was a private company that did not disclose its figures. One of the agency's new owners subsequently agreed to disclose figures, but no information was, in fact, forthcoming. The best sources for UPI's finances are the limited partnership offer and bank reports drawn up during the sale negotiations, though these are now somewhat dated.

1. In my own experience, the fact that Reuters in Paris was far ahead of the other agencies with news of the agreement to open four-sided peace talks on Vietnam enabled the agency to attract subscribers for its business news service in the United States. There have been many similar examples since.

2. See *Financial Times* (London), May 16, 1984.

3. United Press International limited partnership prospectus, 1979.

4. Ibid. The subscribers were not named.

5. The principle of state support never seems to have been questioned. One postwar head of Agence France-Presse, Paul-Louis Bret, ranked a news agency with public utilities as a service that the state should be ready to subsidize.

6. For a full account of Reuters' flotation, see John Lawrenson and Lionel Barber, *The Price of Truth* (Edinburgh, 1985). Reuters' prospectus in *Financial Times,* May 16, 1984, gives details of share structure. House of Commons debate on Reuters' independence and the government's refusal to intervene are reported in *The Times* and *The Guardian* (London), January 28, 1984.

7. *Financial Times* (London), May 29, 1984.

Chapter 8: Agencies, Clients, and Governments

1. Interviews, again, formed the basis for this chapter, together with questionnaires sent out to agency subscribers. Most respondents did so on condition that they were not named. Views about the major agencies were gathered from 29 news organizations in 21 countries: 12 of these were in Europe (East as well as West), 6 in Asia, 4 each in Africa and North America, 2 in Latin America, and 1 in New Zealand. The Europeans seemed readier than news organizations in other parts of the world to reply to my questionnaires. Still, the resulting sample of subscribers' opinions appears representative. Of the respondents, 14 were national news agencies, 11 were newspapers, and 4 were broadcasting organizations. For the United States, the Associated Press Managing Editors' Association *Red Books* contain much valuable material on the attitude of members to the service they receive, and the outlook of AP executives.

2. Denis MacQuail, *Analysis of Newspaper Content*, Research Series 4 (London: Royal Commission on the Press, 1977), p. 271.

3. George Thomson, *Blue Pencil Admiral* (London, 1947).

4. TASS runs a special service, for instance, whose circulation is restricted to picked officials and that contains much more news from Western agencies than the service issued to the Soviet media.

5. W. Phillips Davison, "News Media and International Negotiation," *Public Opinion Quarterly* (Summer 1974), p. 175.

6. Letter to author.

7. A more detailed picture of harassment and the limited extent of press freedom can be gained from the annual reports on the subject issued by the International Press Institute in London and Freedom House in New York.

8. This account of the ANA/RNS episode is based on the recollections of some of those involved and papers in the British Public Records Office. A British writer, Richard Fletcher, wrote a paper submitted to UNESCO in 1979, which went into the RNS case as "an example of certain undesirable practices by British news organizations." In 1981, UNESCO said that this paper was being edited for publication, but it has not so far appeared. An

article in the London *Observer* on December 20, 1981, reported the RNS case as one of several instances of British media having links with "a former Secret Service network of 'front' news agencies." The story quoted Gerald Long, then recently departed from Reuters to the managing directorship of Times Newspapers, as saying:

I do not think those projects were worthwhile. I think that most secret activities are for the birds. . . . The trouble with secret services and all parallel activity is that they put a certain amount of money, influence and authority into the hands of clever, silly people. I think these activities are extremely danger-ous. . . .

9. I wrote to Snepp seeking further information on his allegation. No reply was received.

Chapter 9: Secondhand News

1. For information on national news agencies, see monographs written for the UNESCO International Commission for the Study of Communication Problems.

2. In the case of Ethiopia in the mid-1970s, Reuters was told by the authorities in Addis Ababa that the Reuter correspondent there would be beheaded if the agency ran any information from anywhere in the world that displeased the Ethiopian government. This, and a previous experience in which the agency's correspondent was held in detention for several hours with a cocked submachine gun pointed at him, led Reuters to withdraw its correspondent. (A local stringer in the Ethiopian city of Asmara had also been detained, held without food for several days, and then flown to Addis Ababa in the cargo hold of a plane.) A few months after the withdrawal of the correspondent, Reuters received messages expressing the dismay of the Ethiopian authorities that the agency was not represented in their country and urging that a new correspondent be sent. I declined to take up the invitation.

Chapter 10: Under Fire

1. There is a large literature setting out the criticisms of the present world news system and of the agencies. See particularly Mustapha Masmoudi, *The New World Information Order* (Paris: UNESCO, 1980); D. R. Mankekar, *Media and the Third World* (New Delhi, 1979); Herbert Schiller, "Now, a New International Information Order," *Mass Media,* April 1977; Agence Tunis Afrique Presse, *Conférence des Agences de Presse Africaines et Ar-abes, Rapports et Documents* (Tunis, 1975), and *Conférence des Agences de Presse Euro-Arabes* (Tunis, 1976); Non-Aligned News Agencies Pool, *Non-Alignés sur l'Information, Documents* (Belgrade, 1979). For general background to UNESCO position, see Amadou-Mahtar M'Bow, *Building the Future* (Paris: UNESCO, 1981), and Report of International Commission for the Study of Communication Problems (Paris: UNESCO, 1980).

2. See Voices of Freedom, *Working Papers* (Talloires: World Press Free-

dom Committee, 1981 and 1983), and Note by Henri Pigeat of AFP in *Federation International des Editeurs de Journaux (FIEJ) Bulletin* (Paris, 1984).

3. Wilbur Schramm, et al., *International News Wires and Third World News in Asia* (Hong Kong, 1978), table 8.

4. Reuters has subsequently stopped this service, judging it not to be financially worthwhile. A sign of the times came in October 1983, when the International Monetary Fund decided to use Reuters as its main communication channel with central banks for collecting and distributing rates of its special drawing rights (SDRs) (see *Reuters World,* October 1983). At the World Bank, Reuters had been supplying news for development. The IMF agreement concerned world monetary movements.

5. It was, for instance, striking at a 1977 conference in New York on news and the Third World how the Nigerian representatives attacked the agencies for not covering Africa sufficiently and for not employing Nigerian staff. At the time, Nigeria had expelled all except the Agence France-Presse correspondent and refused to allow Nigerian journalists employed by Reuters to send copy out of the country. See Philip Horton, ed., *The Third World and Press Freedom* (New York, 1978).

6. As has been shown earlier, there is no doubt that the major news agencies are the main channels through which news flows. The question is the extent to which their news and values are aggressively Western and the extent to which they are forcing alien values on the developing nations.

7. See, for instance, the exaggerated statistics on agency wordage in UNESCO, International Commission for the Study of Communication Problems, *Monographs I-II-III,* working papers nos. 13–15 (Paris: UNESCO, 1977–78).

8. Extracted from studies mentioned in note 3 to chapter 5.

9. Wilbur Schramm, *Mass Media and National Development* (Paris: UNESCO, 1964).

10. David Weaver and Cleveland Wilhoit, "Foreign News Coverage in Two U.S. Wire Services," *Journal of Communications* (Spring 1981).

11. Fernando Reyes Matta, *News Values and Principles of Cross-Cultural Communication* (Paris: UNESCO, 1980), pp. 45–46.

12. See, for example, lecture by UNESCO Director-General Amadou-Mahtar M'Bow to Lagos Institute of International Affairs, Nigeria, January 1984, summarized in UNESCO press release no. 2, 1984.

13. North Carolina study cited in note 3 to chapter 5.

14. Mankekar, *Media and the Third World,* p. 27.

15. Letter to the author.

Chapter 11: Alternatives

1. See Deutsche Press-Agentur, *Portrait of an International News Agency* (Hamburg, n.d.), and *25 Jahre Deutsche Presse-Agentur* (Hamburg, 1974); and Efe, *History and Organization* (Madrid, 1980).

2. See TASS, *News Agency of the Soviet Union* (Moscow, n.d.).

3. This account of Latin is based mainly on interviews with those involved in running the agency from its foundation to 1980, and on the author's own experience when editor of Reuters' World Service.

4. See article on Latin by J. Nichols in *Gazette* 21, no. 3 (1975).

5. This account of the Caribbean News Agency is based on interviews, the author's own observation, and reports of UNESCO missions to the Caribbean.

6. In material submitted to UNESCO International Commission for the Study of Communication Problems.

7. This account of IPS is based on interviews, study of IPS service, and Phil Harris, "People in the News," *Population and Communication* (Rome: Inter Press Service, n.d.), *Directions for Understanding* (Rome: Inter Press Service, 1979), and *The International Information Order: Problems and Responses* (Rome: Inter Press Service, 1979).

8. Harris in above documents.

9. Jacques van Aernsbergen and Hans van der Veen, *Interpress Service: News from the Third World* (Nijmegen, 1979).

10. Figures supplied by Dr. Roberto Savio, chief executive of IPS.

Chapter 12: News Exchanges

1. See Gunnar Naesselund, *Collaboration Between News Agencies in Nordic Countries* (Paris: UNESCO, 1980), for best account of Nordic cooperation.

2. The resolutions of the 1976 meeting of Arab and African agencies in Tunis make this aspect of the appeal of pools quite clear. See Agence Tunis Afrique Presse, *Conférence des Agences de Presse Africaines et Arabes, Rapports et Documents* (Tunis, 1975), *Conférence des Agences de Presse Euro-Arabes* (Tunis, 1976), and *Symposium International sur les Moyens de Développer l'Information entre les Pays Non-Alignés* (Tunis, 1976).

3. See Ghana News Agency, *Twenty Years in Existence* (Accra, 1977), for early African agency plans.

4. See PANA statutes, at agency headquarters in Dakar. For PANA communications costs, see *IPTC News*, International Press Telecommunications Council (London), September 1984, p. 38.

5. Latin American sociologists and media observers have been in the forefront of calls for change. Much of their work has been centered on the ILET institute in Mexico City headed by Juan Somavia.

6. Internal study.

7. Quoted in *UK Press Gazette* (London), September 8, 1980.

8. Main collection of pool documents is noted in Bibliography. D. R. Mankekar, *Media and the Third World* (New Delhi, 1979), also gives pool viewpoint fully. This account is also based on conversations with the first pool chairman, Pero Ivacic, and others involved in launching the experiment.

9. Mankekar, *Media and the Third World,* p. 26.

10. Survey carried out by author for this book.

Chapter 13: Present and Future

1. Voices of Freedom, *Working Papers* (Talloires: World Press Freedom Committee, 1981).

2. At UNESCO meetings on regional information systems in Paris in 1982. At the time this book was completed, no such study had been published.

3. See International Programme for the Development of Communication, *Collection of Basic Texts* (Paris: UNESCO, 1981), *Intergovernmental Council Session, Final Report* (Paris: UNESCO, 1981), and *Intergovernmental Council, Second Session, Final Report* (Paris: UNESCO, 1982). See Garbo, quoted in UNESCO press release no. 95, November 1983.

4. See lists of projects in International Programme for the Development of Communication, *Collection of Basic Texts, International Council Session, Final Report*, and *Intergovernmental Council, Second Session, Final Report*. (IPDC conference documents Paris, Acapulco, Tashkent, 1981–83.)

Bibliography

The following bibliography does not pretend to be exhaustive. There is a huge amount of literature on subjects that connects with the major news agencies in one way or the other. Much of this is in monographs, magazine articles, and papers written for UNESCO and other organizations concerned with international news. To have listed each individually would have resulted in an unselective list. Those who wish to do so can consult the detailed list of publications issued by UNESCO and the indexes of journalism reviews, particularly *Gazette* and *Journalism Quarterly,* where much extremely valuable material has appeared. Most national news agencies have information booklets on their activities. I have not listed these individually, except for some of the more substantial or those particularly relevant to the major agencies. Again, such information can be obtained through a request to the relevant national agency. Nor have I included in the bibliography works on general politics, history, and current affairs, though these, obviously, set the general context within which the major agencies operate.

Aernsbergen, Jacques van, and Veen, Hans van der. *Interpress Service: News from the Third World.* Nijmegen, 1979.
Agence Tunis Afrique Presse. *Conférence des Agences de Presse Africaines et Arabes, Rapports et Documents.* Tunis, 1975.
———. *Conférence des Agences de Presse Euro-Arabes.* Tunis, 1976.
———. *Symposium International sur les Moyens de Développer l'Information entre les Pays Non-Alignés.* Tunis, 1976.
Archambault, François, and Lemoine, Jean-François. *4 Milliards de Journaux.* Paris, 1977.
ASIN, *Action of National Information Systems.* Mexico City, n.d.
Assemblée Nationale. *Rapport sur le Projet de Loi de Finances, Culture et Communication.* Paris, 1973–83.
Associated Press. *APME Red Books.* New York, 1973–83.
———. *Green Books,* annual corporation reports. New York, 1973–83.
Ayar, Farid. *Les Agences de Presse Arabes.* Paris: UNESCO, 1980.
Baillie, Hugh. *High Tension.* London, 1959.
Barnes, Margarita. *The Indian Press.* London, 1940.

Barnes, Peter. *The Wire Services from Latin America*. Nieman Reports. Cambridge, Mass., March 1964.

Bartholomew, Frank. "Putting the 'I' into UPI." *Editor & Publisher,* September 25, 1982.

Barton, Frank. *The Press of Africa*. London, 1979.

Bourges, Hervé. *Decoloniser l'Information*. Paris, 1978.

Boyd-Barrett, Oliver. *The International News Agencies*. London, 1980.

————, and Palmer, Michael. *Le Trafic des Nouvelles*. Paris, 1981.

Braestrup, Peter. *Big Story*. Garden City, N.Y., 1978.

Brot, Isabelle. *Les Archives de l'Agence Havas*. Paris, 1969.

Cholmondely, Hugh. "CANA." *Media Asia,* no. 3, 1976.

Cohen, Bernard. *The Press and Foreign Policy*. Princeton, N.J., 1963.

Collins, Henry. *From Pigeon Post to Wireless*. London, 1912.

Cooper, Kent. *Barriers Down*. New York, 1942.

Desmond, Robert. *The Information Process*. Iowa City, 1978.

Deutsche-Presse Agentur. *Portrait of an International News Agency*. Hamburg, n.d.

————. *25 Jahre Deutsche Presse-Agentur*. Hamburg, 1974.

Dioudonnat, Pierre-Marie. *L'Argent Nazi à la Conquête de la Presse Française, 1940–44*. Paris, 1981.

Documentation Française. *L'Agence France-Presse*. Paris, 1976.

Documents of the Gatherings of Non-Aligned Nations. Belgrade, 1978.

Efe. *History and Organization*. Madrid, 1980.

Frédérix, Pierre. *Un Siècle de Chasse aux Nouvelles de l'Agence France-Presse*. Paris, 1959.

Gans, H. J. *Deciding What's News*. New York, 1979.

Ghana News Agency. *Twenty Years in Existence*. Accra, 1977.

Gramling, Oliver. *AP: The Story of News*. New York, 1940.

Gunter, Jonathan. *The United States and the Debate on the World "Information Order."* Washington, D.C., 1979.

Halberstam, David. *The Powers That Be*. New York, 1979.

Hall, Peter. "What's All the Fuss About IPS?" *Columbia Journalism Review,* January/February 1983.

Hamelink, Cees. *The New International Economic Order and the New International Information Order*. Paris: UNESCO, 1980.

Harley, William. *The New World Information Order: Confrontation or Cooperation with the Third World—An American View*. Medford, Mass.: Tufts University, 1979.

Harris, Phil. *Directions for Understanding*. Rome: Inter Press Service, 1979.

————. *The International Information Order: Problems and Responses*. Rome: Inter Press Service, 1979.

————. "People in the News." *Population and Communication*. Rome: Inter Press Service, n.d.

Havas Archives. Archives Nationales, Paris.

Hester, Al. "An Analysis of News Flow from Developed and Developing Countries." *Gazette* 17, no. 1.

———. "The News from Latin America." *Gazette* 20, no. 2.

Hill, Laura. "The Mystery Mavericks of Troubled UPI." *Washington Journalism Review,* July/August 1983.

Hoggart, Richard. *An Idea and Its Servants.* London, 1978.

Hohenberg, John. *Foreign Correspondence.* New York, 1964.

———. *Free Press/Free People.* New York, 1971.

Horton, Philip, ed. *The Third World and Press Freedom.* New York, 1978.

"How We Get Our News." *Harper's Monthly,* 1866.

International Press Institute. *Annual Reports on Press Freedom.* London.

———. *The Flow of the News.* New York, 1972.

———. *Strengthening the Press in the Third World.* Paris: UNESCO, 1980.

Inter Press Service. *Putting the New International Information Order into Practice: The Role of Inter Press Service.* Rome: IPS, 1981.

———. *Working Paper for UNESCO Symposium 27–30 October 1981: Inter Press Service.* Paris: UNESCO, 1980.

Iwanaga, S. *Story of Japanese News Agencies.* Tokyo, 1980.

Jolly, W. P. *Marconi.* London, 1972.

Jones, Roderick. *A Life in Reuters.* London, 1951.

Kieve, J. L. *Electric Telegraph: A Social and Economic History.* Newton Abbot, England, 1973.

Keyserling, R. H. *Media Manipulation: The Press and Bismarck in Imperial Germany.* Montreal, 1977.

Kitchen, F. Harcourt. *Moberley Bell and His Times.* London, 1925.

Knightley, Philip. *The First Casualty.* New York and London, 1975.

Kruglak, Theodore. *The Two Faces of TASS.* University of Minnesota, 1962.

Kulle, Gerd, et al. *Paul Julius v. Reuter.* Kassel, 1978.

Lawrenson, John, and Barber, Lionel, *The Price of Truth,* Edinburgh, 1985.

Lees-Milne, James. *Another Self.* New York, 1970.

McIntosh, Pat. "Communication Principles: A Critical Analysis of the Impact of the Caribbean News Agency on the Print Media of the Region." Unpublished research paper, 1977.

MacQuail, Denis. *Analysis of Newspaper Content.* Research Series 4. London: Royal Commission on the Press, 1977.

Maddox, Brenda. *Beyond Babel.* London, 1972.

Mankekar, D. R. *Media and the Third World.* New Delhi, 1979.

Masmoudi, Mustapha. *The New World Information Order.* Paris: UNESCO, 1980.

Massing, Michael. "Inside the Wires' Banana Republics." *Columbia Journalism Review,* November/December 1979.

Mattelart, Armand. *Multinational Corporations and the Control of Culture.* Brighton, England, 1979.

M'Bow, Amadou-Mahtar. *Building the Future*. Paris: UNESCO, 1981.

Morris, Joe Alex. *Deadline Every Minute: The Story of the United Press*. New York, 1957.

Mousseau, Jacques, ed. *Les Communications de Masse*. Paris, 1972.

Naesselund, Gunnar. *Collaboration Between News Agencies in Nordic Countries*. Paris: UNESCO, 1980.

Ng'weno, Hilary. "All Freedom Is at Stake." *The Weekly Review* (Nairobi), November 8, 1976.

Nicols, M. E. *The Story of the Canadian Press*. Toronto, 1948.

Non-Aligned News Agencies Pool. *Non-Alignés sur l'Information Documents*. Belgrade, 1979.

Organization for Petroleum Exporting Countries. *Statement of 54th OPEC Conference*. Vienna, June 28, 1979.

Paige, Glenn. *The Korean Decision*. New York, 1968.

Palmer, Michael. "De l'Information Étrangère dans la Presse Quotidienne Française: Les Agences de Presse et le Journalisme Anglo-Saxon 1878–85." *Revue d'Histoire Moderne et Contemporaine* 22 (April–June 1976).

Phillips Davison, W. "News Media and International Negotiation." *Public Opinion Quarterly,* Summer 1974.

Pinch, Edward. *A Brief Study on News Patterns in Sixteen Third World Countries*. Medford, Mass.: Tufts University, 1978.

———. "The Flow of News: An Assessment of the Non-Aligned News Pool." *Journal of Communication* 28, no. 4 (1978).

Pinto, Roger. *La Liberté d'Information et d'Opinion en Droit International*. Paris, 1984.

Pool, Ithiel de Sola, and Dizard, Stephen. *International Telecommunications and the Requirements of News Services*. Medford, Mass.: Tufts University, 1978.

Rachty, Gehan. *Foreign News in Nine Arab Countries*. A Murrow Report. Medford, Mass.: Tufts University, 1978.

Radolf, Andrew. "UPI Says Finance Secure for Turnaround in 1984." *Editor & Publisher,* July 1983.

Reuters. *Annual Reports*. London.

Reyes Matta, Fernando. "The Latin American Concept of News." *Journal of Communication* 29, no. 2.

Righter, Rosemary. *Whose News?* London, 1978.

Rivers, William, and Schramm, Wilbur. *Responsibility in Mass Communication*. Rev. ed. New York, 1969.

Rosenblum, Mort. *Coups and Earthquakes*. New York, 1979.

Sanders, James. *Dateline NZPA*. Auckland, 1979.

Saxon Mills, J. *The Press and Communications of the Empire*. London, 1924.

Schiller, Herbert. *Communication and Cultural Domination*. New York, 1976.

————. "Now, a New International Information Order." *Mass Media,* April 1977.

Schramm, Wilbur. *Mass Media and National Development.* Paris: UNESCO, 1964.

————, et al. *International News Wires and Third World News in Asia.* Hong Kong, 1978.

Schulte, Henry. *The Spanish Press.* Urbana, Ill., 1968.

Schwarzlose, Richard. "Harbor News Association: The Formal Origins of the AP." *Journalism Quarterly,* Summer 1968.

————. "The Nation's First Wire Service." *Journalism Quarterly,* Winter 1980.

Scott, George. *Reporter Anonymous.* London, 1968.

Scott, J. M. *Extel 100.* London, 1972.

Seldes, Georges. *The Truth Behind the News.* London, 1929.

Selser, Gregorio, and Roncagliolo, Rafael. *Trampas de la Información y Neocolonialismo.* Mexico City, 1979.

Sington, Derrick, and Weidenfeld, Arthur. *The Goebbels Experiment.* London, 1942.

Smith, Anthony. *The Geopolitics of Information.* London, 1980.

————. *Goodbye Gutenberg.* New York and Oxford, 1980.

Smith, Janet Adam. *John Buchan.* London, 1965.

Sreberny-Mohammadi, Annabelle, with Nordenstreng, Kaarle; Stevenson, Robert; and Ugboajah, Frank. "The World of the News: The News of the World." Unpublished report. Paris: UNESCO, 1980.

Stern, Fritz. *Gold and Iron.* London, 1977.

Stone, Melville. *Fifty Years a Journalist.* Garden City, N.Y., 1921.

Storey, Graham. *Reuters' Century.* London, 1951.

TASS. *News Agency of the Soviet Union.* Moscow, n.d.

Times. *History of "The Times."* Vol. 2, The Tradition Established. London, 1939.

Tolkunov, M. L. "Communication for Peace and Mutual Trust." Paris: *UNESCO Features,* no. 69 (1984).

Tunstall, Jeremy. *The Media Are American.* London, 1977.

Twentieth Century Fund. *A Free and Balanced Flow.* New York, 1978.

United Nations Educational, Scientific, and Cultural Organization. "Address by Mr. Frederico Mayor, Deputy Director-General." International Press Institute General Assembly, Athens, June 1979.

————. *Declaration on Fundamental Principles Concerning the Contribution of the Mass Media to Strengthening Peace and International Understanding, to the Promotion of Human Rights and to Countering Racialism, Apartheid and Incitement to War.* Paris, UNESCO, 1978.

————. *Intergovernmental Conference for Co-operation on Activities, Needs and Programmes for Communication Development, Final Report.* Paris, UNESCO, 1980.

————. International Commission for the Study of Communication Problems (ICSCP). *Many Voices, One World*. Paris, UNESCO, 1980.

————. ICSCP. *Monographs I-II-III*, working papers no. 13–15, Paris, UNESCO, 1977–78.

————. International Programme for the Development of Communication (IPDC). *Collection of Basic Texts*. Paris, UNESCO, 1981.

————. IPDC. *Intergovernmental Council Session, Final Report*. Paris, UNESCO, 1981.

————. IPDC. *Intergovernmental Council, Second Session, Final Report*. Paris, UNESCO, 1982.

————. *Moving Towards Change*. Paris, UNESCO, 1976.

————. *Recommendation sur le Nouvel Ordre International de l'Information*. Paris and Baghdad, UNESCO, 1980.

————. *Thinking Ahead: UNESCO and the Challenges of Today and Tomorrow*. Paris, UNESCO, 1977.

————. *World Communications*. Paris, UNESCO, 1975.

Voices of Freedom. *Working Papers*. Talloires: World Press Freedom Committee, 1981 and 1983.

Wadda, Joe. *Developing Countries Seek Greater Voice in Communications Decisions*. New York: United Nations Development Program, 1978.

Weaver, David, and Wilhoit, Cleveland. "Foreign News Coverage in Two U.S. Wire Services." *Journal of Communications*, Spring 1981.

White, David. "The Gate-Keeper." *Journalism Quarterly*, Autumn 1950.

Winkler, John. *W. R. Hearst, an American Phenomenon*. New York, 1928.

Wright, Denis. *The English Amongst the Persians*. London, 1977.

Wynter, Andrew. *Our Social Bees*. London: Robert Hardwicke, 1861.

Index

269